# The Great Debate

## OUR SCHOOLS IN CRISIS

*Edited by*

C. Winfield Scott
*Director of Advanced Study*
*Rutgers, The State University*

Clyde M. Hill
*Sterling Professor Emeritus of Education*
*Yale University*

Hobert W. Burns
*Assistant Professor of Education*
*Rutgers, The State University*

A SPECTRUM  BOOK

## SPECTRUM 📡 BOOKS

©—1959, BY

PRENTICE-HALL, INC.

ENGLEWOOD CLIFFS, N. J.

LIBRARY OF CONGRESS
CATALOG CARD NUMBER: 59–15369

PRINTED IN THE UNITED STATES OF AMERICA
36351

# Preface

Throughout the length and breadth of our land, public education is being debated today as never before. Most of the discussion has to do with fundamental issues and some of it is well reasoned and pointed. A considerable portion is much more emotionally charged than it is reflective. All of what is being said and written seems to indicate that our schools are indeed in a period of crisis.

The gravity of the situation cannot be overestimated. If we fail to educate the present and immediately future generations appropriately and well, we may lose the current conflict with the Soviet powers and cease to be free to educate and live as we see fit. This is the grim prospect before us.

In the final analysis, laymen more than educators will determine the educational issues that now confront us. This collection of criticisms of public education and related materials has been prepared to help them see both sides of questions and to stimulate them to think before they act. It provides only a sample of the debate that rages about us, yet this is adequate for the reader to understand the general nature of the whole and to sense the urgency of the problem.

This book differs from a previous one edited by Scott and Hill (*Public Education Under Criticism,* Prentice-Hall, 1954) in that it relies more heavily on material from popular magazines, is much shorter, and concentrates pretty much on specific criticisms and responses thereto. The previous book, after presenting both criticisms and defenses, gave considerable attention to the analysis of criticisms and to proposals for handling them.

In the preparation of this anthology, as was true previously, the editors derived support for their own convictions and welcome encouragement from the responses of publishers to their requests for materials to study and for reprint privileges. No publisher failed to grant a specific request for permission to reprint material. For this necessary assistance and the interest in public education that it implies, the editors wish to express their sincere appreciation.

Although the book was prepared for laymen, the editors are cognizant that it may prove interesting and useful to professional educators. If such proves to be the case, this by-product will be welcome.

The editors would like to acknowledge the aid received from Raymond Bacchetti, a graduate student in the School of Education at Rutgers, The State University, who assisted in the initial title search and helped to collect materials. The collection of materials was facilitated by the full co-

operation of the library staff at Rutgers, The State University, particularly
that of Mrs. Ellen C. Kelley, Mr. H. Gilbert Kelley, Mr. Oliver K. Westling,
and Miss Rose E. Sieber.

*New Brunswick, New Jersey*                          C. WINFIELD SCOTT
                                                     CLYDE M. HILL
                                                     HOBERT W. BURNS

# Contents

III. NEGLECT OF FUNDAMENTAL SUBJECTS, *continued*

IV. THE CHALLENGE OF SOVIET EDUCATION, 59

V. DO WE DO ENOUGH FOR THE GIFTED CHILD? 77

VI. ARE SCHOOL BUILDINGS TOO FANCY? 92

VII. CAN TEACHER TRAINING AND CERTIFICATION
     PRACTICES BE JUSTIFIED? 106

*To laymen, who as school patrons, school board members, and tax-paying citizens play the most important role of all in determining the content and form of public education.*

# Bird's-Eye View
# of the Great Debate

## BACKGROUND

Since Soviet Russia launched its first globe-circling satellite in the fall of 1957, shrill criticism of public education has reached a new crescendo. The unexpected achievement of the Russians has been attributed largely to their educational system; conversely, our failure to be the first launcher of a successful satellite has been laid at the door of public education. To a large extent, criticism has focused on the comparative emphasis of basic subjects, particularly mathematics and science, in the schools of the two countries. This approach has tended to create the impression that public education in the United States neglects fundamental subjects and gives too much attention to "life adjustment" problems which, many critics say, should be mainly or altogether the concern of the home and other non-school agencies.

The current wave of criticisms is but one phase of a debate that is probably as old as formal education itself. For instance, Aristotle made the following observation in Athens about 300 B.C., presumably as he reflected on existent confusion as to the purposes of education:

> There are doubts concerning the business [of education] since all people do not agree in those things which they would have a child taught, both with respect to improvement in virtue and a happy life; nor is it clear whether the object of it should be to improve the reason or rectify the morals. From the present mode of education we cannot determine with certainty to which men incline, whether to instruct a child in which will be useful to him in life, or what tends to virtue, or what is excellent; for all these things have their separate defenders.[1]

Some 2150 years later, in 1856, the school committee minutes of a New England community contained this lament:

[1] Quoted by Mark Van Doren in *Liberal Education* (New York: Henry Holt & Company, Inc., 1943), pp. 2-3.

Our schools are in a feeble and backward state. We think the modern mode of instruction is decidedly bad.[2]

A final example from the past is the following excerpt from an editorial that appeared in the *New York Sun,* October 5, 1902:

When we were boys, boys had to do a little work in school. They were not coaxed; they were hammered. Spelling, writing, and arithmetic were not electives, and you had to learn. In these more fortunate times (1902), elementary education has become in many places a vaudeville show. The child must be kept amused, and learns what he pleases. Many sage teachers scorn the old-fashioned rudiments, and it seems to be regarded as between a misfortune and a crime for a child to learn to read.[3]

Current criticisms differ from those of yesteryear primarily in volume, intensity, and to some extent in emphasis. In the period since World War II, public discussion of public education has been more extensive than ever before and the emotional content of the debate has often been very high. The topics, however, have been either the same as, or similar to, those of the past. For instance, the quotation from Aristotle indicates that mankind has long been trying to determine just what is *basic* in education. The charge that modern public education is undermining our democratic form of government and encouraging some type of socialistic organization was quite common during the last years of the preceding decade and the first years of the present one. But this criticism was not new as is shown by the fact that public education in the United States originally had to overcome opposition which held that it was indefensible to tax one man's property to educate the children of other men.[4] The persistence of criticism itself and of most, if not all, of the common charges is a fact that both educator and layman may well keep in mind as they try to maintain balance and perspective in the present or any future crisis period.

## TYPES OF CRITICS

Critics whose opinions attain wide or fairly wide attention may be divided into five groups: scholars, professional educators, public figures, professional writers, and outright enemies of public education. In the first group, one finds mainly college professors and administrators who have had no formal training in education but who have given much serious thought to educational problems. Arthur E. Bestor, some of whose writings appear in this text (e.g., pages 26-27) is easily the best known and most prolific of this group at present.

---

[2] Quoted by William H. Burton in "Get the Facts: Both Ours and the Other Fellows!" *Progressive Education,* January, 1952, p. 89.

[3] Quoted by Marian G. Valentine in *School and Society,* June 7, 1952, Vol. 75, No. 1955.

[4] Elwood P. Cubberly, *Public Education in the United States* (Boston: Houghton Mifflin Company, revised and enlarged edition, 1934), p. 160.

Professional educators tend to be professors and administrators in colleges and schools of education, with a sprinkling of representatives of other types of institutions. Parenthetically, it should be noted that this group has probably been more self-critical than any other group of professional workers in the country. Two vocal and scholarly examples from the professional educator group, both of whom have writings in this volume are William Clark Trow (pages 27-28) and Harold C. Hand (pages 139-140).

Public figures, especially scientists at present, often seem impelled to speak out on public education. Hyman G. Rickover, also represented in this book (pages 146-151) is a good example. The topics they cover are usually important and their motives above suspicion, but at times their views seem to reflect only limited knowledge and consideration of educational problems.

The professional writers' group includes newspaper columnists, producers of magazine articles, such as those by John Keats (e.g., pages 7-15) and George B. Leonard, Jr. (e.g., pages 41-43) in this anthology, and authors of books, of whom Mortimer Smith, whose *The Diminished Mind* is debated herein (pages 24-28) is an outstanding example. Some of the staunchest supporters of education and some of its most thoughtful critics are to be found in this group, as well as some critics whose insights and appreciations appear to be severely limited or dubious.

Finally, there are the individuals and organizations who, under the guise of friendly interest in education, actually try to undermine it. Their motives are seldom, if ever, clear to the outsider, but they seem to be actuated in part by a doubting attitude toward democracy and a desire to reduce the costs of public education. While the number of true enemies of education is doubtless very small, their influence and ability to confuse issues are such as to warrant continued vigilance on the part of the profession, for instance, of the type maintained by the Commission on the Defense of Democracy through Education of the National Education Association. Also, an alert, questioning attitude toward critics of education should be adopted by all laymen interested in this subject.

## PURPOSE

This anthology is intended primarily for the layman who pays school taxes and sends children to schools. There are three simple reasons why the editors developed it.

They have been strongly impressed by the waves of criticism that have swept over the country in recent years and concerned that the negative currents may not meet in open, adequate conflict the countercurrents that exist. Implicit in their concern is a belief that if issues are freely debated, workable solutions of merit will emerge which will probably be better than those that could be produced by any other means. Finally, they hold even more firmly to the conviction that the public schools belong to the people and that the public should, on the basis of knowledge and sound deliberation, determine what they will be.

Although criticisms are plentiful, the public has difficulty in obtaining a comprehensive view of the situation with respect to areas, or topics, and a balanced presentation of *pro* and *con* arguments. Both magazine articles and books tend to concentrate on specific topics or to emphasize certain ones more than others, and both tend to be adversely critical. This collection is designed to provide the lay reader an over-all picture of the current debate with views from opposite angles whenever these could be obtained. Limited space precluded any explanation of the situation or presentation of evidence on possible effects of criticisms, but a number of suggestions for improvement of public education are included.

Insofar as possible, the editors relied on consumer, or popular magazines for their material, reasoning that such sources would yield interesting, readable discussions of most, if not all, important issues. Approximately 80 per cent of the final content originally appeared in consumer publications. The editors also felt that defenses of education by laymen, such as the article by Herbert L. Brown, Jr. (pages 15-24), would carry more weight with laymen than defenses written by professional educators. As they expected, most defenses have been written by professional educators and been published in educational journals. The editors freely used such materials whenever they appeared to be the only ones available or the best of their kind.

While not intended primarily for use as a textbook in education courses, the editors have tried to produce a book that professors and students of education will find helpful. The lay writings at least wear no "ivory tower" halo.

## PROCEDURES

Writings of possible interest and value were identified primarily by use of indexes and bibliographies. The *Education Index* was the principal index source and the *Reader's Guide to Periodical Literature* was an important secondary source. Bibliographies issued by the National Education Association were more helpful than any others.

In an effort to introduce group professional judgment into the identification and evaluation of materials, Dr. Clyde M. Hill asked some 50 of his former students and professional friends to send him references for current criticisms that they considered most important. This procedure, although not highly productive, contributed some titles that might otherwise have been overlooked, and also confirmed or strengthened the editors' judgment with respect to a number of articles.

The *National Education Association Research Bulletin* (1958) provided both an example of a good classification system and also important references. As the editors' thinking crystallized, they found themselves categorizing criticisms somewhat as the *Bulletin* does and seeking material on certain topics for which their supply seemed inadequate.

Once references were identified, the next step was scanning them to determine which ones should be retained for careful evaluation. Some titles were examined in the main Library of Rutgers, the State University, but most were reviewed after they had been supplied by publishers. The request to publishers called attention to the problem, explained the nature of the project, and invited them to contribute specific articles and any suggestions they wished to make. This procedure resulted in the collection of about 350 articles for the study.

All articles were initially evaluated by Hobert W. Burns and classified into two groups: *accepted* and *rejected*. C. Winfield Scott then read the accepted ones, eliminated some and forwarded the remainder to Clyde M. Hill, who made judgments concerning all that he received. A simple rating system was used by the three editors, and also informal comments. Final decisions were made by the senior editor, C. Winfield Scott.

As has already been indicated, articles from lay magazines were preferred and coverage of topics considered most important, rather than a strict sampling of the most prevalent types of criticism, was sought. A determined effort was made to identify the most vocal and presumably influential lay critics and to obtain for use articles that represent them well. In some cases, the most suitable writings seemed to be reviews, usually in debate form, of popular books by the critics. Such articles, presented herein, cover a good proportion of the most important critical books of the last six or seven years.

## LIMITATIONS

Material in this anthology is limited entirely to articles and excerpts from lay and educational magazines published since 1952. Timeliness was an important consideration, so the bulk of the material is from the latter part of the period covered. Outstanding books are represented only by reviews, and coverage of such books, although good, is not complete.

Public elementary and secondary education is the focus of attention, and teacher education is the only area of college education covered. This one exception was dictated by the close relationship between teacher education and public education practices. All important areas of criticism are covered except school costs and religion, neither of which has been of late an independent and lively controversial topic of discussion in lay and educational journals. However, school expenditures are treated to some extent in the chapter on school buildings; and their importance as a butt of criticism is evident too often in public votes on school bond proposals and budgets. Religion will remain a vitally important area of conflict as long as a sizable minority of citizens implicitly express criticism of public education by supporting private religious schools.

Socially subversive tendencies in public education are not covered because criticism under this head dwindled almost to the point of extinction in the period covered. The most important social issue that faces public education today, namely desegregation of schools, was excluded from consideration because it does not represent an area of criticism but rather a question of social policy.

In selecting articles and excerpts, the main consideration was representativeness of criticisms, critics, and respondents. This narrowed the choices in some cases to the point where not much, if any, weight could be given to the quality of the writing. Whenever possible, however, judgment was exercised with respect to both composition and content. In most areas, the editors had ample material to choose from, and were able to develop what they consider to be satisfactory coverage of major questions in brief, popular fashion.

Both the concept of the project and the small size of the contemplated book limited selections pretty much to the great debate itself. While there is a brief classification of the critics (page 2-3), there is no attempt to analyze their motives as a group or as individuals. Another and a related limitation of the book is its failure to provide any help on the handling of criticisms, except as suggested programs and practices in the final chapter may constitute aid. These two important limitations are entirely consistent with the main purpose of the project, namely, to stimulate thinking about big issues that confront public education.

The final limitation is a characteristic of all books of readings. No single position is fully developed or defended and continuity is somewhat lacking. Only the individual reader can integrate the whole for his own purposes. However, the editors have tried to ease his task by providing this introduction and short introductory statements for the several chapters.

## PRESENTATION

This microcosmic presentation of the Great Debate begins with a general discussion and moves through debate on five specific topics. As was noted in the previous section, these represent all areas of fundamental criticism except those of finance and religion.

Following the debate itself, there is a chapter that presents the over-all case for public education, with a considerable amount of reassuring research evidence. The final chapter reports a debatable proposal for retooling public education, summarizes three important proposals for improvement of public education and an historic conference on teacher education, and presents a few challenges which, in the main, merit serious consideration by the public and educators alike.

# II

## General Pros and Cons

Much of the current criticism of education, easily a majority of the total output, is of a general type. Negative broadsides are answered by affirmative salvos which cover a wide range of topics, but which tend to emphasize the purpose, content and practices of public education.

This chapter presents two general debates, the second of which centers about a popular book that accuses the schools of promoting mediocrity in education. It also offers a critical review of three other popular books on public education; two items which set forth somewhat contrasting views of the ends of education; and, finally, a rather glowing defense of contemporary educational practices. This fare provides in brief compass a taste of the most fundamental issues involved in current criticisms.

## Are the Public Schools Doing Their Job?*

### No

*John Keats, a free-lance writer descended from an uncle of the poet who bore the same name, is the author of* The Crack in the Picture Window, *a humorous book on housing developments. He asserts that public schools stunt young minds by feeding them insipid lessons in social conformity and "living skills"—instead of furnishing intellectual challenges to develop mature citizens.*

---

* Reprinted by permission from *The Saturday Evening Post*, September 21, 1957. Copyright 1957 by The Curtis Publishing Company.

The public high school in our suburban Washington, D. C., area is fully credited by the Middle States Association of Colleges and Secondary Schools. It is not plagued by split sessions; the classes are not particularly large by today's standards. The school is staffed by intelligent, hardworking men and women whose every thought is of the students' welfare. The teacher pay scale is relatively high and the teachers' morale is excellent. The million-dollar building is brand new. It is light, spacious and completely equipped with everything from a motion-picture theater to an auditorium, science rooms and library. Behind the tremendous gymnasium there are grassy playing fields and a football field encircled by a running track. The school offers sixty-three different courses of study, and professional public-school evaluators give it an excellent rating. There is no question in my mind that the public-school system of which our school is a part compares favorably with any other public-school system in the nation.

These facts might make it seem difficult to explain why we sold the pleasant house that served us so well, and have just moved to a smoky city to spend more than $2000 a year in order to send our three children to a private school this fall.

I do not know how we are going to afford it. I know that we must try, for our children's sake. My wife and I have come slowly and bitterly to believe that our children cannot receive an adequate education in our local public-school system, or in any public-school system of comparable stature.

We believe that most of this nation's public schools now offer America's children an education that is anticultural, anti-intellectual, narrowly utilitarian at best and utterly vapid at worst. We think most of our public schools subscribe to an erroneous educational philosophy. We think most public education is bad in theory, bad in practice and abysmal in its results. We are convinced that the splendid public school building we are spurning, with its staff of dedicated teachers, simply does not, and cannot, offer any student an education that is in any way comparable to the education we both received in the public schools twenty years ago.

These conclusions were not reached quickly. We argued against ourselves every step of the way, because we did not want to believe what, eventually, we were forced to believe.

Our dissatisfaction with the public schools began when our son, now fourteen, entered first grade. At the time, we were merely a little puzzled, but we took for granted that things would have changed since we were in school, and trusted they had changed for the better. As our boy went on in school, however, our puzzlement deepened into something resembling dismay, and then, two years ago, a publishing house asked me to prepare a book on America's public schooling. It would be a book, they said, that would explain different educational points of view, but would not lobby for any one of them. In the course of my research, I studied nearly every book on educational philosophy and technique printed since 1947. I visited public and private schools; liberal arts and teachers' colleges; talked with hundreds of pupils, college students, teachers and professors and examined the school district in which we live. My wife studied with me, and the more we learned, the more we became convinced our public schools were failures. We think the schools have failed because they do not ask children to think. This is not entirely due to the fact that the schools devote less time to the child's mind in order to stress vocational hints and lessons in social conformity. The schools fail because their method of presenting subject-matter courses is an ironclad guarantee of poor quality.

For instance, our high school teaches English to college-preparatory students in terms of How To. Our children learn How To write letters; How To use the library; How To "get up-to-date information about various vocations"; How To make a speech; How To carry on a conversation; How To listen; and How To tell a poem from a short story. Nowhere do our children get the idea that English is a disciplined means of expressing thought. Instead, they can only gather that English is a collection of isolated skills, each somehow different. Poems look like this, and short stories are always short and have snappy endings. Letters are things that begin Dear Sir and end Sincerely and have the date in a corner. Making a speech is being relaxed and speaking slowly and clearly.

Nowhere do our children learn that the basic ingredient of any story, speech or poem is its content. Nowhere do they learn that the important thing about writing a letter is having something to say, and using precise language to say it. Worse yet, our English teachers do not at all times insist on correct usage. Rather, they "attempt to place the accent on accepted usage," as the school catalogue puts it.

The insistence on technique rather than thought begins in the earliest grades. Thirty years ago my first-grade primer was based on story content, which, the authors said, "contributes no small part to the child's mastery." Today, my youngest child uses a primer that stresses "ease," never mentions "mastery" and calls reading a "skill." Instead of stories, children now begin with "Oh, oh, oh; look, look, look," and they are bored silly.

When elementary schools offer arithmetic disguised as How Money Helps Us, the idea is to interest children in arithmetic by showing them examples of its use in real life. They call this "motivation," and say the result is that today's children learn arithmetic better than their parents did. Unfortunately, the teaching technique tends to wag the dog. One elementary school in our area has set up a school bank to help teach what it calls "the social phase" of arithmetic. Forty-five minutes each day are devoted to electing young bank presidents, taking turns being cashiers, and standing in line at the cardboard play bank the children built. I say that school is not making arithmetic "meaningful," but is instead demonstrating just one narrow use of numbers, and is taking the long way of doing it. I doubt if forty-five minutes a day devoted to bank playing is a better use of the time than showing children that numbers are thoughts, and combining this idea with drill in arithmetic.

Emphasis on thought is missing from all subject matter in our local school system. The high-school science programs are nothing more than magic shows of curious facts. They deal with such matters as How To tell one detergent from another by certain chemical tests. They do not deal with understandings of basic relationships or with the historical development of scientific method. All our rigorous courses are presented in terms of techniques to be memorized for special occasions or as something about which the child can learn something in a vague, unspecified future if he ever really finds it necessary. Then, as if this were not enough, original thought and individual initiative are discouraged, as we shall see.

Meanwhile, there are other goodies for our children to nibble. High schools in our area offer lessons in How To answer the telephone, buy a house, buy insurance, dress properly, shop wisely, apply for a Federal job, drive a car, behave on dates, curl hair, typewrite, fly-cast, decorate a living room and budget pocket money. This is not asking children to use their heads as best they can—it's simply giving them formulas.

As I see it, the cause of the schools' failure is not the teacher shortage, nor the argument that a public school must teach the mass, and hence must lower its standards to the level of the plodders. I think the trouble lies in a zany educational philosophy, first seen in full leaf at Columbia University's Teachers College several decades ago, which has now found such general acceptance that it is no longer called "progressive" or even "modern." The cornerstone of this philosophy is the quaint notion that no course of studies can train the mind.

The dean of one teacher factory told me that studying algebra, for instance, leads to nothing but a knowledge of algebra. He said it does not discipline the mind in a way of thinking. Thus, he said, English teaches only reading, writing, listening and speaking skills or techniques. History, he said, does not demonstrate a way of thinking to most children, but merely clutters their memories with a lot of dead facts. Likewise, chemistry teaches only chemistry, and so on.

"That is why," he told me, "we say 'We teach children, not subjects.' "

The next question was, "What do you teach children?" and the teachers-college answer was—and is—"life adjustment." By this, our public-school men mean that whatever a child learns must be up-to-date and immediately useful to that child's getting along in this world. Hence, subject matter is not presented as thought but as vocational technique wedded to present reality. Meanwhile, the schools concentrate on good citizenship and behavior. They try to indoctrinate children with respect for the rights of others. They harp on the need to listen to everyone's point of view, just as though all points of view were valid. They offer behavior-conditioning programs emphasizing conformity. Advanced-learning groups are discouraged or disguised in an attempt to hide from the rest of the class the fact that some children are brighter than others. Our school, in common with too many others, makes life adjustment its chief educational aim.

Now, if a child is obviously maladjusted, I think the school should help him. But I also think making life adjustment for everyone the first aim of public education implies our children are all maladjusted; that our homes, churches and social agencies have failed and that our community is morally bankrupt. There is no reason for this assumption in my community, where, as in yours, the maladjusted child is the exception. One result of life adjustment in our school system is that relatively less time is spent on intellectual matters, and our children come out well-behaved little know-nothings, which is exactly what they were when they entered. Another result is more serious.

Our son, Christopher, put it thus: "I learned how to get along with the group, all right. All you do is shut up or tell them (the teachers) what they want you to tell them. If you don't, the teacher says, 'You're talking back' or 'You're getting ahead' and 'Why don't you just wait?' and either way the class is against you. If you don't do what everybody else does, you're lonely."

Our elementary school devotes the first three hours of its day to a dreary stew called social studies—the intellectual, so to speak, component of life adjustment. Children learn to do everything together, in committees. They study food and transportation. They snip pictures of carrots and trucks out of advertisements. They visit the local dairy to learn to call the milkmen "community helpers." They see movies with little social messages, and the mental result of all this activity could be put in your eye.

The last two and a half hours of the school day—after lunch, when the children are beginning to tire—are devoted to reading, writing, spelling and arithmetic.

Our elementary school is a happy place. Together with educator Wilbur A. Yauch, author of How Good Is Your School?, it believes "the task of education is to make children unselfish and interested in others." It claims to teach children better than ever, thanks to the elaborate lifelike motivation techniques. This is simply not true. Our elementary school fails to give children good individual work habits and it fails to give them mastery of the fundamentals. I'll let one of our junior-high-school teachers sum it up for me.

"Children come here unprepared," he said. "They don't know their three R's. They can't work by themselves. We make junior high a transition for them. We tell them there are no more committees. We say two or three can collaborate on their work if they need to, but they'll each receive a lower grade than if each did his own work. We tell them there's no collaboration at all in high school. You'd be surprised how much this upsets many of them, because they've been taught to do things together."

As our son breezed through elementary and junior high school making straight A's, we wondered if the work wasn't pretty simple, because Christopher is not talented. The answer was that Chris was never asked to think; he simply relied on his good memory. When he read Dickens'

Christmas Carol in sixth grade, he was asked to retell the story in his own words, rather than being asked to write a paper on the meaning of the story. His examinations consisted of true-false and multiple-choice tests. Neither test requires a child to prove his grasp of the thing learned, as written answers would. Such tests do not ask children to think; they merely ask them to guess.

Moreover, we found Christopher falling into sloppy work habits.

"Why bother with that?" he'd ask, when we'd suggest his information on any subject seemed a bit sketchy. "All I have to do is get an A, and I already know enough for that."

All in all, we suspected our school was not asking children like Christopher to use their brains, but we had no idea how deeply it underestimated children's ability to do mental work until friends returned this spring from three years in England. Their son, just Christopher's age, had in those same three years completed two years of Latin, two of French, a year of algebra, a year of geometry and more work in history and English composition than our high school offers.

I refuse to admit English children are that much brighter than our own. The difference is one of attitude. The English school required students to attempt hard mental work, while our school does exactly the opposite. Not only does our school system postpone establishment of advanced-learning sections until high school, but once there, each child receives printed advice not to select the college-preparatory program unless he feels able and willing to do hard work. This is a curious statement in more ways than one, for it falsely implies there is real meat in our college-preparatory program. At any rate, a good many of our children take warning, and select the general course and driver training and girls' chorus instead. Thus, one school in our area dropped European history because not enough students elected it. Thus, too, our high school will not offer French next year unless ten students sign up for it.

It hurt us to see Christopher sliding through a school that never asked him to think about the meaning of a story or about the meaning of anything else. We experienced in our school system what Adm. H. G. Rickover, chief of the Navy's atomic submarine program, finds true of the nation's schools in general.

Admiral Rickover told the Edison Foundation last November twentieth that "the above-average child is kept from advancing at the speed appropriate to his ability, with the result that many lose interest in learning as such, others develop sloppy work habits, and some build up a false sense of superiority which convinces them that they are so smart they will never need. to apply themselves to anything. The deadly routine sets in on these young and malleable minds . . . children whose minds are not challenged become frustrated and often turn into poor pupils from sheer boredom."

Over and over again, our children—yours and mine—hear teachers say,

"Don't get ahead of the class." Our elementary-school children are told not to take their readers home, for fear they might read ahead. Christopher's junior-high arithmetic class was taught to use a table to find square roots. Two of his friends loved arithmetic and did outside reading. They found a way to extract square roots without a table, and that the method was easier and made more sense to them than the teacher's. Delighted, they took their discovery to class. Instead of complimenting them for enterprise, the teacher squashed them.

"How did I tell you to do it?" he demanded. "Don't you think you ought to do it our way? Don't you think you shouldn't get ahead of the group? We'll get around to your way later on."

"They always say, 'Don't you think,' " Christopher reported. " 'Don't you think you should go along with the group?' 'Don't you think,' 'don't you think.' They always mean 'Don't you think you shouldn't think what you think?' "

This is not an isolated example of a poor school and a poor teacher. Given space, I could prove it typical. I have mentioned that ours is considered a good school and that our teachers are good people. This really says nothing, because the school is judged by accreditors who seem to think a million-dollar plant guarantees educated graduates, and who believe in the life-adjustment program. Our teachers-college technicians of education have elected themselves judge and jury of their own work. Our classroom teachers have no choice of what to teach or how, and some of them resent this.

Children go through twelve years of our public schooling and emerge still shaky in the simplest things. Our senior high-school English class is clear proof. "Chiefly," our school says, "the senior English course is a review of the language *skills* (italics mine), the skills of listening, speaking, reading and writing. . . . Although teachers provide opportunities for longer compositions, they concentrate on the sentence and the paragraph; the pupil need is still in this area."

Thus, in the last year of higher learning that most of our children will ever know, they are still trying to learn how to listen, still trying to learn how to write sentences. Somewhere in those twelve years, it seems to me, someone has failed.

That children leave Maryland high schools unprepared for college work is evidenced by complaints from the University of Maryland, an institution never particularly distinguished for its intellectual accomplishments. That the nation's high schools have failed generally is shown by Doctor Conant's statement: "If a layman really wishes to hear eloquent evidence to the inadequacies of our public secondary schools, let him talk to the professors on almost any campus."

Pitifully enough, our schools produce children unable to meet the Army's modest demands of its enlisted men. The captain of one of the Nike batteries defending Washington from atomic attack told me he simply didn't know how anyone could expect him to rely on the kind of teen-agers the draft sent him.

"They can't even add or subtract," he said. "I have to read their mail for some of them and write their letters home for them. And outfits like mine are supposed to be getting the cream of the crop. God knows what the rest are like if mine are the cream."

The failure of our public schools cannot be explained away by our schoolmen, who argue "We have to teach everybody these days." They say this in a hurt tone that implies everybody's child is a dithering jackass, but I have not yet been able to discover this is indeed the fact. As I read the schoolmen's own statistics, the number of juvenile jackasses is exactly as small as the number of geniuses among us. What I find in practice is that our schools pamper the jackasses, stuff the geniuses under the rug, and meanwhile envelop everyone in that fatuous diaperism they call life adjustment.

My wife and I believe the school should at least ask children to try to think if it can't train them to think. We believe every child from the nitwit to the young Einstein needs to be asked to use his head as best he can, and if the school makes this its first aim, then we say the school has made a greater contribution to that child's adjustment to life than if it has merely taught him how to curl hair, behave himself in the back seat of a car, buy a pair of pants and type a letter.

Therefore, we think the schools should insist that all children stub their mental toes on rigorous subjects presented as thought. No doubt this will result in some failures. On the other hand, who is to say a failure learns nothing from his course? As a schoolboy, Sir Winston Churchill flunked everything in sight.

This fall our children will attend a rickety building set among busy city streets. The classrooms are dingy, the floors creak, and generations of educands have left their initials in the old-fashioned desks. We doubt whether our children will be aware that the walls are not gaily tinted, because they'll be too busy working with golden things. They will become acquainted with the cultural heritage of mankind, because the school believes, together with Sir Arthur Bryant, "the key to a nation's future is in her past. The nation that loses it has no future. . . ."

In private school our children will study the liberal arts—those arts which, if mastered, set man free. In senior year they won't concentrate on trying to write sentences nor will they be reviewed in how to listen. Instead, they will read Conrad, Eliot, Thoreau, Veblen, Benedict, Lewis, Huxley, Swift, Forster, Joyce, Fitzgerald, Jesus, Plato, Shaw, Anderson, Silone, Crossman, Mill, The Bill of Rights, Machiavelli and Hardy. Then they will write essays on these questions: What is the relationship of man to the state? What is the source of our values? How valid are they? What is the nature of tragedy? Is man progressing? Toward what? What is the good life? What right has the individual to disagree? How much must he conform? What is loyalty?

Here is life adjustment, if you will, but a real adjustment based on understandings rather than on manipulative technique or mass indoctrination in good group behavior. The children at this school are not all geniuses. They are ready to read such authors and write on such questions because the fundamentals have been presented to them not as skills, but as thoughtful means of expression, and they have been asked to think about the meaning of everything they've studied from first grade up.

We are not sending our children to this school in order that they may go to college. If they master the private-school work, they will be prepared for college. If they want to go, they can take themselves.

What our children will do in later life does not concern us. We can't lead their lives for them. We are certain, however, that whatever they do they will do better if they have been asked always to use their heads and have had some practice in the matter. The real reason we are sending our children to private school is that the school we have selected will require them to use what brains they have as best they can, and that our public school does not.

My wife and I have thus made our expensive separate peace with our educational system, but we do not leave the field with light hearts. We think continually of those whom we have left behind; of children as bright as or brighter than our own; of children whose potentialities will never be realized by a school system which puts conformity ahead of accomplishment, which substitutes techniques for understandings, which underestimates children's desire and ability to do hard mental work and which—there are no other words for it—defrauds our youth of their right to a decent education while pretending to adjust them to life.

We have no doubt that our teachers-college schoolmen are well intentioned, but the way to hell is paved with such intentions, and when we consider that a nation's schools are the bulwark of its freedom, and then look at our schools in the context of the hydrogen-bomb age, we fear we see that well-paved path stretching out before us all. Thoughtful men may save themselves; robots—no matter how well adjusted—never will.

## YES

*Herbert L. Brown, Jr., managing editor of* Changing Times (*The Kiplinger Magazine*), *is a former Rhodes Scholar. His concern about our schools and local government has prompted him to file as a candidate for his county board in the elections this fall. This parent declares that the American public-school system is demonstrating a notable superiority over private schools in equipping youngsters to meet the demands of the complex age in which we live.*

My two children, a boy of thirteen and a girl of ten, go to public school. My wife and I intend to keep them there. We believe they are now getting the best possible total education. This conclusion is based solely on what we think is most desirable for them. We want the best and are lucky enough to be able to afford any school we might choose. We still choose public school.

Yes, I am familiar with all the horrendous charges against public-school education. I have heard them in my own community, in Arlington, Virginia, just across the Potomac from Washington, D. C. The public schools, it is said, have gone to the dogs. They don't teach the fundamentals any more; kids get out without having learned to read, write or do simple arithmetic. They are full of "life-adjustment" nonsense that turns them into well-adjusted morons. They don't really know anything. They can't think. They are unprepared for college, for jobs, for citizenship. They have learned to strive for an easy conformity. The devil responsible for all this is something called "progressive education."

These charges, played on various strings, come from a scattering of parents, clergymen, businessmen, educators themselves and taxpayers. Some reflect sincere concern over the goals and methods of modern education. Some are no more than the snorts of a few professional cynics and blowhards. A good many start from an isolated instance, get magnified by rumor, and then are presented as wholesale indictments of all public education.

The United States public-school system embraces 30,000,000 youngsters in some 150,000 schools, all administered more or less locally. I have no doubt that in this immense network there are substandard schools. I know that some of the teachers in this country are less than competent. In view of what we pay them, it's a miracle we have so many good ones. Some school systems have gone haywire on their curricula. The only 100-per-cent-safe generalization is that there are good schools and bad schools—public and private. Some schools, public and private, are "traditional" in their approach, while others lean to the "progressive." Two of the most prominently "progressive" schools in the Greater Washington area are private schools.

Another point or two that must be remembered about public schools: Accelerated birth rates, particularly since World War II, have dumped into our schools vast hordes of youngsters. Building programs, halted by the war, have just begun to catch up. Many schools are overcrowded. Certified teachers are in short supply. The public schools must nonetheless continue to take all comers, the bright ones and the dumb ones, the quick and the slow, the kids from normal homes and the kids from troubled homes, the boy who will be an atomic scientist and the boy who will sell neckties, the girl who will be a dress designer and the girl who will marry early and have six young ones of her own. Nowadays, almost everybody goes to high school. Not so far back, it was only the brighter 10 per cent.

Today's world is nothing like the world of a generation ago. Changes of almost imponderable magnitude have been wrought by the automobile, TV, atomic energy, the Cold War, the trend toward greater specialization, automation, the need for managers, the creation of more and more leisure. The public schools are supposed to accept our children—all our children— and to teach each of them to live usefully in this world.

The public schools must absorb a growing list of chores. Draft rejections in World War II raised demands that the schools emphasize anew physical education and health programs. The alarming increase in divorce has led to an insistence on more family-life education in the schools. Poor turn-outs in elections have resulted in a clamor for more extensive teaching of citizenship. Traffic fatalities have brought demands for effective driver training.

But I do not mean to defend the public schools by weeping over their problems. Let me tell you something about our schools in Arlington and how my children are doing. This community is typical enough to provide a reasonably good example of what today's good public schools are like.

Arlington County is primarily a bedroom for people who work for the Federal Government in Washington. We have few of the very rich or the very poor. Median family income is around $7500, maybe higher. The adult-education level is compartively high.

Our schools are financed primarily by local real-estate taxes. We have virtually no industry to help broaden the tax base and help foot the bill— and this hurts. There is some compensation in payments we receive from the Federal Government for being a Federally impacted area. We also get some money from the state of Virginia, but nothing like what we pay to the state in income and gasoline taxes.

Some factors in Arlington thus favor a good school system; others militate against one. Net, we are probably in better shape to have good public schools than many other communities, and our school system is, in fact, considered to be among the top half hundred in the nation. But we weren't born with it; we had to fight like dogs to get it. The present system is only ten years old. Prior to 1947 a political machine indifferent to the growth of the community refused to modernize and expand what was essentially a second-rate, rural school system. A Citizens' Committee for School Improvement organized itself, campaigned for an elected school board, spearheaded a drive to pass bond issues for new construction, and kept applying pressure for adequate school budgets.

The crucial element here was the collective will of the citizens of Arlington. They got a sound, up-to-date school system because they wanted it and were willing to work for it.

My son, Herb, is now in the eighth grade, in junior high school. He has gone through the Arlington elementary schools. My daughter, Carolyn, is in the fifth grade. My wife and I feel easier about her than we did about our son, because we did our pioneering with the boy.

I think most parents pass through a similar experience when the oldest child hits the first grade. Things have changed since we went to school. Much of the confusion and misunderstanding about contemporary schools stems from changes that most of us have been unware of because we have been out of touch.

There have been changes in the practice of medicine, too, but in this and most other areas of living we have all seen and digested change as it has occurred.

Schooling is an exception. We got out, and that's the last we saw of the inside of a school until our firstborn entered one. Suddenly we notice that they don't do things the same way. Classes are less formal. Children are encouraged to ask questions. They may be split up into three or four groups. Textbooks are colorful and actually look interesting. The rigidly departmentalized subjects have yielded to more fluid organization.

At best, we are surprised; at worst, angered. Our egos rise up to confuse our judgment. What goes on here? Why the fancy changes? Do these school people think we parents weren't decently educated? Waves of nostalgia then pass over us, and we remember in a rosy haze all those nice teachers we had, how wonderful school was, how we really had to work, how we really got our lessons down pat and no fooling, and how, by golly, this molded our characters, which, of course, are quite high.

"No doubt about it," we think, "the public schools aren't what they used to be."

Said a Citizens' Committee in Madison, Wisconsin, after visiting certain classrooms: "Almost universal lack of distinct articulation, proper pronunciation and correct spelling." This is a common criticism.

The report is dated 1901.

I receive in my work a spate of letters from businessmen and parents deploring the failure of today's children to master the fundamentals. Actually an impressive number of tests have been run by educators. Old examination papers have been dredged up and given to contemporary children. The present-day youngsters almost invariably outscore their counterparts of former years in arithmetic, grammar, geography and reading.

Many new insights into the learning process have been acquired in recent decades. Teachers generally know a great deal more about their jobs than their predecessors did. This knowledge is backed up by a vast body of research.

It has now been pretty well demonstrated, for example, that individual children mature at different rates. One six-year-old may be ready to read: another child may not be ready until he is eight, not because he is lazy or "bad," but because he just doesn't have the skill yet.

Real learning, the psychologists have also discovered, requires some kind of motivation or interest on the part of the learner. This interest may be provided by rewards or by punishment. At an early age rewards are probably more effective than punishments.

Drill as an instrument of learning, it has been found, has limitations. Everybody knows the story of the boy who kept saying, "I have went." The teacher made him stay after school and write "I have gone" 500 times on the blackboard. Next day she found the 500 statements plus a note. "I have writen it 500 times. It is six o'clock. I have went home."

Learning is more meaningful if it is "adjusted to life." The so-called "life-adjustment" approach does not spurn the basic skills or discard academic subjects. It merely tries to make education more lifelike. My son was led into the study of fractions and percentages by being shown how to compute the batting averages of baseball players. He also checked prices in newspaper ads to see what percentage could be saved by buying a bicycle from one store rather than another. Percentages to him are real.

Some people maintain, nevertheless, that the schools should junk all this "modern nonsense" and return to the good old ways of teaching.

I realize there are some educators who have perverted the newer insights into all kinds of absurdities. In a few schools, public and private, there is the "child-centered" curriculum where the kids do pretty much as they please, where there is little discipline, where some subjects may even be discarded if the children are not interested in them. Some of the more extreme examples of this sort of "progressive education" have been represented as typical. In fact they are not.

My daughter, Carolyn, is an alert and imaginative child, with a marked desire to do every job well. During her first year in school she just could not read—just as she could not run 100 yards in ten seconds. A generation or two ago she would have flunked the grade. As it was, she was encouraged to keep trying. The next year she began to pick up slowly. A handful of other children were in the same boat. These children read one text while the more advanced children went on to a more difficult one. The children in Carolyn's group received special coaching.

In the third grade, and again last year, Carolyn began to move ahead rapidly, and she now reads on the "normal" fifth-grade level. The way her situation was handled makes sense to me. To say she was spoiled or inculcated with a disregard of proper standards does not.

It is the public high schools that really are catching it for a whole parcel of supposed shortcomings. The argument runs that the traditional academic program is being crowded out by vocational subjects and diluted to meaninglessness by frilly electives in such subjects as glee club and dating techniques. The kids who want to study such quaint subjects as mathematics, languages and science allegedly must go to private schools if they are to get a decent education or get into a respectable college.

Let's see. My son is taking the following required eight-grade courses: General education—a combination of English and social studies whose area of study this year is United States history and geography—mathematics, general science, physical education and health. He had a choice of one elective from these: home economics, art, newspaper production, industrial arts, choral music, instrumental music, general speech and library methods. His elective—which his parents elected—is instrumental music.

Yes, the choice of electives is broad, and will stay fairly broad throughout high school. Some of these electives may be considered quite nonessential to some folks, but quite important to others. Herb will get no chance to fritter away his high-school days. He has been observed and tested to see what his interests and aptitudes are, and his program will be set jointly by his teachers, guidance counselor and parents.

In the college-preparatory program which Herb probably will follow in senior high school, these courses are available: French, German, Spanish, Latin, algebra, geometry, trigonometry, biology, chemistry, physics, English, social studies, art and music.

This youngster of ours has turned out to be above average in general ability. He is quick—and for several years his teachers have occasionally graded him down for being careless. He shows high aptitude for arithmetic. He was among a small group of seventh graders who late last year were given the eighth-grade-arithmetic text and special instruction by the teacher. This sort of advanced individualized instruction is typical of good modern schools.

Herb got all A's last year, except in industrial arts—the kind of elementary course in shopwork that was called manual training in my day— in which he got a B. When we asked how come, he said he had been goofing off. He has learned that he will be penalized for not working up to his standard.

As I said before, a few folks in Arlington charge that our high schools don't do a first-class educating job. There is concrete evidence that this charge is not true.

About 1000 youngsters were graduated from the Arlington high schools last June. This senior class garnered 172 college scholarships worth about $270,000. Eight seniors received appointments to West Point, Annapolis, the Air Force Academy and the Coast Guard Academy.

The scholarships were to such representative institutions as University of Virginia, University of Chicago, Brown, Duke, Dartmouth, Oberlin, Cornell, Princeton, Stanford, California Institute of Technology, Yale, University of Wisconsin, University of Pennsylvania, Carnegie Tech, Massachusetts Institute of Technology, Vanderbilt, Harvard.

The Director of Admissions at Massachusetts Institute of Technology recently wrote the principal of our Washington-Lee High School:

"I have reviewed the record of Washington-Lee High School students. Since 1941, 17 students have entered M.I.T. from Washington-Lee, and their aggregate record is an excellent one. Of the 7 who have been here long enough to graduate, 6 have actually graduated and 2 have, in addition, received masters' degrees."

Reports the Office of Admissions, California Institute of Technology:

W-L students have made the highest grades after entrance of any secondary-school youngsters enrolled.

The records of Arlington public-high-school graduates in these notoriously tough institutions are eloquent—particularly in light of the common charge that public-school youngsters are ill-trained in math and science.

Perhaps the most significant evidence, however, is revealed in results of College Board examinations. The purpose of these tests, given by a large group of colleges, is to test the applicant's intellect. As the College Board says, the only preparation for its Scholastic Aptitude Test is "a lifetime of intellectual challenge." Achievement tests, says the board, are based on knowledge of facts plus the ability to reason with them.

College Board scores run from 200 to 800. The bulk of the youngsters who take the tests are public-school pupils. However, the percentage of all public-school enrollees who elect to take College Boards is smaller than the percentage of all private-school enrollees who elect to take them. That's mainly because lack of money keeps a lot of public-school kids from planning on college.

Here are the most recently tabulated complete results of College Board scores. The figures, noting the comparative grades of public-school and private-school boys and girls, average the work of some 45,000 students.

|  | Public | Private |
|---|---|---|
| Scholastic Aptitude Test (Verbal) | 484 | 482 |
| Scholastic Aptitude Test (Mathematical) | 514 | 492 |
| English composition | 521 | 523 |
| Achievement Tests |  |  |
| Social studies | 525 | 511 |
| French | 506 | 526 |
| German | 509 | 492 |
| Latin | 557 | 530 |
| Spanish | 486 | 500 |
| Biology | 508 | 491 |
| Chemistry | 540 | 522 |
| Physics | 549 | 518 |
| Intermediate Math | 530 | 495 |
| Advanced Math | 582 | 575 |

The public-school youngsters thus outscored the private-school youngsters in both aptitude tests and in all subjects except English composition, French and Spanish.

A general comment from the Director of Admissions of a major Ivy League college is revealing:

"Since 1949 we have had a gradual increase in enrollments from the public schools. This has not been by design, but simply has evolved from the nature of the qualifications of the individuals who have applied and, obviously, from the relative growth in public-school populations.

"We have, however, kept some data on the academic work of the public-school groups and the independent-school groups on succeeding classes with the same results discovered in an earlier study; namely, that on the average, graduates of public schools perform academically better than do the boys from the private schools."

If there is no substance to the generalized charges against the quality of public-school education, how come all this pro-private-school talk?

Let me say again that in some places a particular private school may be noticeably better than the local public school. Some parents feel they are trapped in a desperate situation where reconstruction of the public school is too big a job, and they conclude they should send their children to a private school.

Other parents favor private schools because that has been the family tradition. It is difficult and a bit impertinent to try to psychoanalyze somebody's belief in a given tradition. It may reflect generations of pride in a high-minded way of life. It may reflect a desire to maintain social status and prestige. There are still other parents who prefer that their children be in a more select or refined environment.

Private schools all cost money. They all cost more than public school, and some cost a whale of a lot more. For most American families, a private boarding school is prohibitively expensive, and even the cost of most private day schools comes high. This means that private schools are required to take only the sons and daughters of families who can afford to pay the price. The few scholarship students in private schools hardly dilute the attendance. Enrollees in most private schools are silver-spoon kids.

The heads of the better, highly responsible private schools deplore this fact. They would like to select, solely on merit, those youngsters who are fit for the superior education they wish to give. But they still must run their schools on a price basis. The second- and third-rate private schools operate without qualms on a price basis.

The last place in the world I want my children is in an institution where membership depends on a comfortable thickness in papa's wallet—where the principal requirements for getting along are the expensive car and the expensive wardrobe.

I hate to see so much money and effort drained into private schools. And it isn't only the direct drain of money. Private schools have another debilitating and even dangerous effect on the public schools. When a parent pays a special tab for a private-school education, he usually is not too willing to vote for higher taxes to support public schools in which he has no personal interest.

I do not question anyone's right to maintain or support a private school, but I do say that support of public education is a basic obligation of citizenship. I cannot shake the conviction that private schools in twentieth-century America may be an anachronism.

The link between private school and parents is usually weaker than the ink between public school and parents. The private school represents a service that is bought; the public school is a community institution which the citizens support and can control. This intimacy of relationship among home, community and public schools—which accounts for P.T.A.'s and all the other apparatus of co-operation—is extremely desirable, it seems to me. After all, the child at home, the child in the neighborhood and the child at school are all the same child, one and indivisible.

My wife and I think our children deserve whatever time and effort we can contribute to the schools, and we have learned that the schools are grateful for the contribution. This contention that the "school people" want to "take over" and don't want any "interference" from the parents is quite ungrounded, at least in our schools in Arlington.

Some years ago I happened to ask our principal why she thought narrative report cards were superior to the ABC cards; this was just an inquiry— I was curious. The following year she asked me to be chairman of a study group on report cards. This was a local school group composed of a dozen parents, of various points of view. We hashed it out and wrote a report. The next year I was asked to be chairman of a similar county-wide committee. This group subsequently made a report to the school board recommending certain changes. The changes were made. I cite this as ordinary procedure in Arlington.

The school board appoints advisory committees of parents for each school and names advisory councils in such areas as libraries, personnel policies, textbooks, art and home economics. Some 400 Arlington parents serve on these bodies. They are another reason why we have good, strong schools here.

Those of us who do take part in these activities are not professional educators or professional busybodies. We believe that a little constructive participation in school matters is less wearing and more useful than grousing or throwing stones from the side lines.

Yes, our children are where we want them—in our local public schools. My wife and I have heard all the criticisms; we have investigated and have found them basically without truth. We know the Arlington public schools are excellent, and we have no reason to indict the public schools of a great many thousand other communities.

What is it that a parent wants for his children? For Herb and Carolyn I think what I want most is that they will learn to think, and to think responsibly. I want them to have a chance to develop all the ability they may possess. But as they learn to think with their heads, I want their feet to be planted solidly on the common ground which nurtures all of us. I want them within, not above or alongside, the course of events.

I want them to have a fair and equal start, but no head start prearranged for them by their parents. Like every other parent, I think my children are smarter and nicer than many other children, but to make an important distinction, I don't think they are any better. I want them to learn—and they will learn in the microcosm which is the public school—that this is a world full of good and evil, of energy and slothfulness, of greed and honesty. I want them to understand that there is no necessary correlation between virtue and money, between decency and the circumstances of birth I want them to mix, as they do, with the children of the Ph.D., the iron-worker, the man who runs the grocery. I want them to learn to achieve and also to be tolerant and humble.

I want my children in no hothouse, no headmaster's private preserve, no snob factory. If they want to go to an elevated private college later on that's fine. By that time they will be proof against being made prigs or jerks I will keep my children in public school, and will continue to stew around, along with my neighbors, to make those schools the best possible. "The common school," said Horace Mann, "is the greatest discovery ever made." He was right.

# "Mediocrity" in Our Schools*

EDITOR'S NOTE: *Ever since the end of World War II, as readers of SR's Annual Accent on Education issues have frequently been reminded, the schools have become one of the most keenly fought-over battlegrounds in American life. In P-T-A meetings, in magazine articles, in books the question is raised and debated: Are our children being properly taught? One recent and widely read book that addresses itself to this question in spirited and partisan fashion is "The Diminished Mind" (Henry Regnery), by Mortimer Smith, a retired Connecticut businessman.*

## THE BOOK

Mr. Smith's "The Diminished Mind" is subtitled "A Study of Planned Mediocrity in Our Public Schools," and its thesis is that the country's schools are stifling the development of the student as an individual and that, instead, they are concentrating on his development as an unthinking member of a group. The educators, according to Mr. Smith, insist that they are trying to teach modern children to cope with real life and to grow thereby. But, asks Mr. Smith, "Growth toward what?" and it is with this question that his book is chiefly concerned. "I think," he says, making liberal use of italics, "the *primary* function of the *school is to transmit the intellectual and cultural heritage and knowledge of the race, and in the process to teach young people to think and to buttress moral values.*" But, unfortunately, according to Mr. Smith, things are not going this way. He argues that, though "the personal pronouncements of leading educators and the ukases of their professional associations pay lip service to formal knowledge

* Reprinted by permission from *Saturday Review,* June 25, 1955.

and the cultural tradition . . . their *practice* shows that this has been pushed to the periphery of educational aims while they are busy devising courses in trade skills, personal grooming, smoke abatement, and social adjustment." These new courses, he says, cannot take the place of intellectual and moral training.

Today, according to Mr. Smith, there are two fashionable theories of the purposes of education. One of these is known as the Life Adjustment movement; the other is known as the Social Reconstruction movement. Both, according to Mr. Smith, are bad. To advocates of the Life Adjustment movement, says Mr. Smith, the country's students are divided into three groups. The first of these groups consists of that 20 per cent who are mentally capable of meeting the requirements of college preparatory courses; the second consists of another 20 per cent who are able mentally to meet only the educational requirements of preparing for a vocation; and the third group consists of the remaining (and the largest) 60 per cent who, according to the Life Adjustment educators, are incapable of either of their fellow students' achievements. It is on this third group that the Life Adjustment movement, according to Mr. Smith, has focused all its educational philosophy. "The advocates of Life Adjustment," says Mr. Smith, "believe that . . . the best that can be done (with this 60 per cent) is to adjust them to their environments"—environments which, again according to Mr. Smith, are tending to be lowered more and more by the replacement of such basic subjects as reading, writing, and arithmetic with such ridiculous new (but supposedly practical) courses as "How to Have a Successful Date" and "A Group Study of the Cost of Corsages." Now unhappily, says Mr. Smith, this educational philosophy is coming into favor for all pupils, not just for those in the lower 60 per cent group. The brighter students have been forced to conform to the mass pattern and they have been denied the opportunity of learning to make their individual moral and ethical and intellectual judgments. Instead, the primary aim of each individual student has tended to be one of trying to adjust to the group. More unhappily, the colleges are beginning to sanction such an educational philosophy: in one state, according to Mr. Smith, 121 high schools and thirty-eight colleges have signed an agreement by which the colleges will "disregard the pattern of subjects of high-school graduates who are recommended for college entrance."

Though the purposes of the Life Adjustment movement are bad, those of the Social Reconstruction movement are even worse, according to Mr. Smith. The philosophy of this latter group—a group which Mr. Smith claims is still active though small in numbers—is based on an attempt to establish a "collectivist society" whose education would be molded by what the majority of people think it should be. In reality, Mr. Smith says, this works out to an education molded on what the majority of the advocates of Social Reconstruction want. As an extreme example of the ends to which this educational philosophy has gone, Mr. Smith cites the case of

students who were given an examination in which they were marked down
as "illiberals" if they denied that certain statements in the examination were
true. Among the statements:
  "What this country needs is more TVA's."
  "Income taxes on the rich should be greatly increased."
  "If European countries want to establish left-wing governments . . . we
should support them."
  Of such educational philosophies, Mr. Smith asks, "Are they democratic?" His answer: No. And he adds, the educators have got a stranglehold
on American education—a stranglehold which has become so well organized that it can defame its critics as reactionaries or even Communists
through the American press.
  "The American public-school education," says Mr. Smith, in summing up,
"will throw off the incubus of these two false philosophies by restoring the
centrality of the individual in education. We must adopt again the idea that
the purpose of education is the improvement of the individual and when
we achieve this we can be assured that the quality of the group (in which
the advocates of these two movements are so interested that they tend to
exclude the individual) will rise and society will be sounder."

## PRO

*Arthur E. Bestor*

  The time has certainly come for a fresh and disinterested appraisal by
the public at large of American educational policy. During the past quarter
century the schools have experienced the effects of depression, conscription,
inflation, and cold war. They have faced rapidly expanding enrolment and
major shifts of population. They have had to feel their way through a
storm of conflicting ideologies: individualism *vs.* collectivism, pragmatism
*vs.* neo-Thomism, isolationism *vs.* internationalism, and the rest. American
educators have dealt with these problems and issues in a frankly empirical
spirit. The American people have been willing that they should and have
postponed the embarrassing questions about ultimate purposes and long-
term consequences.
  These questions, however, cannot permanently remain unasked. There
is no such thing as experimentation unless there is some final evaluation
of results. And evaluation is impossible unless we know clearly what our
purposes are and ought to be. To define the purposes of public education
is a public responsibility. It cannot be delegated to professional "experts" if
the public schools are to remain under effective public control.
  Mr. Smith is asking no return to the past, but he is demanding a school
system that will face the intellectual problems of modern life instead of
retreating from them into the infantilism of "Life Adjustment education."

He rejects such programs as the latter not because they are "practical," but because they are the opposite. As he shrewdly observes, "A school program which teaches little beyond how to fix a fuse, drive a car, set the dinner table, and enhance your personal appearance *isn't useful enough* if your aim is the development of maturity and citizenship." (Italics mine.)

In his sober and thoughtful book Mortimer Smith recognizes, of course, that modifications of the curriculum must be made for the slow learner, but he insists "the revision needs to be in the direction of discovering new and better methods and techniques for reaching this group with the values of the cultural heritage." Any alternative plan, Mr. Smith points out, is at bottom anti-democratic. To shove the slow learner "into a variety of non-academic courses devoid of real content" is to treat him "as a second-class citizen of the educational world," doomed for the rest of his life "to intellectual and cultural subservience." He reminds us that the safety of society as a whole is involved: "If we expect the boy with an I.Q. of 90 to become a citizen and make the judgments required of a citizen we ought to be busy devising ways of making him understand the ideas which have shaped his country and world and we ought to be teaching him how to 'communicate' intelligibly."

That Mr. Smith is almost certain to be venomously denounced as an "enemy" of the public schools by certain professional educationists is sad but true. The concluding chapters of his book discuss the obstacles that lie in the path of educational reform. Greatest of these, in Mr. Smith's opinion —an opinion with which I concur—is the virtually uncontrolled power that professors of education exercise, in direct and indirect ways, over the nominally public educational system. That the inertia of such a great vested interest should stand in the way of educational improvement is natural enough. A sinister development of recent years is the ruthless use of this power to stifle criticism, to vilify critics, and to discredit any citizens' group that might take an independent position on school matters. The evidence of this is marshaled by Mr. Smith in a chapter entitled "Putting Parents in Their Place." It is one of the most impressive as well as one of the most frightening sections of the book.

# CON

*William Clark Trow*

This little book is another one of those attacks on the public-school program by its literary-minded critics. Even those who are inclined to share the author's point of view will no doubt regret that his exposé adds little to what has gone before. Nor will careful readers be misled by the jacket-blurb writer into thinking that the book is "closely reasoned and well-documented."

If they do not read too hastily they will recognize the familiar campaign oratory, the exaggeration and distortion, of which the book is as full as a museum. Mr. Smith slides from *some* to *all* with the greatest of ease, attempts to make the unusual seem typical, misinterprets quotations and makes the worse appear the better reason if it gives support to his own view. He also enjoys playing with the two favorite animals of the literary critics: the scapegoat and the *bête noir*.

The scapegoat is the educational profession, on which he unloads a pitiful burden of acrimonious vituperation. And as an educational philosophe Mr. Smith's views are somewhat naive. He describes himself as a "traditional humanist," presumably because he favors "disciplined knowledge" (*sic*) and also "the discipline of the exposure to the cultural heritage." He gives no criteria for selection from this culture and to Spencer's famous question "What knowledge is of most worth?" his easy answer, for stupid as well as bright pupils, is "real education . . . especially English and History."

The *bête noir* is the "Life Adjustment program," which, whatever its excesses, can hardly be accused of teaching any more useless information per school day than is to be found in the traditional curriculum. The British philosopher and mathematician Alfred North Whitehead expressed the concern of many when he wrote in "The Aims of Education and Other Essays": "There is only one subject-matter for education, and that is Life in all its manifestations. Instead of this single unity, we offer children— Algebra, from which nothing follows; Geometry, from which nothing follows; a couple of Languages, never mastered; and lastly, most dreary of all Literature, represented by plays of Shakespeare, with philological notes and short analyses of plot and character to be in substance committed to memory. Can such a list be said to represent Life, as it is known in the midst of the living of it?" The effort of those to whom has been assigned the responsibility for running our schools is not resulting in a decrease but in an increase in the volume of pupil learning, Mr. Smith to the contrary notwithstanding. They are gradually succeeding in making the content less esoteric, more meaningful, and more visibly related to actual living. They are not "anti-intellectualistic." They recognize other values too, which they are striving to incorporate in the school program in order to develop the good individual in the good society.

If anyone is going to "deal a body blow to the stranglehold of the educationists," as Mr. Smith recommends, let us hope it will be dealt by someone who spends less time hunting through educational writings for statements that support his position and more in exploring the findings of research in education, mental hygiene, child development, and social psychology from all of which stem many of the changes Mr. Smith so bitterly deplores

# The Fate of Pedagoguese*

Quackery in the Public Schools, *by Albert Lynd (Little, Brown)*, Educational Wastelands: The Retreat from Learning in Our Public Schools, *by Arthur E. Bestor (University of Illinois Press)*, *and* Let's Talk Sense About Our Schools, *by Paul Woodring (McGraw-Hill)*, *take three differing positions on one of the subjects Americans are now heatedly debating: their public schools. The books and the implications of their arguments are discussed below.*

*Fred M. Hechinger*

Never has so much been written about education by so many within so brief a period as this fall. One educator, who did not look kindly on this number of new books, recently called it an "epidemic." I'd rather think of it as a harvest, and though all the fruit may not be perfect, it should be welcome. For the first time in a long while serious thought is being given to the *content* of public education, not just to buildings, salaries, and tax elections. This is progress. It may signal the end of one phase and the beginning of another, and since none of the books recently published advocate less public education, or less money spent for it, it would appear that the basic battle has been won. Now that we seem agreed that we want public education, and ought to pay for it, there is nothing wrong with a critical, hard-hitting discussion of what we want the schools to teach.

Albert Lynd, author of "Quackery in the Public Schools," one of the three major works published this fall, used to teach history in college. He is now a businessman. He is a member of the school board in Sharon, Mass., believes in the public schools, thinks public education ought to have much better financial support, and is sure that the teachers' colleges and professors of education are ruining the schools. Mr. Lynd is alarmed, and he registers his alarm sometimes brilliantly, sometimes amusingly, and always with the kind of overstatement which will delight or outrage the reader, depending which side of the fence he is on.

Arthur E. Bestor, who is professor of history at the University of Illinois, shares Mr. Lynd's alarm. Like Mr. Lynd, he is against the domination by pedagogy over education. Pedagogy, he writes in "Educational Wastelands: The Retreat from Learning in Our Public Schools," "tells *how* something can be taught most effectively, but it provides no basis whatever for deciding *what* should be taught." He objects to specialists in pedagogy making the decisions on what is to be the content of public-school instruction.

Finally, there is Paul Woodring, who taught in many places, including

---

* Reprinted by permission from *Saturday Review,* December 12, 1953.

high schools, and is now professor of psychology at Western Washington College of Education. In "Let's Talk Sense About Our Schools" he makes it clear that he would agree with many of the complaints registered by Messrs. Lynd and Bestor; and yet, I believe, he would disagree with their books largely because they overstate and oversimplify. Using the title of his own book, he might even say something about talking sense about our schools.

The extremists, writes Mr. Woodring in his concluding chapter, have a very real advantage. They have either their backs or their faces to the wall, and so they can be attacked only from one direction. The moderates, on the other hand, stand right out in the exposed center and are therefore vulnerable from all angles. To make things worse, moderate books on controversial issues—books which don't say that what they oppose is all black and what they propose is all white—don't sell very well. Therefore they don't publish very well. And consequently not many writers spend much time over moderate books. "But it so happens," Mr. Woodring observes, "that some things *are* middling gray. One of these things is public education in the United States as of 1953."

It might have helped things all around if Mr. Lynd and Mr. Bestor had had a chance to read Mr. Woodring's book before they respectively got down to writing their own volumes. For while the three authors are critical of many of the same aspects of modern education, Mr. Woodring seems to be the only one who knows how to consider the relationship between cause and effect, and how to look at the world in perspective.

"The best thing about contemporary education," says Mr. Woodring, "is that a great many classroom teachers ignore the gobbledygook and the pedagoguese and go right ahead and do a sensible job of teaching. If one visits the classrooms instead of reading the journals he may well conclude that the schools are not so bad after all. It depends on which classroom you visit; but I for one, if I again had to face the prospect of twelve years as a pupil in a public school, would far rather take my chances in a school of today than return to the schools I attended between 1913 and 1925."

Neither Mr. Lynd nor Mr. Bestor seems to accept this view. They would say, indeed they do say in their books, that it is not good enough for the schools to claim they are doing a somewhat better job than the schools of twenty years ago. With the greater amount of time and money (though the latter is, at least in proportion, debatable) spent on the schools they ought to be doing a far better job.

Where is the problem and the real disagreement? Messrs. Lynd and Bestor tried to pinpoint the blame for everything that seems wrong with public education today, and in pinpointing they picked the teachers colleges as their target. There is a measure of truth in Mr. Lynd's amusing, sharp satire of the super-administrators, the group dynamicians (if I may coin a new word that is only slightly more absurd than many of the ones now in use), and the miserable jargon. He is justly scornful of a teachers college ourse on "urban cities." He detests, with good reason, the bargain basement collection of courses and sub-courses in methodology. There is probably no good excuse for a master's thesis on "The Effects of Coaching on the Acquisition of Skill in Baseball Free Throw," though I am sure that a pretty devastating list of topics could be assembled from the files of the academic departments of the universities, too. (In all fairness, furthermore, it should be added that this gem of an example originated not at a teachers college, but at the University of Wisconsin. But that may be quibbling and, anyway, I am not a teachers college man myself and need not be partisan in either attack or defense.)

There is also just cause for the complaint, contained in all three books, that too much stress on methods and the omission of real knowledge of subject matter are both an indication of shallowness and a boost to the trend of anti-intellectualism. It is quite right to say—as do our authors—that pragmatism, the philosophy made noted and notable by John Dewey, is a dangerous idea in education because it sticks too closely to "what is" and threatens to ignore "what should or might be." (Dewey himself would not have accepted pragmatism as the philosophy of things as they are. He was too deeply interested in social reform—so deeply that Mr. Lynd, who emphatically clears him of any Communist charges, still considers him a Socialist. But he would have insisted that theories are not much good unless they can be made to work, and this is a point of view not entirely alien to the American industrialist and businessman.) It is certainly fair to say that our schools and our colleges—teachers colleges as well as liberal arts institutions and, especially, the great universities—have offered too varied, too scattered, too confusing a diet. Since many teachers have grown up on that diet, their intellectual constitution may be found wanting. The worst of them may actually suffer from malnutrition.

But the real error of these critical views is their insinuation that pragmatism was foisted on the American people by the educationists. This is historically nonsense. America was a pragmatic, anti-intellectual country by virtue of its pioneering, frontier background—long before the first teachers college exerted its influence. When the public high schools began to drop the "academic subjects"—Latin, foreign languages, etc.—the pressure to do so had usually been exerted by the "practical" men on the school boards, not by educators. Those were the days when businessmen attacked as "frills" not the modern subjects which are today associated with progressive education, but rather "all that useless stuff" which is generally known as the humanities. This does not clear the educators of all blame. But the most serious charge that can be brought against them is that, instead of exerting educational leadership, they followed too closely the climate of public opinion.

These are some of the charges. All of them have some basis in some facts. But they are stated in absolutes and sound as uncompromising and self-righteous as they claim to have found their opponents. And that, while it may be a good way of starting a revolution, is hardly a useful approach to improving a system.

"The most far-reaching changes which have occurred on the educational scene in recent decades are ones which cannot be attributed to Dewey or to the progressive movement," writes Mr. Woodring. "The most important of all changes has been the extension of universal education upward through the high school." This is unquestionably the key to almost everything that has happened—good and bad. To pretend that it has not made any difference, or ought not to make any, is absurd. Messrs. Lynd and Bestor keep insisting that any lowering of standards for the great mass of pupils reflects an undemocratic or even antidemocratic attitude on the part of the public schools. It is true that the schools may at times be underestimating the intellectual capacity of some pupils; but it is unrealistic to say that a highly academic program in the classical tradition of the selective old academies could or should be absorbed by all children.

As for the teachers, while there is good reason to complain that many of them are insufficiently educated and that the teachers colleges are overdoing the "technique" courses, nobody ought to overlook the fact that practically every teachers college graduate is better trained and better educated (there *is* a difference!) than every former normal school graduate. I would be the first to admit that the great deficiency in the education of many teachers is the solid liberal arts foundation which many teachers colleges have slighted. But to look at the problem in perspective it should be remembered that originally the liberal arts colleges looked down on teacher training and failed to include in their curriculum the kind of method courses which all but the rare "natural teacher" need. (There aren't enough "natural teachers" to go around, and so some of the less naturally qualified must be given help and shown shortcuts.) It is all right to say rhetorically that Socrates needed no teachers college. One might add that a great many lesser disciples became acceptable teachers because they studied the methods handed down by Socrates.

What will eventually save the day, I believe, is the increasing "infiltration" by the liberal arts into the teachers college curriculum and of good and essential education courses into the liberal arts colleges. This has been happening for a number of years, and though it may not have been a sufficiently rapid and thorough trend, it is not wise to overlook it. It is always useful to set up a straw man and knock him down if you want to make a very complete and radical point; but it is not a very constructive procedure. That it was the procedure often adopted by the lesser "progressives" (their straw man being the "traditional" school) does not make it either wise or helpful for the leaders of the counter-movement to be equally misguided and misleading.

But, even at the risk of being accused of the straw-man technique myself, it seems necessary to recall that the "old" school was much worse than most critics of the new school are willing to admit or capable of remembering. Curriculum and methods were not even very suitable for the selected group of pupils who then went to high school; they would have been disastrous had they been applied to the great mass of pupils (who did not then go to high school at all). There were, of course, good teachers who were immune to the absurdities of the "old" school just as there are today good teachers who have benefited from the liberalization without succumbing to the follies of the "new" school.

One of the errors of the critics—and it should be said that Mr. Bestor recognizes that error and writes very effectively about this problem—is that they often overlook the difference between elementary and secondary school. It is absurd to argue that the application of a wealth of new psychological knowledge to the teaching of the elementary grades has not been beneficial. It has without question been the most startling step forward that education has taken in this century. Contrary to Mr. Lynd's observation, this has been a development which has profoundly influenced teaching far beyond the borders of the United States. It is today a world trend, not an American experiment, and it is not considered nearly as controversial in other countries as it is here.

The real problem is to realize that the purposes of elementary school and of high school are quite different. "The procedures that will kindle interest in the elementary school will not do so in the high school," Mr. Bestor writes quite rightly. "They may even destroy interest, for nothing is more repellent to the youthful mind than something he considers childish. . . . Experts in pedagogy, however, seem blithely unaware of their ignorance concerning the higher stages of the learning process." This is a valid charge, and the sooner corrections are made the better. But improvement is not going to come from a blanket attack on new methods and on the new school.

It will do no good to pinpoint the attack on any one source of the schools' shortcomings. Mr. Lynd quite rightly points out that many of the ills of our present education system could be remedied by adequate financial support of the schools and of the teachers. Many of the worst outrages in the training colleges would disappear if only more intelligent young people were to enroll. The ridiculous, time-wasting course would simply go unattended and would soon be dropped. This is important. And the criticism of bad teaching in some teachers colleges is important. So is the strait-jacket confinement by some of the most rigid accreditation rules. Nor should we overlook the "alumni" pressure to spend so many hours on varsity athletics, or on "driver" education, or on any other pastime or subject which this reader, that writer, or some citizen happens to think are a waste of time. This list could be continued for quite a few pages, and if the schools are to be improved a long list of shortcomings ought to be considered. Such criticism is constructive. But to blame everything on one cause is misleading and not very helpful.

Mr. Bestor writes some very important words: "Genuine liberal education is not a course in first aid. It is a serious effort to train men to recognize symptoms, to trace them to fundamental causes, and to deal intelligently with the latter." This is an excellent definition (though its author does not always trace the schools' shortcomings to their fundamental causes). When Mr. Bestor looks for a remedy he asks for the establishment of a permanent "federation of the learned society" and a "Permanent Scientific and Scholarly Commission on Secondary Education" which would deliberately exclude from membership the educational associations and the "professional educationists." Then there would, in addition, be a third group of organized laymen.

The danger of this kind of "remedy" is obvious. I admit that the exclusiveness of some of the educationist groups is harmful to education; but I also recognize that their present exclusiveness is the result of past exclusion—of being snubbed by the academic world and of not being accepted by the universities. If there is educationist isolation today, it is not voluntary but enforced by the events of yesterday. Moreover, in many important places across the country the isolation has begun to wear thin. Many teachers colleges have accepted more and more liberal arts content as part of their curriculum.

Setting up more rival professional groups with closed-membership rules, such as Mr. Bestor recommends, would signify a relapse into isolation. It would not, I believe, lead to the kind of give-and-take collective bargaining that Mr. Bestor seems to expect to take place between these groups and associations. (Even if it did I am not convinced that this is the way to arrive at educational policy, not to mention philosophy.) It would be far more likely to lead to the permanent splitting up into hostile camps, sniping at each other instead of working together to improve education.

There are no final solutions in sight—in education as little as elsewhere. There can only be good trends and harmful currents. There can be no absolute, monolithic answer to "what is needed." To say that *only* the liberal arts, *only* the humanities, *only* the teaching of the academicians can offer salvation is as misleading as to claim that *only* vocational training or *only* the catering to "present needs" can lead us ahead. That there should be argument—heated, sometimes angry and shrill argument—between the many "schools" of education is inevitable, welcome, and essential. The clashes will lead to compromise. Compromise will show the way to better, more reasonable ways of teaching.

# The Deeper Problem in Education*

## It Is to Dig Out Educationists' Debris and Rediscover Learning's True Nature

It is still a shock to realize the penalties a good teacher must pay, just to do his country's most important job. . . . We must do something quickly about improving teachers' salaries, training and status. But teachers and the public must also get together on a problem less tangible but more basic—how to straighten out the debris left by 40 years of the progressive educationists. It is a legacy of distended play facilities, substandard curricula and principals whose intellectual confusion can no longer be disguised by the compulsory smile on their faces.

American schools have done a tremendous job in educating people at a rate beyond the dreams of most nations. Such a quantitative achievement was bound to hit some snags on the quality side. And it serves no purpose to polarize the educational debate by shouting "un-American" at the late John Dewey's bones (a distinctive Americanism, in fact, was one of Dewey's intellectual boasts), or by making blanket denunciations of "frills" in education (if How to Run a Beauty Shop has no place in a general high school curriculum, a good challenging music appreciation course very definitely *has*). The problem underlying all our confusion is—to use words long out of favor in pedagogical circles—a matter of tradition and philosophy. Only by grasping this can we figure out where and how our education system went wrong.

Until the arrival of Dewey and his disciples, American schools had the stated objective of educating individuals in an inherited and enlarging body of learning. Confident of their own established values in ethics, law and culture, the old-fashioned teachers deliberately set out to pass down these values as part of a living tradition. They held that it was all one cultural heritage—everything from Boyle's Law to Cicero's First Oration against Catiline—and the more of it you learned the wiser and more mentally alert you would be.

Dewey and his disciples revolted against this certitude, which had indeed grown more than a little ossified in its teaching methods. But history records no more egregious case of throwing out the baby with the bath. Instead of modernizing the oldtimers' teaching methods, the new educationists went deeper and denied tradition in anything.

"We agree," Dewey once said, "that we are uncertain as to where we

---

* Reprinted by permission from *Life* magazine, March 31, 1958. Copyright 1958 Time, Inc.

are going and where we want to go, and why we are doing what we do."
In a kind of country club existentialism, Dewey and his boys genially contended that the traditional ends of education—and indeed of human life—
like God, virtue and the idea of "culture" were all debatable and hence
not worth debating. In their place: enter life adjustment. The alternative
to educating the individual thus became, as John Keats puts it in his
excellent new book, *Schools without Scholars,* "to bring the individual by
a process of conditioning, to a realization of his functional role in society."

The Deweyites thus transformed conditioning techniques into ends in
themselves. As they tracked through U. S. education, teachers' colleges
assumed the dignity of lamaseries. They called their system science, but
they worshiped its doctrines like a cult. In thousands of schools teachers
were denied the chance of learning more about their subjects in favor of
compulsory education courses in how to teach them.

Within the schools discipline gave way to increasingly dubious forms of
group persuasion. "With teen-agers," one high school principal said
proudly, "there is nothing more powerful than the approval or disapproval
of the group. . . . When the majority conforms, the others will go along."
It would not easily occur to the modern educationists that such blind
fostering of group pressure is a travesty of free democracy. Such criticism
honestly puzzles them, as do suggestions that they might concentrate more
on dry "learning" subjects, like mathematics and languages, to the exclusion of teen-age problems, beauty care, flycasting. But they try to "understand" their critics, for "understanding" is part of the progressive code—
a recently popular educational tract is titled *Helping Teachers Understand
Principals.*

By their own trusted empirical test, the poor performance of their students has proved the educationists wrong. U. S. high school students are
plain ignorant of things grammar school students would have known a
generation ago. Years of barren discussion courses in English have made
a whole generation chronically incoherent in the English language (the
mutterings of a U. S. teen-ager trying to discuss his beliefs generally sound
like a sanitized version of Elvis Presley). By substituting "projects" for
study, the educationists have soothed students' curiosity, but left them with
little intellectual patience for solving problems. Cut off from any but the
most obvious contact with his tradition, *e.g.,* an occasional project visit to
the local courthouse, the student has lost his sense of history, at a time
when his country needs this most. Surely the history of the Crusades can
give a young American a better grasp of the problems implicit in the U. N.
or NATO than dressing up as a Pakistani delegate in an imitation U. N.
assembly at school.

With Dewey's world so demonstrably in tatters, one might think the
educationists would run up the white flag. Far from it. Entrenched in public
school administrations, they defend with the adhesiveness of a band of
brothers every article of their gobbledygook canons. In Holland, Mich. the

Christian High School, a respected institution of impeccable academic standards, has recently been denied accreditation by the North Central Association of Colleges and Secondary Schools because it refused to dilute its academic standards with shop and cooking courses. A sample of the canons by which such schools are judged: "Is the control and atmosphere of the individual's rooms and classes based upon teacher authority or group self-control and group defined standards . . . ? To what extent are opportunities provided for children to develop moral and spiritual values through the process of direct experience in working with each other . . . ?"

We cannot expect to cure such lopsided standards just by giving teachers the pay they deserve, building the schools we need, and ordering up more science courses. A few important steps *can* be taken by state and local authorities. For one thing, most of our state teachers' colleges should be abolished as such and converted into liberal arts colleges, with subordinate education departments. There must also be some drastic upgrading of curriculum requirements.

But most of all we need to do some thinking about the true ends of education. The worthwhile innovations in method brought by Dewey's educationists should be kept. But their exclusive devotion to techniques and group adjustment should never again be allowed to hide the fact that American education exists first of all to educate the individual in a body of learning, with a tradition and purpose behind it. A man so educated is far better equipped as a democratic citizen than the merely "well adjusted." For he will have not only the social ease to make his civilization comfortable, but the intellectual discipline to help save it.

# John Dewey and the Luce Ends of Education*

*A philosopher of education attempts to distinguish between warranted criticism and accusation designed to bring into being reactionary or authoritarian institutions.*

*Frederick C. Neff*

Public education, like every other institution that is public, needs critics. Thoughtful reaction to public policy is indispensable to the survival of democratic processes. There is a substantial difference, however, between warranted criticism, formulated for the purpose of strengthening democratic institutions within their own framework, and planned accusation, ostensibly meliorative, but ultimately designed to bring into being reactionary

* Reprinted by permission from *Phi Delta Kappan,* December 1958. Mr. Neff is a professor of education at Rutgers University.

or authoritarian institutions. The American public needs to be cautioned against a failure to distinguish between the two. Current attacks upon public education in which the Luce publications have taken an active part are especially in need of discriminating review.

In a hard-breathing editorial, *Life* magazine recently exercised its generous capacity for indignation by reviling John Dewey, state teachers colleges, and public education in general. Dewey is criticized, first, because he saw a characteristic precariousness in life and universal processes and because he failed to proclaim absolute certainty where he found none to exist. Apparently overlooked was the fact that the cultivation of doubt and the exercise of inquiry have usually typified the great minds of history, while unexamined belief and passive orthodoxy have for the most part characterized the reactionary and the ignorant. "The trouble with the world today," says Bertrand Russell, "is that the stupid are cocksure, while the intelligent are full of doubts." Even *Time* magazine, in another connection, describes with apparent approval the Harvard conception of what education should consist of: "a progression from cocksure ignorance to—at least—thoughtful uncertainty."

The criticism that Dewey advocated something called "life adjustment" and an implied "group pressure" is especially revealing, for it plainly indicates either a loose-ended reading of Dewey or simply a state of being misinformed. Dewey has said that if unqualified adjustment were all that was needed, it could best be achieved by going to sleep or by dying, and that complete adaptation to the environment was equivalent to death. Regarding the matter of conformity to "group pressure," Dewey in fact urged more than anyone else an attention to, in his words, "the *diversity* of capacities and needs that exist in different human beings," and he criticized traditional education for assuming that "all human beings are as much alike as peas in a pod."

Dewey is derided for advocating aimlessness in education. What he actually said was that "acting with an aim is all one with acting intelligently." Whereas it is claimed that Dewey de-emphasized subject matter, he in fact said that "What is needed in the new education is more attention, not less, to subject-matter and to progress in technique. But when I say more, I do not mean more in quantity of the same old kind."

In respect to the Luce proposal that most state teachers colleges be abolished, it requires no philosophical depth to detect the innuendo that schools and colleges of education in general and, indeed, such courses as are designed to prepare young people for the profession of teaching should likewise be abolished. Let us consider for a moment what state of affairs would result from such a move.

Teacher-training institutions have been designed primarily to elevate teaching to the status of a profession by equipping their graduates with a competence in understanding the nature of the learning process, in dealing with the philosophical alternatives that confront the educational enterprise, in recognizing the human differences that make each individual unique, in devising ways of administering to the distinctive capacities of learners, in preventing the pitiful phenomenon of "square pegs in round holes," in planning learning experiences so as best to implement the democratic ideal that an individual is an end in himself and not a mere instrument of institutions and ideologies—in short, they have been designed to make of education a respectable and humane profession.

What is the alternative? It is to presume that a method of teaching and a philosophy of education are of no particular consequence; that "if he knows he can teach"; that knowledge is something that a teacher "shoots" at pupils like buckshot in the hope that some of them will "get hit"; that a teacher can be indifferent to the varying needs and capacities of learners and, when problems arise, take refuge behind a textbook—in short, it is to degrade education from the level of a profession to that of a series of menial chores, a matter of parceling out bits of information, with little or no concern for the development of attitudes and ideals whereby life is endowed with purpose and meaning.

## While We're at It, Some Other Victims

While we are about it, why not urge the abolition of our law and medical schools? Why not hold that the prospective lawyer needs no particular training in arguing a case, no special knowledge of legal processes? Why not turn him loose with nothing more than a set of books and some memorized cases and let him sink or swim? He may have to repeat all the mistakes that his predecessors have made, it may take him a lifetime to do it, his clients may suffer accordingly, and he may never succeed in earning a living—but at least he will have been spared the nuisance of mastering the techniques and procedures of his profession.

Why not present the prospective physician or surgeon with a series of liberal-arts courses in the history of medical lore and forego training him in the techniques of how to make an adequate diagnosis, how to administer an anaesthetic, or how to perform a successful operation? No sane person would seriously consider permitting a medical man to practice without a license or to engage in his profession without a mastery of whatever techniques are necessary for the successful performance of his professional duties. Yet, if teacher-training institutions and, by implication, teaching certification are to be abolished, then any housewife, truck driver, or degreeholder who has accumulated an arbitrary number of "subject-matter credits" would be permitted to practice in our schools, regardless of whatever harm might come to youngsters from his teaching ineptness. It seems just a bit odd that such a proposal in law or medicine would be laughed out of court, while an analogous proposal in education can receive so serious a hearing.

## YOUNG MINDS AND BROKEN LEGS

We are led to believe that thorough training in the practice of law and medicine is quite essential, but that thorough preparation in how to educate is not very important—in fact, might even be abolished. The way that we treat impressionable young minds in the process of education is apparently less consequential than the way that we win cases or set broken legs. In view of the hard fact of human differences, can we seriously pretend that knowledge of the Pythagorean theorem or of the Latin gerund—important as it may be for other reasons—can be substituted for a teacher's competence in distinguishing the gifted from the retarded, the mechanical-minded from the academic-minded, the disturbed from the well-adjusted—and in meeting their respective needs? So long as our schools remain public they will continue to remain diverse—as diverse as the needs, interests, and capacities of *all* the youngsters of *all* the people. There can be no doubt that teachers should be well grounded in the subjects they teach. But to suggest that subject-matter proficiency replace competence in educational guidance is to deny by indirection the uniqueness of human personality and to breed a deplorable insensitivity to our historic respect for human worth and human dignity.

## GENUINE INTEREST—OR PROPAGANDA

Criticism of public education is salutary as far as it evinces a genuine interest in education as a public concern. But propaganda is something quite different, and it often moves people to act in haste and repent at leisure. Perhaps the time has come for asking ourselves a rather solemn question: Are we able to distinguish constructive criticism—honestly designed to further the hard-won aims of American free, public education—from subtly disguised schemes for undermining America's confidence in the free, public school system and paving the way for an eventual return to the day of the private school, with all the economic, religious, and social divisiveness that it represents? If not, then we may have something to be concerned about.

# Adjustment vs. Knowledge*

*George B. Leonard, Jr.*

* Reprinted by permission from *Look,* June 11, 1957. Copyright 1957 by Cowles Magazines, Inc.

Schools like Birney Elementary in Rivera, Calif., have been under sharp attack for several years. At Birney, as at most American schools, the children are happy, the parents are happy and the teachers are happy. Still, the critics howl and harass.

Who are these critics and what do they want? Some of them feel the schools are trying to accomplish too much—and spend too much money doing it. They complain about handsome new school buildings, argue the uselessness of courses in music and art, band together to oppose each new school-bond issue. When they speak of "frills," they really aren't concerned with the effect so much on the children as on their own pocketbooks. Another group attacks the schools for the same reason it would attack anything or anybody that represents change or liberalism. For hidden psychological reasons which masquerade as political philosophy, the individuals who make up this group prefer the narrow curriculum, the boss-teacher, the hickory stick.

If these two groups made up the total opposition to current American educational practice, The Big School Controversy would be less cloudy and confused than it is. But there is a third group of critics, for the most part men of intelligence and conviction, who believe American education zigged where it should have zagged. Last July, a group of these men— college professors, industrialists, writers—joined together in a Council for Basic Education. To date, they have provided a fairly reasonable, if still vehement, voice of dissent on the educational scene. Council members charge that the professional educators, bewitched by progressive education, have led the schools astray. The basic subjects, the Three R's, are being woefully neglected, say these critics. Teachers are being taught *how* to teach but not *what* to teach. Firm standards of actual accomplishment are lost in a haze of concern for the child's emotional well-being. Poor students are promoted in the name of education for all, thereby creating a situation of real education for none.

Most damning is the charge that today's children mainly are being schooled in "how to"—how to have a successful date, how to get along on the job or with the family, how to drive, how to be attractive, how to be happy. In short, according to the more constructive critics, adjustment to life has replaced the absorption of knowledge as the highest goal of a public-school education. Bearing the first thrust of all the attacks is an organization that this year is celebrating its 100th anniversary. This is the National Education Association, a professional group of teachers and educators, 700,000 strong. It is a sort of fact-finding association, union and lobby, often starry-eyed, but always dedicated to the welfare of the teacher, to freedom of expression in the classroom, to progress and to a democratic education for all. ("It's very difficult," said a critic of the NEA, "to be in conflict with an outfit so allied with sweetness and light.")

At its centennial convention next month, the NEA will be congratulating itself on a century of remarkable and very real accomplishment. It will be pointing out that in our schools we are very near to realizing one of mankind's oldest dreams: universal education. In no European country are more than 15 per cent of the 16-year-olds in school; here, the figure climbs close to 90. Gone is the little red schoolhouse, NEA speakers will say, and likewise the boss-teacher. Today, the best scientific knowledge on child development is being brought to bear in teaching a wide and useful variety of subjects. And while no NEA spokesman is likely to tell you that adjustment to life is more important than the acquisition of basic knowledge, neither is it likely that any will deny the importance of courses which give practical experience in citizenship, group co-operation and just plain human happiness.

For a year and a half, this reporter has been visiting schools throughout the country with no particular ax to grind, no particular point to make. Approaching the current controversy from this position, he found a surprisingly large amount of middle ground. Educators and critics are not so far apart as they think. Here is what the visits showed:

## PROGRESSIVE EXTREMES HAVE BEEN ABANDONED

*Extreme progressive education is a dead duck.* Those who have written recently about the perils of progressivism have had to go out of their way to find the beast. In visits to well over 100 classrooms, I did not find one where, for example, the pupils decided what they should study and how they should study it. Nor have educators shown me any enthusiasm for this darling of the 1930's.

"Progressive . . . traditional . . . permissive . . . authoritarian"—these terms are more ominous on the speaker's rostrum and in ax-grinding literature than they are in America's classrooms. For every high school that offers a course in dating, 100 would have no part of it.

*Modern teaching methods are sound.* No school turned up any kindly Miss Dove with eyes of steel and a heart of gold who rams knowledge down the throats of her students with admirable results. The teachers pointed out as being "old-fashioned" or "traditional" were often merely bad teachers. To sit at the front of the class and meter out facts in an inflexible, one-way stream is to take the lazy—and ineffectual—way. The best modern teaching insists that the pupil participate in the learning process; it takes into consideration individual differences and rates of growth, and it infuses facts with meaning. Significantly, these methods are most effective when brought to bear on the basic subjects.

As for the extremes: "It's distressing," U. S. Commissioner of Education Lawrence Derthick said, "some of the things I've seen done in the names of either authoritarian or progressive teaching. The great teachers of all ages have used the sound methods that the majority of our teachers are being taught to use today."

*A return to the Three R's is sheer nonsense.* By this is meant any drastic curtailment of the expanded curriculum. The trend toward diversification has ceased, and there has been a swing back toward the basic subjects, due to a general public reaction as well as the outcries of the critics. But the schools cannot discontinue training in hygiene, safety, citizenship or even happiness; the parents would not stand for it. The critics are wrong when they blame a small group of educators for expanding (or diluting) the curriculum. The schools are a true expression of our national spirit, our tenacious belief that any idea or philosophy must be judged by its practical results. And most parents feel that the schools are getting good results in their efforts to help children find their way in today's complex society.

On this point, the critics are gentler than they sometimes seem. "We're not asking for a revolutionary end to nonbasic subjects," said Dr. Harold Clapp, executive secretary of the Council for Basic Education. "We think we're working with a trend."

*Our schools lack a healthy respect for excellence.* Here, the critics' attacks strike home with the most impact. In its enormous task of schooling an entire populace, American education, perhaps more out of desperation than design, tends to slip into the role of a mere baby sitter. Weighed down by sheer numbers, the schools sometimes give more attention to their "custodial" function than to the job of education. They often view children as social ciphers, may look for what is normal rather than what is exceptional, and try perhaps too hard to make all children "average" and "happy." But the insidious, creeping trend toward mediocrity and conformity is not found only in the schools. It may also be observed on the political podium, in the home, the church, the factory and the executive suites of many businesses.

Here, it seems to objective observers, is a worthy challenge for our schools—and for the NEA as it starts out on its second 100 years. Modern education has as an underlying principle a respect for individual differences. This belief, it is said, needs reaffirmation. Many educators already are aware of the challenge; their awareness is reflected in the many recent conferences, committee meetings and experiments on education for the gifted child. But the forces of conformity and mediocrity are strong. To beat them back will take the same grand effort that brought American education out of the little red schoolhouse.

*The Big School Controversy is not a bad thing,* when conducted constructively and with intelligence. It has forced educator and layman alike to take a fresh look at that wonderful, if ponderous, miracle: free education for all. The controversy would become harmful if it should force a turning back of the clock, if it should "make us throw out the baby with the bathwater," as NEA members often say. And while discussion of trends is often useful, frightening words and phrases should not obscure a school's essential ingredients: a teacher, a child and a place to teach. This is where each parent's evaluation must begin, and end.

# III

## Neglect of Fundamental Subjects

To some extent, public education is always under criticism for neglect of subjects considered to be fundamental. In recent years, such criticism has been either of the general kind presented in the preceding chapter or it has had to do with poor teaching of reading, and with neglect of foreign languages, mathematics, and science. A great stir about instruction in reading was caused by the publication of *Why Johnny Can't Read*, which is described and then discussed approvingly and negatively in one of the articles in this chapter. The material presented on foreign languages, mathematics, and science is limited, but it gives the flavor of pertinent criticisms and responses.

## Teaching Johnny to Read *

EDITOR'S NOTE: *The popular misconception that books which deal with the subject of education are all dull, albeit well-meaning, was dramatically exploded by a book published by Harper & Brothers early last spring.* Why Johnny Can't Read *by Rudolf Flesch, a Ph.D. from Columbia University's Teachers College and author of many books on writing is a scalding attack on the methods by which the subject of reading is being taught in American schools. The book has been angrily attacked by schoolteachers and just as angrily defended by aroused parents. Unlike any other educational book in our time, it has popped up week after week on bestseller lists, has been syndicated in newspapers throughout the country, and has been the cause of a host of articles now appearing in national magazines.*

*A month ago SR published an objective summary and two opposing reviews of another recent controversial book about education, Mortimer*

---

\* Reprinted by permission from *Saturday Review*, July 30, 1955.

*Smith's* The Diminished Mind. *This week we publish a summary (which is as objective as we can make it) of* Why Johnny Can't Read, *together with two opposing opinions of it. William Morris, who takes the affirmative side in the debate, is the editor-in-chief of a leading publishing house, the editor of a dictionary, and the author of a nationally syndicated newspaper column called "Words, Wit, and Wisdom." He is also, he assures us, an "aroused parent." Emmett Albert Betts, who has written the review which opposes the book, is professor of psychology at Temple University and director of the Betts Reading Clinic in Haverford, Pa.*

*Methods currently being used to teach reading in American schools were described in detail in "The ABCs of the Battle Over the Three Rs" (SR Sept. 11, 1954).*

## THE BOOK

*Why Johnny Can't Read* is a short, well-organized book, divided into two distinct sections. The first section contains Mr. Flesch's analysis of why he thinks schoolchildren today are incapable of reading as well as he would like them to read. The second contains Mr. Flesch's own primer of phonics for teaching children to read. Both sections are highly critical of educators for using "modern" methods of teaching reading.

"Let me spell out in so many words what I am trying to say in this book," Mr. Flesch writes in the first section of his book. "Your child's trouble with reading comes solely from the fact that in school he has been taught word guessing instead of reading—and by reading I mean getting the meaning of words formed by letters on a printed page, and nothing else.

The trouble with modern methods of teaching children to read, says Mr. Flesch, is that they are taught to memorize words, not to read them letter by letter. "We have decided to forget that we write with letters and learn to read English as if it were Chinese," he says.

"If a child isn't taught the sounds of the letters, then he has absolutely nothing to go by when he tries to read a word. All he can do is guess. Suppose a child tries to read the sentence, 'I saw a kangaroo . . .' If he has been trained in phonics, he simply 'sounds out' the [letters] and reads 'kangaroo' as easy pie." But says Mr. Flesch, today's schoolchildren are not being taught the sounds of letters. They have to guess at them. As proof of his argument, he cites the examples of children in some schools he visited while he was writing his book. These children, he says, could not tell the difference between the words "ancient" and "accident." One girl read "said" instead of "jumped" and one boy, who was learning to read in a class where flash cards were used, recognized the word "children" only because the particular card with the word "children" on it had a smudge at the corner.

To bolster his theory of the need for phonics, Mr. Flesch also visited a school where old-fashioned phonics were taught. "These children," he says, "did *not* go through the ritual that I had seen performed dozens of times in another school. They did *not* chant words, one by one, laboriously and insecurely, in a monotonous, one-word-after-another sing-song. Instead, they did something that I have seen done in no other classroom. *They read the story.* They went through the pages at a pretty fast clip, with completely natural intonation, laughing spontaneously at one place, expressing surprise at another, following the thread of the story with animated suspense."

Mr. Flesch proposes that parents teach their five-year-old children to read before they enter school in order to offset the disadvantages of the present-day teaching methods, and the second section of his book is devoted to a series of seventy-two word lists which the child should sound out as he copies them from the book. The words are grouped by phonic elements, the first list, for example, containing ninety three-letter words containing the short vowel *a*. For parents who are uncertain of their own ability to teach reading to their children, Mr. Flesch says, "You paint your living room. . . . Why not take on instruction in reading? Surely you can do a simple job like that." And, as proof that a parent can do so, he includes some sample material from the type of primer used in today's schools. The implication: that anybody can teach reading to a child better than such gibberish can teach him. The sample material which, according to Mr. Flesch, is supposed to achieve its effect by repetition:

*Father said, "I want something. I want to get something. Something for the car. We can get it here."*

*"Oh, Father," said Sally. "What do you want? What do you want for the car?"*

*Father said, "You will see. You will see."*

*Up, up went the car. "Oh, oh," said Jane. "See the car go up. The car can go for a ride. It can ride up."*

*Sally said, "Oh! See Tim! He went up, too. He and Spot and Puff went up."*

*Sally said, "Look, Father! Spot and Puff want to jump. Please make the car come down. Can you make it come down?"*

*"Yes, Sally," said Father. "We can make the car come down. We will get Spot and Puff and Tim."* . . .

Though Mr. Flesch has quoted the above story without benefit of the pictures which accompanied it in the actual textbook, he still considers it gibberish. It is a wonder says Mr. Flesch, in an educational system where such "stories" are regarded as necessary because no basic phonics have been taught, that our Johnnies are not considerably less adept at the art of reading than they actually are.

# PRO

*William Morris*

This year a major state university in the Midwest has had to schedule forty-three classes in Remedial English—which can only mean that it can fill forty-three classrooms with pupils of college age and intelligence who cannot adequately read, write, and spell. Is it any wonder, then, that parents the length and breadth of the country have been perplexed and angry at the failure of the schools to teach otherwise intelligent children how to read and write? Is it to be wondered at that after receiving from their child's teachers bland and condescending rebuffs—usually couched in academic gobbledygook—they have greeted with such enthusiasm the appearance of Rudolf Flesch's "Why Johnny Can't Read"? For here they find a lucid and thoroughly documented explanation of the origin of this shocking situation—and the reasons why it will persist unless and until the entrenched educators start to pay some heed to the protests of aroused and informed and suffering parents.

Mr. Flesch has done a more than reasonably thorough job of documenting his work—frequently quoting passages from educational journals and from the published monographs of the reading "experts." One suspects that the authors of some of the passages quoted by Mr. Flesch are now smarting at the revelation of their fundamental nonsensicality when exposed to the light of public print. As an example, note this statement from a university "expert" on reading: "Current practice in the teaching of reading does not require a knowledge of the letters [of the alphabet]. . . . In remedial work such knowledge is helpful." In other words, try to teach the child to run before he walks. After he has fallen down sufficiently often that it becomes obvious that he needs "remedial work," teach him to take one step at a time.

Among advanced English teachers and on college faculties Mr. Flesch has many supporters. A professor of linguistics at a leading Eastern university writes: "Flesch has given the public a clear, well-reasoned, convincing account of the present mess in reading and how we have gotten there. It was about time somebody did just this." And the children's librarian in a major Southern public library writes: " 'Why Johnny Can't Read' makes articulate in understandable language to the lay reader what thousands of intelligent people have been trying to tell educators for many years." Indeed, it sometimes appears that the aspect of this book which rankles the reading "experts" most deeply is the fact that its author is himself a Ph.D. from Teachers College, Columbia University—the fountainhead from which the "sight" and "word-recognition" theories were first enunciated.

More important, however, are widespread indications that Flesch's book has already begun to have a remedial effect on educators. I have before me a clipping from *The New York World-Telegram* headed "Reading Instruction Everyone's Business" and containing this paragraph about a meeting of New York City public-school principals: "The controversial matter of teaching reading by phonics instead of word recognition came in for considerable discussion on the program." Without retreating completely from support of the "sight-reading" method, the conclusion was that "for most children the teaching of phonics should start in the first year."

The second part of Mr. Flesch's book, headed "What You Can Do About It," consists of a series of exercises and phonic drills designed for use by the parent with his child, preferably before the child enters school. What each parent should do is to study this teaching material with care and then work it regularly into daily play with the preschool child. When your youngster asks how to spell his name or the names of his friends and pets help him learn the value of each letter by teaching him to enunciate each syllable as he writes. "Reading readiness" experts to the contrary, any reasonably intelligent child is ready and eager for this simple word-play at age four or five, providing he has learned his alphabet from an "old-fashioned" mother or grandmother.

If enough American parents read and follow the precepts that Mr. Flesch so effectively sets forth "Why Johnny Can't Read" may well be ranked the most important contribution to the betterment of public-school teaching methods in the past two decades. Hundreds of thousands of parents, inarticulate in the face of the pompous and condescending "explanations" of the educators, have at last found a highly articulate and very well-informed spokesman. The sparks have begun to fly, and unless I miss my guess the results will be beneficial to every educator, pupil, and parent of every pupil.

## CON

*Emmett Albert Betts*

In this book journalist Flesch reports his "absolutely fantastic" finding: "The teaching of reading—all over the United States, in all the schools, in all textbooks—is totally wrong and flies in the face of all logic and common sense." With supreme confidence, he assures his reader that while working with one pupil he "knew of a way to teach reading that was altogether different from what they do in schools or in remedial reading courses or anywhere else." He offers a very simple formula for everyone: "Learning to read means learning to sound out words."

Mr. Flesch—a master of histrionics—has written a readable book on phonics for parents and teachers. Probably none of his readers can remain unmoved by his condemnation of "our Chinese word-learning system," "the frighteningly idiotic work of educational drudges," and "this deadly warfare between the entrenched 'experts' and the advocates of common sense." His use of emotive language is very effective.

In his effort to present his case for phonics Flesch has introduced confusion regarding what reading is. He quotes a dictionary definition, to "get the meaning of writing or printing." He twists this definition by insisting that "reading means getting meaning from combinations of letters." He tells a native of Prague that he could not "understand a word" of the Czech newspaper—"I can only read it." Throughout his book he says he teaches the child to "read words" when he means to identify, or pronounce them. He drills home his idea that reading is merely the identification of words by means of phonics: "Teach the child what each letter stands for and he can read." If the teaching of reading could be reduced to this simple formula and if this formula could be applied to *all* children Mr. Flesch could become the Albert Einstein of reading instruction.

In a few pages Mr. Flesch outlines his natural method of teaching phonic skills which he calls "teaching reading." He begins by teaching the short sounds represented by *a, e, i, o, u* and the sounds represented by "all consonants spelled by single letters." Quite logically but not psychologically, he then drills Johnny on the pronunciation of lists of isolated words, presented and reviewed in groups of ninety words on each of nine consecutive pages. Since his idea of reading is word pronunciation he is not concerned with the fact that his five-year-old may not know *mass, jazz, hag, van, sin, fib, mutt,* or *huff.*

The first step is completed when Johnny is drilled on isolated words beginning with *c* and *k* and words ending with *ck*—all representing the sound of *k.* At this point these rules are given: (1) "before *a, o,* and *u* this sound is spelled *c";* (2) "before *e* and *i* it is spelled *k";* after a short vowel it is spelled *k."*

During the second step Mr. Flesch teaches thirty-two combinations of letters, including *x,* used as word endings; five combinations used as word beginnings; *tch* and *ch* used as word endings and *ch* used as a word beginning—a total of thirty-nine phonograms. At this time Johnny is given another rule regarding the *s* and *z* sounds of *s* at the end of a word. In addition, Mr. Flesch introduces a page of two-syllable words, representing compounds, inflectional endings, and at least three different types of syllabication situations. But he does not give systematic help on syllabication and other word-analysis skills because he rules out "another method of word attack."

In the third step Mr. Flesch "teaches" thirty-four phonograms—"vowels and vowel combinations spelled with two letters." He tells the child about two rules for knowing when to expect *oi* or *oy* and *ou* or *ow.* This step is concluded with one page of "mixed" drill on two-syllable and three-syllable words, without any mention of either syllabication or accent.

For the fourth step the child is given forty-five more phonograms plus nine combinations of silent letters. During this time he learns three more rules. For the last step Johnny gets eleven more phonograms and a page of ninety three- and four-syllable words.

Mr. Flesch gives "a reasonably complete recipe" for teaching a five-year-old 151 phonic elements and six phonic rules. For the author, drilling Johnny in phonics is all there is to reading: "Everything else will come to Johnny automatically, because he can now read anything." Furthermore, "this method is guaranteed."

Critical readers, of course, will expect Mr. Flesch to publish information on why he implies his natural method is linguistically sound. For example, a phonetician would accept the sound value assigned to *ea* in *break* and *head* but could he accept *ea* rather than *ear* in *learn?* Also, why would Mr. Flesch omit systematic guidance on syllabication and on the analysis of prefixes and suffixes, which, for good reason, are included in all basic reading programs?

Critical readers also will expect Mr. Flesch to publish his data to demonstrate the psychological validity of his natural method. Experimental psychologists have demonstrated the value of set, meaning, and grouping of elements as stimuli in visual perception, but Mr. Flesch apparently does not consider these factors to be worthy of mention.

Unfortunately, Mr. Flesch fails to mention even one limitation of his simple formula for teaching reading or, for that matter, for teaching word perception. For example, he does not tell his reader how many beginners will be confused by his natural method. He does not tell how many word callers, or word-by-word readers, he will produce. He merely states that after many months of drill on words in isolation Johnny can pick up anything and read it.

## Foreign Languages Neglected Grievously*

*Douglas Bush*

One thing that has suffered grievously and conspicuously in this last generation has been the study of foreign languages. The usual reason given is again the pressure of numbers, the numbers who are not going beyond high school, but again a positive reason has been open or quiet hostility. Languages have been pretty well crowded out of the school curriculum, and of course there has been a corresponding decline in college study. Nothing has been commoner in recent decades than the applicant for admission to a

* Excerpt from Douglas Bush, "Education for All Is Education for None," *The New York Times Magazine,* January 9, 1955. Reprinted by permission.

graduate school who has had little or no acquaintance with any foreign language except possibly a year or two of Spanish.

Serious study of a foreign language means work, and a first principle of modern pedagogy has been the elimination of work. Thus, during the years in which we have all become conscious of one small world, and in which this country has become the leader of that world, educational theory and practice have retreated into cultural parochialism. There is no need to argue how necessary for the ordinary citizen is some knowledge of a foreign language and a foreign people.

In the last few years a good many parents have been aroused, and the Modern Language Association has been putting on a vigorous campaign, so that progress has been made; but there is a long way to go. It is encouraging that in some cities successful experiments have been conducted in the teaching of languages in elementary schools, where, for good psychological reasons, they ought to begin. I wish there were something encouraging to be said about the ancient languages, but we are concerned with actualities.

## Decline in Language Teaching*

*Arthur Bestor*

Q. Has there been an actual decline in teaching languages, too?

A. Yes. The figures I gave a while ago for science and mathematics can be matched for foreign languages. In 1900 nearly three quarters of all high-school students were taking some foreign language. Today less than 22 per cent are doing so.

Q. Is this because Latin is being given up?

A. No, all foreign languages are suffering. Over these same years, French has dropped from 7.8 per cent of all students to 4.7 per cent, and German from 14.3 to less than 1 per cent.

Q. Those figures on languages would seem to indicate that somebody has an idea that languages are not worthwhile in the modern world. What do you think?

A. I consider this view part of the retreat from the facts of modern life.

Q. Is the study of languages a form of mental discipline, or is it a background to education—or what?

A. I would say that the first argument for foreign languages is essentially

* Excerpt from Arthur Bestor, "We Are Less Educated Than 50 Years Ago." Reprinted from *U. S. News & World Report,* November 30, 1958, an independent weekly news magazine published at Washington. Copyright 1958 United States News Publishing Corporation.

practical. The United States is deeply involved in world affairs and needs men and women who can understand the language and get the ideas of both our allies and our potential enemies.

Moreover, studying a foreign language is an essential part of learning to use one's own language. It was Goethe, I believe, who said that no man knows his own language until he knows another. One of the reasons for the decline in effective use of the English language is that so few students today have any knowledge of the principles of language in general.

Q. What do you think is to be said for the idea that, when you study other languages, you study the literature and culture of other peoples and therefore you begin to understand how their minds work, so that in this world of misunderstanding we can bring about some form of understanding? Is there anything to that theory?

A. I think there is a great deal to it. I subscribe to it wholeheartedly.

# Russia Emphasizes Foreign Languages*

*Kenneth Holland*

A significant development in Soviet education is a clear recognition of the international interests of the Soviet Union. Every student begins the study of one foreign language in the fifth year, continuing through the 10th. If his native tongue is not Russian, he begins Russian in the third grade. I was told that about one-third of all the fifth-year students begin the study of English; one-third, French; and one-third, German. Some 65 per cent of the students in institutions of higher learning study English. It is estimated that at present 7,000,000 Soviet students of all ages are studying English. At most, possibly 7,000 American students are trying to learn Russian.

Here again, I was impressed with the quality of the instruction in English in the fifth grade. In the school which I visited in Moscow, the students in the fifth-grade classroom already had started to speak and read English. The accents were Russian, of course, but the concentration was most impressive.

* Excerpt from Kenneth Holland, "The Current Challenge of Soviet Education," *School and Society*, June 7, 1958. Reprinted by permission of Stanley Lehrer, Managing Editor.

# Geographical Location and Foreign Languages*

*Byron S. Hollinshead*

Aside from the difference in philosophy I have been discussing, the difference in geographical location explains much in motivation and interest. For example, from where he lives, the French boy, of course, has a different view of the importance of Latin. He can go to Provins and see the tower of Caesar, he can see ancient Roman churches as far north as Paris, he can see old Roman arenas at Nimes and Arles. His own mother tongue is very close to Latin and probably he goes to a Roman Catholic church every Sunday where he hears a Mass in Latin. In nearly every French town he can see relics of European history left by the Romans, Franks, Visigoths, Germans, English, Dutch, Moors, Spanish, or others, as they have fought up and down his fair land. One cannot expect an American boy to have the same interest as the French boy in Latin and European History.

Or take modern languages. The Dutchman is usually no more than fifty miles from the nearest border on the other side of which few speak Dutch. To survive, he studies languages almost from birth so that he can understand the German language to his east, the French to his south, and the English to his west. The Swiss boy has to learn languages to get along within his divided state of German-Swiss, French-Swiss, and Italian-Swiss, not to speak of the need to make a living by understanding the tourists who speak English.

The American youngster, on the other hand, can go three thousand miles on land east and west and at least one thousand miles north and south without any concern about another language, so why should he worry about it. Isn't English, he says, becoming the great international language anyway? Or at least the great second language?

Please do not misunderstand me. I believe everybody is greatly enriched by speaking at least one language other than his own. I also wish American diplomats were better trained in foreign languages. All I am saying is that necessity and geographical location play a large part in language learning. Even of the larger countries in Europe—France, Germany, and Italy—the people in the interior don't have the same interest or ability in languages as those near the borders.

* Excerpt from Byron S. Hollinshead, "Is European Education Better?" *The Educational Record*, April 1958. Reprinted by permission.

# Do Schools Neglect Science and Mathematics? *

*Arthur Bestor*

Q. Are the schools paying less attention to the teaching of science, mathematics, history and foreign languages than they used to?

A. Yes, they are. In fact, lots of American high schools don't even offer courses in the basic sciences and advanced mathematics, that is, geometry and algebra. And an increasing percentage of American students aren't taking the courses even when they are offered.

Q. How bad is that situation?

A. Well, more than half of the high schools in the United States offer no physics; roughly a quarter offer neither physics nor chemistry. And even geometry is missing in 23 per cent of our high schools.

Q. Is the situation getting better or worse?

A. Worse. A responsible estimate is that last year some 1,500 high schools reduced the number of their courses in science and mathematics, or dropped them entirely.

Q. Is there a relationship, do you think, between the shortage of scientists you hear so much about today and what we have been doing with education in the last 30 to 50 years?

A. A very obvious relationship. The figures of the U. S. Office of Education show that in 1900 nearly 84 per cent of all American high-school students were taking some science courses. That has dropped to only 54 per cent today. In mathematics the drop has been from 86 to 55 per cent.

Q. Where does that put us in comparison with other nations?

A. Behind the eight ball, I should say. What we know about education in the Soviet Union is causing real alarm in scientific and military circles. The Russians are giving intensive training in these fields. In the upper grades of their secondary schools, 40 per cent of the time is spent on the sciences and mathematics. And they aren't playing at it. The school day has more hours, and the school weeks and terms are longer. The competition among students for academic honors is intense.

* Excerpt from Arthur Bestor, "We Are Less Educated Than 50 Years Ago." Reprinted from *U. S. News & World Report,* November 30, 1958, an independent weekly news magazine published at Washington. Copyright 1958 United States News Publishing Corporation.

## Neglected Issues in the Science Subjects Enrollment Controversy*

*C. Winfield Scott*

In his "Black Horses Eat More Than White Horses," in the June, 1957 *Bulletin,* Harold C. Hand did a thorough and excellent job of setting the record straight with respect to current high school enrollment in science subjects. An earlier account, in a periodical of wide circulation, had quoted Arthur E. Bestor, Jr., to the effect that 84% of all American high school students were taking some science courses in 1900, against 54% today.[1] Unfortunately, these data seemed to indicate that 46% of present day high school students study no science. Hand showed that at least 90% of any high school graduating class will study some science during their period in high school and that the proportion of any high school age group or generation who receive some formal high school instruction in science today is several times greater than in 1900. While Hand and some other disturbed educators[2] have proved that the situation is much better than Bestor's data seem to imply, they have consistently ignored some issues that are of greater importance.

The first of these has to do with the amount of formal science instruction that high school students now receive. Data available cannot be used to derive comparative statistics; so any conclusion must be inferred. However, since proportional enrollments by grades and subjects do not change radically from year to year, one may assume that the typical high school graduate in 1900 had completed considerably more work in science than is true of the typical graduate of today. To be sure, today's graduate is representative of a much larger proportion of his age group, and presumably has lower aptitude for learning, but this does not mean that he needs less science instruction than his counterpart of 1900.

A second crucial question has to do with the total amount of science education youth of today receive. Since education is a process that goes on constantly, one must consider out-of-school educational stimuli as well as school activities in any effort to determine the educational status of any group. It would be very difficult, if not impossible, to make any valid comparison of the science education status of today's youth and those of 50 years ago. However, the superiority of today's environment for providing science education stimuli seems self-evident.

---

* Reprinted by permission from *AAUP Bulletin,* December 1957.

[1] *U. S. News & World Report,* November 30, 1956, p. 68.

[2] For instance, Walter C. Eells in "Let's Talk Facts," *School Executive,* March, 1957. pp. 41-46

Products of science and simple explanations of scientific phenomena surround and influence modern youth. Television, air conditioning equip ment, and automobiles are good illustrations of science products; popular science magazines and articles, and radio and television programs are omnipresent explanatory or instructional media. Furthermore, there is a distinct possibility that some science education filters through nonscience school subjects; for instance, the social impact of science may be got to some extent in social science courses, and some biological understanding through health instruction. Another possible source of formal science instruction that is not so labeled is core curriculum programs. The net result of all formal and informal science-education influences today may well be an adolescent who, in terms of available science knowledge and skills, is more sophisticated than was his predecessor in 1900.

Even if today's youth stand higher on science education, the question still remains: *Are they as well educated as they should be?* This is the crucial neglected issue. To answer it, educators and the public should seriously consider further man's need to understand his environment and to be able to cope with it.

Currently, the major concern seems to be with control of the environ ment, particularly with the Western world's ability to maintain itself in competition with Communism. Although this is basically a conflict of ideologies, the determination of whether the two will coexist or one dominate the other may well rest on their relative success in promoting and using science. The question of how much science education is necessary for satisfying personal living is a more difficult and philosophical question Neither educators nor laymen will find answers to either of these major questions in enrollment data, but setting the record straight was a desirable preliminary to further work on much more basic questions. Perhaps now everyone can get on with the main job.

# How Much Mathematics and Science? *

*Byron S. Hollinshead*

And now let us look at mathematics, physics, and chemistry. The post-Sputnik critics say that we are behind Europeans in these subjects. This seems strange since many of the recent discoveries in physics and chemis try have been made here and certainly the applications of knowledge in these two fields are much more advanced in the United States than any-where else in the world. However, this begs the question somewhat. What

* Excerpt from Byron S. Hollinshead, "Is European Education Better?" *The Edu cational Record*, April 1958. Reprinted by permission.

he more exact critics say is that the European schoolboy is further ad-
anced in mathematics, physics, and chemistry at a certain age than his
merican counterpart. Let us grant the truth of this, although it is equally
rue that the American youngster is more advanced in certain other respects.
o be fair, the question of comparison should be as follows: In a certain
ubject, say mining engineering, at the end of the course, say at age twenty-
wo, are European students of a given native ability better prepared in
heir field than American students of the same native ability? This would be
very hard question to answer because the European might be ahead in
ome respects, the American in others, but the question does, at least,
ndicate how difficult such comparisons are.

The real questions are far different ones. Agreed that we need to im-
rove American secondary education in all respects as much as we can,
he questions are: What should be the minimum knowledge of mathematics
nd science we might expect students who do not go to college to have?
Vhat knowledge should the student who goes to college but is not expect-
ng to major in mathematics or science have? What knowledge should the
tudent who is expecting to continue these studies in college have when he
nters?

Obviously what is necessary is to differentiate these studies in the high
chool so as to deal properly with these three general categories as well as
ariations of them. American educators have been saying this for years and
racticing it insofar as their budgets would allow. Because of the small
roportion of European students in secondary school, nearly all of them
reparing for the university, the Europeans have not had the same need
o differentiate by abilities and interests. However, in the future, as a higher
roportion of their students have an opportunity to attend secondary school
nd college, Europeans will face the same problems we now have. While
he analogy is not perfect, they are also going to find that their road system
vill become more complicated and expensive when a higher proportion of
heir people have automobiles.

What worries me on this subject is what is either an unscrupulous or an
nsophisticated use of statistics. May I illustrate. A columnist in a reputable
news magazine says that in 1900, 56 per cent of American high school
tudents took algebra and in 1949 this percentage had decreased to 27.
Then he quotes approvingly of someone who speaks of this as a de-emphasis
of mathematics. But these percentages are of pupils in school, and in 1900
the percentage of the age group in school was not only very small but also,
n most secondary schools, only the college preparatory course was offered.
The only statistics which mean anything in this context are the percentages
of the secondary school age group studying algebra in 1900 compared with
1949.

Since the percentage of the age group in secondary schools increased by
almost ten times from 1900 to 1949, the correction needed in these statistics
is quite startling. If the percentage of those in the pupil body studying

algebra decreased by 50 per cent in those fifty years, and at the same tim
the percentage of the pupil body to the total age group was multiplied by ten
then the percentage of the secondary school age group studying algebra in
creased by five times.

But there is an even larger question than faulty statistics. It is, wh
should everybody pursue algebra, physics, and chemistry? There is ver
good psychological evidence to show that not much more than 25 per cen
of the population have any high degree of ability in the abstract though
which advanced work in mathematics, physics, and chemistry requires
If this be so, why must everybody study these subjects? Must everyone pla
the piano, or play football? Granted that a knowledge of arithmetic an
general science is essential, how far beyond that are low-ability student
supposed to go, or, indeed, can they go? Science and mathematics courses
at least as now taught, are usually designed to be sequential—brick or
brick. For those who continue, there is finally a real structure of knowl
edge. Those who do not continue may simply possess some loose bricks

Again, suppose the individual has high ability, but he wants to paint a
picture, sing an opera, write a book, or be an anthropologist. Why mus
even the gifted who do not expect to specialize in mathematics or science
master these subjects beyond the point required for intelligent citizenship
The article I referred to earlier says that "when a Russian graduates from
high school he has had five years of physics, four years of chemistry, one
year of astronomy, five years of biology, ten years of mathematics and
trigonometry, and five years of a foreign language." I don't know what
percentage of Russians graduate from high school. Evidently it is very
small. But if this is the educational diet of the Russian student I think we
need have no great worries. He will be a lopsided fellow indeed and I
should think he would be consumed with irritation and frustration because
of the imbalance of his studies. In all seriousness, is there anyone with
even a modicum of knowledge about education who thinks that we should
imitate such a curriculum? Or, to put it differently, is this a curriculum
which prepares for citizenship in a modern democracy?

Just as I hope my comments about foreign languages will not be mis-
understood, I hope these observations about mathematics and science will
not lead to misunderstanding. A modern society such as ours has increasing
needs for people well trained in mathematics and the natural sciences. Without such persons it cannot exist. We do need to improve our teaching in
mathematics and science. We need to have a richer offering of courses in
large high schools and solid courses in small high schools which are now
neglecting these subjects. Above all, we need to encourage by every possible
means those who are interested and talented in mathematics and science to
go on with their studies. But this does not mean that we should try to force
everybody into a similar educational mold.

# IV

# The Challenge
# of Soviet Education

Soviet education, as a topic of study and as a basis for unfavorable comparison of public education in the United States, blazed its way through popular and educational literature following Sputnik I. Generally speaking, the informative and critical discussions tended to place our schools in a negative light with respect to purpose, efficiency, and emphasis of foreign languages, mathematics, and science. By implication, if not outright suggestion, a good number suggested that we pattern our educational system after those of the Soviet Union and European countries.

A brief comprehensive treatment of Russian education, with recommendations for our schools, opens this chapter. Reputedly, this article was the first to dramatize the Soviet educational challenge in a large-circulation publication. Then follow two pieces that support our educational system and a closing item which reports a recent drastic change in Soviet educational policy. The combined effect should be conducive to neither hysteria nor complacency.

## Now the "Cold War" of the Classrooms*

*Soviet leaders have boasted that Russia's 'gold reserve' consists of trained technicians for the future. Here is a challenge flung to our educational system.*

*William Benton*

\* Reprinted by permission from *The New York Times Magazine*, April 1, 1956. William Benton, a former U. S. Senator from Connecticut, is the publisher of the Encyclopedia Britannica. He visited the Soviet Union last fall to prepare a report on Communist indoctrination behind the Iron Curtain for the 1956 Britannica Book of the Year.

Leon Bloy, the French philosopher, once referred to what he called "th good news of damnation." His theory was that none of us might behave a Christians if we were not afraid of perpetual hellfire.

My recent trip to the U.S.S.R. suggests that the Soviet educational systen can prove to be the good news of damnation for American education— the spur which may rouse us and propel us toward salvation. If so, this wil sustain Arnold Toynbee's thesis that the competition provided by the Sovie system will force us to live up to our own great ideals.

Technical experts form the Soviet Union's "gold reserve," Premier Nikola Bulganin told the recent Communist Party Congress in Moscow. Further four million new specialists are to be trained before the current Five-Yea Plan ends in 1960; this exceeds the combined output of the two previou plans.

Nikita Khrushchev, party chief, shouted at the Burmese in December: "We shall see who has more engineers, the United States or the Sovie Union." He and Bulganin offered to build and staff a technological institute in Rangoon "as a gift to the people of Burma from the people of the Soviet Union."

This is the new "cold war" of the classrooms. And it is very dangerous. I have seen for myself the vast technocratic Sparta that is burgeoning in the U.S.S.R. I have talked to the topmost Soviet educators. I returned con- vinced that Russia's classrooms and libraries, her laboratories and teaching methods, may threaten us more than her hydrogen bombs or guided missiles to deliver them.

The new propaganda of the Kremlin, emphasizing economic, political and ideological competition, clearly reveals the long-range Soviet plan—a plan so potent as to make military and political maneuvering seem by comparison tactical and even diversionary. Central to it is the schooling for export of scores of thousands of indoctrinated and capable engineers, scientists, schoolmasters and technicians of all kinds. These are being trained to help develop the resources of countries outside the present Soviet orbit, and to help convert the world to communism. The advance guard is now in India, to which a technical institute has also been offered; and enticing induce- ments have recently been advanced to Egypt, Afghanistan and Latin America.

Even more formidable is the spectacular example set for underdeveloped countries by the Soviet Union's mass-training for its own industrial needs. For without the present outpouring of trained experts within the U.S.S.R., the sixth Five-Year Plan could not promise by 1960 a 60 per cent increase in the national product of the U.S.S.R. and a 70 per cent step-up in its heavy industry.

If we Americans are now complacent about our own educational prob- lems, at a moment when whole galaxies of our own educational neglect are coming into head-on collision, then we stand in mortal danger of being outwitted, outtalked, outmaneuvered and outbuilt throughout the world. We re not preparing to cope with the surging flood of youth that looms ahead, emanding to be educated. The Soviet threat may now be the only thing that can shake us out of our sleep-walk—on the educational brink.

\* \* \*

What is it that most impresses a foreign observer about the Soviet school system? In less than forty years, starting with a population about 50 per cent illiterate, the Soviets have built a seven-year primary school system rivaling our own in universality, with nearly 100 per cent enrollment.

Since World War II, the Soviet secondary school system has mushroomed amazingly. By 1960 the basic ten-year school is to be compulsory everywhere. In spite of acute labor shortages, all children are to be kept in school from 7 to 17. Every Russian youngster is to be given an education —a Communist education of course, but comparable in its high standards of study and learning to an English public school or a French lycée, though without the same emphasis on the humanities.

Further, the U.S.S.R. is on the road to surpassing the U. S. both in the number and percentage of students enrolled in institutions above the secondary level. Indeed, when high-level extension-correspondence students are included, the Soviet total of 4,300,000 enrolled in 1955 is already 70 per cent over our 2,700,000. The Soviet Union offers as much training to every boy and girl as his or her talents and abilities will absorb.

Russian youngsters today go to school six days a week, and more hours per day and more weeks per year than ours do. Discipline is strict, study hours are long, the curriculum is demanding, and examinations are severe. At all levels the Soviet students, like European students in general, work much harder than do our American youngsters.

Wearing military-looking uniforms, Soviet children for the first four years of the ten-year school concentrate on reading, writing, arithmetic, and Russian. In the last six years, more than 40 per cent of their time goes to science and mathematics. During these years they must take algebra, geometry, and trigonometry. Also compulsory are four or five years of physics, four years of chemistry, two years of biology, a year of astronomy, and a year of psychology.

Finally, each student is supposed to take six years of a foreign language. English, the new language of science, is said to be the favorite in the U.S.S.R. Russian is favored in the satellites.

The contrast with our American secondary school curriculum is startling. Lewis L. Strauss, Chairman of the Atomic Energy Commission, recently told the Thomas Alva Edison Foundation: "I can learn of no public high school in our country where a student obtains so thorough a preparation in science and mathematics, even if he seeks it—even if he should be a potential Einstein, Edison, Fermi, or Bell." *Indeed, last year, for the 28,000 high schools of the United States, we produced only 125 new teachers of physics. I repeat: only 125.*

When I was in Moscow last fall Pro-Rector Vovchenko of the Universit of Moscow told me that, above the ten-year schools, there are now mor than 2,000 *"tekhnikums."* Later I learned that the number probably ex ceeds 3,500. These have an enrollment of two and a half million student: We in the United States have no parallel for them. They are a kind o vocational college, giving two-and-a-half and four-year courses. They pro duce "middle-trained" specialists in scores of fields. I visited a *tekhnikun* for the coal-mining industry in Kiev, and was astonished at the extent an value of its equipment.

Then there are the 800 institutions of higher Soviet education. Thirty three of these are universities. The balance are the specialized institutes fo doctors, engineers, lawyers, aeronautical experts, electrical specialists, agri cultural experts, etc.—all the specialized skills in such demand throughou the world. The universities concentrate largely on the training of teachers scientists, scholars and professors. All universities and higher institution provide five-year programs, except the pedagogical institutes, which ar four years, and the medical, which are six. These top institutions have a estimated enrollment of 1,825,000 students.

Eighty to 90 per cent of all students at Soviet higher institutions have been on state scholarships, which included stipends rising slightly from year t year. In February we learned from the Party Congress that beginning thi autumn all education is to be free. Every Soviet student can now keep go ing upward in the Communist world at the state's expense so long as h can make the grades. Indeed, he is pushed, prodded, pressured and entice to reach the limit of his capacity for training.

The University of Moscow, dominating the city with its gleaming nev 33-story central tower dedicated to the sciences, enrolls 23,000 students The recent investment of three billion rubles for this new building, com pleted in 1953, is astounding by our standards. It is equivalent to at leas $150 million. Thus this building costs more than has been spent for the completed physical plant of all but a very few American universities.

It contains 1,900 laboratory rooms. Here work most of the 2,000 pro fessors of the University of Moscow who teach students. Here, too, are the 500 scholars dedicated to research from whom no teaching is expected Original and creative research is demanded from all 2,500.

Pravda recently reported that 60,000,000 are enrolled in educational courses, including those taking evening and correspondence courses. Fo most students, of course, graduation from a ten-year school or *tekhnikum* marks the end of formal education. But many continue to struggle and strive for another chance and still another.

This is why one sees teenagers in bookstores buying books on nuclear physics. This is why in the Leningrad library I found every desk occupied in the great science reading room. The silence was absolute; the concentrated zeal of the students was breathtaking. I asked my librarian guide, "Are these university students?" He replied, "Oh, no, the University has its own

brary; these are workers from the night shifts of the factories; we keep the
brary open at night for the day-shift workers."

The Soviet educational system has, of course, grave and tragic weak-
esses by our standards and goals. There is no academic freedom or tenure
or teachers or professors. No criticism of the regime, or of official dogma,
s permitted. Classroom discussion is not encouraged. Heavy emphasis is
iven to rote memorization of texts.

Every advanced student must devote his full time to his specialty except
or 10 per cent to the study of dialectical materialism and Marxism-Lenin-
sm-Stalinism. The student can't change his mind about his profession in
nid-stream; he can't shift. Every graduate must work for three years on
ny assigned job in his specialty.

By our standards, the Soviet system is the training and conditioning of
uman instruments, rather than the education of human beings. It is de-
igned to sharpen human tools for coming Five-Year plans, rather than to
levelop Soviet youngsters to their highest powers as individuals. It is with-
ut human spirit or soul. It is the gospel according to Pavlov.

But I fear the Communists may have found a formula for combining high
quality in scientific and technological training and research with an ac-
eptance and obedience in political, economic, philosophical, and moral
natters. Whether this formula will hold up over the decades may turn out
o be the crucial question of our historical epoch.

The third generation, for whom Lenin said "two whole generations"
nust be sacrificed, is now coming up. I talked with forty or fifty key ad-
ninistrators of the current generation, most of them men in their forties.
They struck me as men of ability and energy, men who rise to the top in
ny mobile society. They seemed to me dangerously dedicated men—true
elievers in communism, and frighteningly ignorant of the West, of its system
of values, and of its hopes and aspirations.

They went out of their way to talk to me—not about Stalin or even about
the present regime—but about the beauties of dialectical materialism and
the progress that is being made towards world acceptance of Marxism,
Leninism and Stalinism. This last standardizing trio of words seemingly is
about to be condensed into Marxism-Leninism, but we shouldn't take encouragement from this recent revelation that there has been latent opposition to Stalin. For many years interviews with intellectual refugees from the
Soviet Union have revealed more evidence of unhappiness over "miscar-
riages" under the Communist system itself. Surprisingly to many, even the
refugees from the U.S.S.R. haven't complained too much about the nature
of the Communist regime.

Some of the figures I have quoted above were given me by the top
Soviet school officials among the men I interviewed. They may exaggerate.
But my checks do not prove the figures invalid. I suggest that we would be
wise to accept them. Americans have for years scoffed at Soviet claims—
only to find that they have outstripped all nations but ourselves in industrial

production. The Communists from the earliest days gave up butter fc guns; but they gave up meat for education.

*          *          *

How can we meet this new Soviet challenge?

First, we require a generous program of scholarships and fellowships fc students of more than ordinary promise who need help. This should b launched at once, both by government and by private philanthropy.

Our high schools abound with talent worthy of such scholarships. Secre tary Folsom of the Department of Health, Education and Welfare recentl cited an estimate that "each year about 60,000 students of high quality dro out of high school before graduation * * * and half of the students in th upper one-fourth of their high school classes do not go on to college. Dael Wolfle, of the American Association for the Advancement of Science tells us that 150,000 pupils from each age and class who could enter th important specialties fail to go to college. These figures show the tragi waste of our talented youth—our own potential manpower.

The frantic competition for engineers now going on in the United State has been reported on the front pages of *The New York Times*. Our industrie and our defense establishment require at least 45,000 to 50,000 new engi neers a year. We graduated 23,000 in 1954 (compared with Russia's 53,00( that year and 63,000 in 1955).

There is also a scramble for physicists, chemists and mathematicians These shortages have obscured the swelling demand for professional an technical experts in many other fields. At the rate we are growing, w can expect shortages of at least 22,000 physicians and 100,000 nurses b 1960. The shortage of teachers may be the most acute of all.

We in this country must begin to educate more scientists and engineers and we must learn to do it without turning our schools into *tekhnikums* or our colleges into factories for producing highly conditioned robots.

I feel that the Federal Government should immediately launch a nationa competitive scholarship program beginning with as many as 20,000 scholar ships a year, each covering four years of college. I would increase this a rapidly as the administration of the program, and the absorption capacit of the colleges and universities permitted, to a level of at least 100,00( scholarships a year. To these should be added 20,000 or more graduate fellowships.

Such a program could require a Federal outlay of perhaps $1 billion a year. But Mr. Bulganin's figure of speech about his "gold reserve" is apt Trained manpower is like money in the bank. It is our most importan national resource.

The second priority is for a program designed to attract and hold the finest instructional corps in the world. That means the development, with out delay and on a bold scale, of new incentives for teachers.

Perhaps the second priority provides us with the key question in two parts:

irst, how can we offer greater incentives to the talented public school and to every teacher who successfully teaches, and to every teacher who successfully seeks self-improvement; and, second, what system of incentives will tempt and hold young prospective teachers of talent? I do not see why we should greatly step up the salaries of hundreds of thousands of teachers who are inferior and who will continue to be inferior. Indeed, one of our national tragedies is that our teachers' colleges do not attract a better caliber of students.

Here again, I fear, we must turn to the Federal Government for leadership. Hundreds of millions of dollars are required at once, to be allocated through state Departments of Education to communities which undertake to attract and keep uncommonly promising teachers. Further, the Federal Government must help establish a pattern of standards. This will cause a hue and cry about Federal control. We must face up to it.

This brings me to the third requirement, the dilemma of the physical plant. The urgent need is for $3.8 billion a year for the next ten years if we are to obtain the 950,000 new classrooms required for the public schools.

Because state and local community outlays for school construction are now at a two-billion-dollar-a-year level, leaving a gap of $1.8 billions, the $250 millions offered annually by the present Administration or even the $400 millions of the Kelley Bill are far too little.

Fourth, and finally, we must re-examine our teaching methods, and our institutional setup. In the latter category are such questions as the need for more junior colleges, 50 per cent of which are today in California.

As to teaching methods, I shall cite only a single example. Our goal of secondary school pupil-teacher ratio has been twenty-five to one; in the university it has been twelve or thirteen to one. These goals now seem to be about to vanish. Soon we shall receive the tide of forty-two million school children.

We must bring technology to the schools. For example, all plans for new buildings should make it easy for children in Maine and Kansas to learn history and science and arithmetic from the Californian or the Britisher who understands them best and can explain them best through films and educational television. One good teacher, with a couple of aides, can learn how to take care of 200 or 300 pupils—and improve the instruction. This makes it profitable as well as easy to raise salaries greatly in order to attract and hold good teachers.

After twenty-six years of pioneering effort the classroom film producers of the United States haven't yet put a projector into more than one out of every fifty classrooms. By contrast, the U.S.S.R., once it began to use classroom films, has made rapid progress. The goal of a projector in every classroom has not yet been achieved in the U.S.S.R. But at present rates of progress the Soviets will achieve this a decade before the U. S. has a projector in every school building.

\*        \*        \*

If we compare the Soviet educational system with our own, it is clear that we can lose the race if we continue to waste our potential talent. But it is also clear we cannot win it on our terms on numbers alone. Our best opportunity lies in educating whole men, rather than mere functionaries. Obviously, America must make a larger investment in training for science. At the same time our technical experts must be educated in the liberal arts. They must understand the history and logic of our great traditions of freedom and justice.

Recently, Marion Folsom said, "Education is basic * * * to our collective strength in the cause of world peace."

Soviet Russia may be the first country to develop free and unlimited schooling for all with talent who are willing to work hard. But we in the United States have tended a brighter fire during the last 180 years. That is our dedication to the advancement and perfection of the individual. It should be far more appealing to all mankind if we now begin to do a better job of building the fire to a blaze.

Education is one area where we in America most surely have nothing to lose if we accept the Red gauntlet. Intercontinental competition in education need be no challenge to an arms race or a war. If the Russians goad us to do a better educational job, then we shall only be doing what our own best traditions call for—what we should be doing even if the Soviet Union were to sink suddenly into the sea.

# Is Russia Really Out-Producing Us in Scientists? *

*Robert J. Havighurst*

We have been hearing from an assortment of admirals, generals, senators, columnists, and university presidents lately a curious proposition: Russia produces more engineers and scientists than the United States; therefore, Russian education is better than American education; and, therefore, American education should become more like Russian education. When we examine the basis for this proposition, we find a very few, ill-chosen facts which easily lead one to faulty conclusions.

There are three basic questions: How do the Soviet Union and the U.S.A. compare in numbers of university graduates and in science graduates? What is the quality of these graduates? How do Russia and the U.S.A. compare in quality of education?

Looking at the question of how many university graduates are produced by Russia and the U.S.A., let us first consider the numbers of graduates

* Reprinted from *School and Society*, April 26, 1958, with the permission of Stanley Lehrer, Managing Editor.

n engineering, mathematics, and in science. It is useful to combine these ields, because a good many Russian engineers do work which is done by physicists or chemists or mathematicians in the U.S.A. According to "Soviet Professional Manpower," written by Nicholas De Witt for the U. S. National Science Foundation, Russia graduated 65,000 people in this category in 1954, while the U.S.A. graduated 48,000. Thus, by this kind of comparison, Russia is currently out-producing the U.S.A. in engineers and scientists.

But let us take account of the numbers of young people from whom these scientists were chosen and thereby introduce the concept of *effort*. The effort of a nation in producing engineers, or any other types of persons, should be defined in relation to the number of young people who are in the basic manpower pool. Thus, if one country has only one-tenth as many young people as another country, it will be equal in effort to the larger country if it produces one-tenth as many scientists.

In *effort* the U.S.A. is superior to the Soviet Union in the production of scientists and engineers. According to the Russian census reports, the Soviet Union had 202,000,000 inhabitants in 1956, when the U.S.A. had about 170,000,000. Furthermore, Russia has almost twice as many young people of university age as the U.S.A. currently, due to differences in the age-structure of the population in the two countries. The Soviet Union has been producing about 4,000,000 22-year-olds a year for several years, while the U.S.A. has been producing a few more than 2,000,000 a year (Table 1).

The U.S.A. has been producing more engineers and physical scientists *per thousand 22-year-olds* than the Soviet Union (Table 1). In 1954, the U.S.A. produced 20 per 1,000 as compared with 17 per 1,000 in the Soviet Union, while in the 1946-50 period, the U.S.A. produced 26 per 1,000 as compared with 11 per 1,000 in the Soviet Union.

At the same time, the U.S.A. has been out-producing the Soviet Union in other fields of training, both in terms of *effort* and in terms of gross numbers. The Soviet Union in 1956 gave the equivalent of our bachelors and first professional degrees to 200,000 young people, while the U.S.A. produced 300,000. Measured in terms of effort, the U.S.A. spent three times the effort of the Soviet Union in producing university graduates in 1956.

In the U.S.A. there has been a wider variety of jobs open to college graduates than in the Soviet Union. The Russians have concentrated on steering their university students into jobs in engineering, medicine, and other applied sciences.

With so much demand and so many jobs for college graduates in the U.S.A., we have produced, nevertheless, the numbers we required until the last few years, when we suffered from a shortage of university-trained people. This is due to a combination of three factors: a great postwar economic boom which has increased the need for university-trained tech-

TABLE 1

"EFFORT" GOING INTO PRODUCTION OF UNIVERSITY GRADUATES

| | U.S.A. | | | U.S.S.R. | | |
|---|---|---|---|---|---|---|
| Year | No. of 22-yr.-olds (thousands) | Univ. Grads. per 1,000 22-yr.-olds | Graduating Engineers & Scientists per 1,000 22-yr.-olds | No. of 22-yr.-olds (thousands) | Univ. Grads. per 1,000 22-yr.-olds | Graduating Engineers & Scientists per 1,000 22-yr.-olds |
| 1928-30 (Average) | 2,000 | 58 | 11 | 2,900 | 12 | 4 |
| 1940 | 2,400 | 77 | 13 | 3,200 | 32 | 11 |
| 1946-50 (Average) | 2,400 | 118 | 26 | 4,000 | 33 | 11 |
| 1954 | 2,150 | 135 | 20 | 3,800 | 46 | 17 |
| 1960 | 2,300 | | | 4,400 | | |
| 1965 | 2,900 | | | 3,700 | | |
| 1970 | 3,600 | | | 4,200 | | |
| 1975 | 3,900 | | | 4,800 | | |

nical experts and executives in business and industry; the low birthrates of the depression years of the 1930's, which give us an abnormally low supply of young adults in the 1950's; and the great upswing in the birthrate since 1946, which has crowded the schools and created an enormous demand for university-trained teachers.

Thus, at present, even though our "effort" is greater than that of the Soviet Union, and even though we have record enrollments in the colleges, we are short of engineers, scientists, teachers, and nurses; and we will continue to suffer from those shortages until after 1960. Then the upward trend of the birthrate, which commenced in 1942, will begin to increase the numbers in the manpower reservoir from which the university graduates are drawn. By 1966 we will have 3,000,000 new 22-year-olds, 50% more than we have now, and by 1975 we shall approach the number of 4,000,000 22-year-olds. Indeed, some people fear that we shall have an oversupply of university graduates by 1975; but our economy may have expanded by that time to need far greater numbers than it uses now.

While the U.S.A. is overcoming its deficit in young manpower, the

Russians may have shortages during the next decade because of their great loss of births during the war years of the 1940's. Russia will have to make much greater efforts in the 1960's to recruit and train her ablest youth, since she will have a substantial decrease in numbers of young adults in the decade after 1960.

Thus, the fact is that Russia produces more engineers and scientists than the U.S.A. only because Russia has a greater population. Nevertheless, the U.S.A. makes a greater "effort" to produce engineers and scientists than Russia does. Furthermore, the U.S.A. will immensely expand its production of university-trained scientists and others after 1960, when the high birthrates of the 1940's and 1950's have their effect on the population of young adults.

There is no danger in America of our not having enough men and women to build and guide our machines. We soon will have 4,000,000 young people coming of age each year. Russia, with a larger population, will have 5,000,000 young adults a year. This is ample for each country for the rest of the present century.

Although the American educational system actually produces more scientists and engineers per 1,000 youth in the population than the Russian system, some critics will argue that we ought to produce even more because we need them and because we have relatively more boys and girls in school and college than the Russians have. These critics point to the greater amount of science and mathematics in the Russian school curriculum and claim that this makes the Russian schools better than the American schools in producing scientists and engineers.

Sometimes these people seem to be saying that the Russian system produces *better* scientists and sometimes only that it produces *more* scientists. The question whether Russian scientists are better than American scientists cannot be answered on the basis of our present knowledge. However, we may ask whether Russian education in science is better than American education in science.

Comparisons of Soviet and American university education in the sciences have been made by De Witt, who thinks they are of about the same quality. A discussion of the quality of Soviet education in science, held by the Thomas Alva Edison Foundation in 1956, indicated that the several American scientists who had compared Russian and American textbooks and courses of study were quite respectful of the Russian system but thought it no better than the American system of science education in the universities.

If the Soviet system of science education is no better than the American system, why did the Russians succeed in launching a satellite first? There can be several answers to this question. One is that American research effort has been spread over a wider variety of problems, including the biological research which produced the vaccine against polio and the research that produces the gadgets which make life more agreeable in the U.S.A. Another is that the organization and co-ordination of American military research has been less effective than that of the Russians.

The discussion might be closed at this point, were it not for the fact that a number of people are saying loudly and repeatedly that the Russian school system, with its greater emphasis on science and mathematics, is somehow *better* than the American system. Many of these critics have long been criticizing the American school system as being too easy on children, as lacking in the sterner virtues, and they are simply using the current concern about Russian satellite and military research as a convenient means of influencing people to blame the schools. However, other people are honestly perplexed by what they read about Russia's schools, and they wonder whether the Russian methods may not be better. For people who want to understand the true differences between Russian and American primary and secondary education and then to decide what is good or bad about these systems, it is first necessary to clear up some misunderstandings caused by inadequate reports on Russian education.

It has been said, for example, that all school pupils in Russia get five or six years of physics, four or five years of chemistry, and 10 years of mathematics. This statement conveys a completely false impression to the American who is not familiar with the European secondary school curriculum.

The Russian secondary school, like other European schools, puts the pupil into some 30 to 33 hours of classes a week, in contrast to the American secondary school which assigns pupils to 22 to 27 hours of classes. The Russian pupil studies 10 or 12 different subjects in a given semester, but his time on these studies varies from one hour per week to six hours per week. Thus, although the Russian pupil studies what is called "physics" for five years, he takes two hours a week the first year, three hours the next two years, and four hours the final two years for a total of 16 hours per week if all were crowded into one year.

The first- and second-year work, which comes at ages 13 and 14, is very similar to what an American pupil gets in "general science" at that age level and would not be called "physics" in American schools. This leaves a total of 11 hours of physics taken in the last three years of the Soviet secondary school. The American pupil takes physics from five to eight hours a week for one year, which means that he spends a half to two-thirds as much time on physics as the Russian pupil. (But many American pupils do not elect to take physics, while all Russian pupils must do so.) This is the appropriate way to compare the two programs, and it conveys a different meaning than to say that "the Russian pupil gets five years of physics while the American gets one year."

In general, the Russian pupil devotes about twice as much school time to science as his American contemporary who takes courses in both physics and chemistry. The Russian pupil spends about the same amount of time on mathematics as the American pupil who elects to take four years of high-school mathematics.

This leads to another difference between the Russian and American secondary schools. The Russian school selects the ablest youth, or aims to do so. Until about 1952, no more than 15% of Russian youth entered the final three-year unit of the secondary school at about age 15. This was in contrast to about 90% of American youth in secondary school at that age. Since 1952 the Russian secondary school has been enlarged to accept about 50% of youth at age 15. This means that many Russian pupils of average ability are now following a program constructed for high-ability students; and already some difficulties are developing in the Russian schools. Some 30% of Russian youth are now graduating from secondary school, while those who fail to do satisfactory work are being shunted off into schools which give a more limited technical training.

Thus, the American secondary school, which graduates 62% of the youth aged 17 or 18, is quite different in composition from the Russian general secondary school, which graduates some 30% of youth. The Russian secondary school program, if it is good for young people who are going to the university and into scientific work, may not be good for American young people, many of whom will not go to a university and few of whom will go into scientific work.

A further question has been raised about the goodness of the Russian school program, even for able pupils who intend to go into science or engineering. Some American educators believe that the Russians over-emphasize science and mathematics in the secondary school—that they "over-teach" it. They feel that the Russians try to teach science too early, before pupils are mature enough to comprehend it. According to this view, a student may learn physics faster and better at age 16 or 17 than if he is forced into it at 14 or 15, when his experience and his mind are not mature enough for certain abstract concepts.

For example, at the Thomas Alva Edison Foundation Conference on "Strengthening Science Education for Youth and Industry" (1956) Prof. John Turkevich of the chemistry department of Princeton University said,

> I frankly do not care how much science the boy knows when he comes to my freshman class. I expect a certain amount of intellectual maturity, but I think one of the very weaknesses of the Soviet system is this insistence on a tremendous amount of factual material. I would never recommend more than one year of chemistry at the high school level. I would not recommend more than three years of mathematics at that level. More than this just stifles because they are not mature enough at that age to appreciate the fine points.

Some of the people at this conference disagreed with Dr. Turkevich, and others agreed. But most American scientists would question the value of putting as much emphasis on science in the secondary school as the

Russians do. There is no evidence that the American university graduate in science is inferior to the Russian graduate, though the Russian has been exposed to more school hours of science than the American.

In any case, a good many Americans will ask: Why hurry with the education of our youth if they are busy and growing with what they get under present conditions? We live longer than we did a generation ago. Why try to prepare in a shorter time for a longer life? If American boys and girls grow up into competent adults with the present education, what gain is there in making life harder for them as adolescents or in hustling them through college a year younger than has been customary?

In fact, some Russians have wondered out loud whether the Soviet school program was not too much of a speed-up for the good of Soviet youth. In May 10, 1956, a group of leading Soviet medical authorities published a long letter in the *Literaturnaya Gazeta* charging Soviet educational authorities with endangering the health of school children by overloading them with lessons and homework. They said, "Chronic over-exhaustion, frequent headaches, weakened memory and vision, proneness to infectious diseases with various complications, result in a general weakening of the child's organism." They wrote of the "unbelievable over-burdening" of school children. Children of 11 to 13 work an average of eight to 10 hours a day (including homework); children of 14 to 17 work 10 to 12 hours. The majority of the upper forms of secondary schools not only have no time left for reading, sport, theater, or amusement, but so little time is left even for sleep than an industrious pupil becomes irreparably exhausted mentally.

The following September the Russian Minister of Education ordered the abolition of end-of-year examinations in all classes but the seventh and 10th, where the examinations are necessary for promotion to other schools. This will lessen the nervous strain and the burden of work toward the end of the school year, though it does not decrease the daily amount of work which has to be accomplished during most of the school year.

This is not to suggest that we should close our eyes to what is going on in Russia and other European schools. No doubt we can learn from them, and they can learn from us. There are several things about Russian education that we might well ponder. For example, there are as many girls as boys in Russian universities, while the ratio of boys to girls in American universities is 60-40. Russia gives more opportunity to women in the scientific professions, e.g., 75% of Russian physicians and 25% of Russian engineers are women.

Although the Russian school program is clearly not the program which most Americans will want to follow, there probably are some improvements in our educational system which can be made under the push of present needs. The present shortage of young adults, due to the low birthrates of the 1930's, rather forces us to get all the trained talent we possibly can from the youth in our secondary schools and colleges. We might do the following things:

1. Help more of the ablest quarter of students to enter and complete a college course. At present two-thirds of the ablest quarter of youth go to college. To improve this record we would have to find ways of stimulating the present non-motivated youth to want a college education. And, having found ways of motivating more able youth for college, we would need to provide scholarship assistance for most of them.

2. Encourage more able students to go into science and mathematics. However, the publicity of the last few years already has dramatized effectively the need for, and the rewards of, scientists and engineers. The majority of winners in recent national scholarship competitions have chosen these areas of work.

3. Teach physics and chemistry more professionally to the abler students in the last two years of high school so that college courses can be built upon the high-school courses. This means that physics and chemistry courses in high school should be different for students of average ability than for high ability students interested in science careers.

4. Teach mathematics more effectively to high-school students who are interested in scientific careers. But there is no point to requiring *all* high-school students to take more mathematics. Few of those who now take little or no mathematics would ever become scientists, and forcing them to take more mathematics would only worsen the present shortage of mathematics teachers.

5. Pay teachers better, and use this and other methods to recruit young people into the teaching profession.

# Comparison of Soviet and U. S. Education*

*Spencer Brown*

Shortage of teachers and professors, shortage of schools and colleges and scholarships, and long-continued failure of the expensive American educational system to teach anything significant—such are the cries heard separately or simultaneously. The food is poison, and such small portions! And the Russians are serving more and better.

The last point, though vital to our political happiness and probably to our national existence, is paradoxically the easiest to discuss, if we do not allow our justified fear of Russian successes to deprive us of reason, and if we avoid the temptation of using these successes to grind our pet pedagogical axe.

Unfortunately few of us can resist this temptation. Doubly unfortunately,

---

* Excerpt from Spencer Brown, "Have Our Schools Failed?" *Commentary*, June 1958. Reprinted by permission.

the spectacular articles in *Life*[1] on the Educational Cold War have made so much noise that the whine of private honing is inaudible to all but sophisticated ears. *Life*'s initial spread was misleading in the extreme: it purported to compare a typical Russian sixteen-year-old with a typical American contemporary. Alexei, the Russian, is finishing his tenth year and will go on to a university next year. Alexei seldom smiles. He is a zealous student, taught by strict, well-trained teachers; he is interested in nuclear physics; he is only beginning to speak a shy word to a girl. He spends three to four hours a day on homework. There is "purpose in his fun" too: he exercises his body with volley-ball and his mind with chess and concerts and piano practice. He is well read in Russian and has read the works of Shakespeare and Shaw in English.

Stephen, his American counterpart, has only just finished Stevenson's *Kidnapped;* he is in eleventh grade and will not go on to college until the year after next. He jokes in class (which is "relaxed and enlivened by banter"); by pure chance *Life*'s photographer caught a girl in the back row reading *Modern Romances*—free advertising that Luce papers rarely give their competitors). Stephen is nearly failing in geometry; he goes steady; he eases through a course in typing. He is the school's star swimmer and a leader in student affairs; he spends his spare time leading prayers as student council chaplain ("students are hushed, reverent") and doing the Rockin' Cha with his steady at the YMCA; and he wasted four hours a week for two months rehearsing for the YMCA centennial.

No doubt this is profitable journalism; it is defensible in that it focuses public attention on a vital problem. But it is no service to focus attention and at the same time to drop belladonna into the eyes. There are differences between Russian and American schools that *Life* blurs. For example: "Though Alexei gets no direct political indoctrination in school, he is constantly reminded of his duties toward the state"—the neatest formulation for Soviet Russia since Henry Wallace coined the term "directed democracy." Russian schools, as everybody knows, are totally dominated by party politics. As *Life* bravely admits, "For a year after Stalin's death Russian schools stopped giving examinations in modern history, while the party rewrote texts."

In student body as well as ideology, Soviet schools are aristocratic schools. They educate chiefly the children of the oligarchy. *Life* does not specify which of the two kinds of Soviet high school Alexei attends. If he attends an academic high school, for which fees are charged that only the "new class" can afford, he may go directly to the university. If (as seems unlikely in view of the curriculum described) he attends a non-academic high school, where the poor can get scholarships, he has only one chance in seven of going on. In America both types of high school are free. Alexei's mother ("a cost-engineer") and his friend (who lives in "a comfortably

---

[1] *Life,* March 24 and 31, April 7 and 14, 1958.

furnished Moscow apartment") are of the ruling class. Stephen's father, a "painter and decorator," is not. Alexei represents education for selected members of a ruling class. Stephen represents education for everybody. Alexei is above average in his selected setting; Stephen is below average in his unselected setting. The comparison is illogical on nearly all possible counts, and the grinding of preconceived educational axes can be the only motive for drawing it.[2]

# Behind K's "Hard Work" Revolution . . . In Education*

*Leon Volkov*

Taking a full page in Russia's major newspapers, Premier Nikita Khrushchev blueprinted a complete reorganization of the Soviet Union's much-vaunted educational system last week. At a stroke he ripped open the curtain on academic life in the U.S.S.R., revealing his country's stringent manpower needs and the apparent failure of four decades of Communist indoctrination. Nothing as important has happened to Soviet education since Lenin decreed free education for all in 1918. Nothing will so importantly affect Russia's technological future.

Under the present system, basic school has been compulsory for seven years in the rural areas, for ten years in the cities. Under Khrushchev's new system, Soviet youth will be diverted to meet industrial and agricultural demands. What the Soviet leader seeks to create is a method of education that will emphasize practical work—"Teach Russian youth respect for physical labor"—and prepare them for "socially useful work." Russia, Khrushchev argues, has too many intellectuals—a class which he attacked last year for scorning manual labor.

---

[2] Ernest van den Haag sums up the differences between Russian and American school population thus: "1) Education is far less widespread in the Soviet Union than in the United States; 2) the selection of students to be educated is based to a far greater extent on irrelevant discriminations in the Soviet Union (in terms of financial ability, political belief and economic class origin) than is the case in the United States, where a high school education does not require the payment of fees, and where a college education can be obtained for much lower fees—relative to income—than in the Soviet Union (despite discrimination the chance of a Negro sharecropper's son in the U. S. to acquire secondary and higher education is far greater than that of the son of the average Soviet worker or farmer); 3) while the United States has moved in the direction of more education and less irrelevant discrimination in access to education, the Soviet Union has moved in the opposite direction."—Ernest van den Haag, *Education as an Industry*, Augustus Kelley, New York, 1956.

* Reprinted by permission from *Newsweek*, October 6, 1958. Leon Volkov is *Newsweek*'s Contributing Editor on Soviet Affairs.

Manual labor will now be required of even the children in elementary school. Upon graduation from the seventh year every youngster will be put to work in the factories or on the farms. If they wish to continue their schooling, they must attend night classes or take correspondence courses. Only a small elite of the exceptionally gifted will be allowed to continue a theoretical education without making a manual contribution.

Why had Khrushchev dealt such a body blow to the system that has looked so impressive to so many since Sputnik I went into orbit?

One key to the startling move seemed to be manpower. The Soviet economy requires an influx of 3 million new workers into the labor force. But the war years, with their dislocation of Russian life, were responsible for a drastic drop in births, and for the next five years the Kremlin can count on an annual increase of only about 800,000 in its labor force. The proposed reforms will help solve this shortage.

Was "hard work" for the youth also intended to damp down student unrest? Some thought so, noting that Khrushchev's plan was readily accepted last week in Poland and Red China—two nations with labor surpluses which have had continuing trouble with students.

What will be the long-range effect of the new plan on Soviet education?

Many Western experts think that it can only be hobbling. The change, in fact, might well give the West a strategic advantage in the desperate race for scientific and technological dominance.

chapter

# V

# Do We Do Enough
# for the Gifted Child?

The negative side of this question is receiving major attention and support in the current debate. Although public education has long been concerned about gifted children and has followed some good practices, the consensus seems to be that the effort has not been great enough. This conclusion, to the editors' way of thinking, should be regarded as a desirable and emerging outcome of the current strife.

In this chapter, a spirited charge that we are not facing squarely our responsibility for the education of gifted children is followed by a "friendly" rejoinder which indicates that we are not as guilty as some critics declare. The final item adds a little lustre to the positive aspects of the total picture.

## Educating the Gifted Child *

*Arthur Bestor*

American education is dedicated to equality of opportunity. This is as it should be. The phrase, however, must be amplified before it can become a safe guide to action. Equality, after all, can be achieved by diminishing as well as by increasing the value of what is given. Unfortunately there is such a thing as equal *denial* of opportunity.

A trustworthy concept of equal educational opportunity must rest upon a broader base than the experience of a single nation. Young Americans are not being offered genuine equality of opportunity unless they can obtain what young men and women elsewhere are receiving. Children of average or less than average ability are not the only ones who deserve consideration

* Reprinted by permission from *The New Republic*, March 4, 1957. Arthur Bestor, Professor of History at the University of Illinois, is serving as Harmsworth Professor of American History at Oxford University during 1956-1957.

in a democracy. The child of high intellectual capacity has his democratic rights, too. He is entitled to receive, in an American public school, an education equal in seriousness, intensity, and comprehensiveness to the education that a child of similar capacity would receive in the best school systems of any other country.

The American public school today does not, by and large, offer this kind of equality of opportunity. Even among professional defenders of the educational *status quo,* few are so hardy as to allege that the superior student is being regularly called upon to work at the top of his capacity in the typical high school, or that he is being challenged by standards as exacting as those imposed without question upon candidates for advancement up the educational ladders of most European countries. In the process of equalizing educational opportunity *among* Americans, we have somehow permitted our ablest students to be deprived of the only kind of equality that really counts for them—opportunity to equip themselves with intellectual training as thorough and rigorous as that which young men and women of comparable ability abroad carry with them into the arena where intellectual distinction is won.

This sacrifice might be tolerable if only it were temporary, if it were merely part of the price of creating, almost overnight, a vast system of universal education. The appalling thing is that this denial of opportunity is being treated by countless professional educationists in this country not as an evil but as a positive good. Many of them have scruples against providing brilliant students with instruction specially geared to their abilities. They are opposed to using public funds to maintain small classes in the specialized fields and at the advanced levels that the ablest high school students alone are likely to need and to elect. They somehow consider it undemocratic to honor and reward students for outstanding academic achievement or to push them ahead faster and farther than their fellows when they demonstrate their ability and their willingness to work.

In recent years, it is true, there has been considerable to-do about making provision for "exceptional children." To understand what the bustle is really about, one has to bear in mind the peculiar, not to say demented, definition which educationists give of this particular term. Allow me to quote, from a standard work of reference, a statement of the matter written by an official of the United States Office of Education:

> A considerable number of children, estimated at about four million, deviate sufficiently from mental, physical, and behavioral norms to require special educational provision. Among them are the blind and the partially seeing, the deaf and the hard of hearing, the speech-defective, the crippled, the delicate, the epileptic, the mentally deficient, the socially maladjusted *and the extraordinarily gifted.*

Equality of educational opportunity, in any defensible sense, cannot exist for an able student in an American public school so long as the authorities in charge persist in viewing him simply as a deviate from the mental and behavioral norm.

The public school has, of course, other responsibilities besides the education of exceptionally gifted children. It has none, however, exceeding this one in importance. The school must face this responsibility squarely. The thorough intellectual training of the able student is a purpose of education not dependent on or subordinate to other purposes. To furnish it in the most direct and forthright manner is a primary obligation of every school—an obligation not only to the student himself but also to the nation, which has a vital interest in the training imparted. To be quite specific, the education of the gifted child must never be looked upon as a mere variant of, or supplement to, the education provided for the child of merely average ability. The relationship is—or most emphatically ought to be—the other way around. The brilliant student is the pace-setter of the school. He is the one for whom its academic program has the greatest significance. The curriculum for the average student is the one to be thought of as derivative. His deficiency, not the brilliant student's "deviation from the norm," is what makes adaptation necessary. To argue otherwise is to enshrine mediocrity.

## On the Worship of Mediocrity

Much of the talk about "enriched programs" for brilliant students is tainted with precisely this worship of mediocrity. Even though a particular program may in itself be sound, this label turns it into a grudging concession. A great many of the programs for enrichment, however, are basically unsound. One characteristic of the brilliant mind is that it learns quickly. It can grasp ideas after performing only a fraction of the number of exercises that are necessary to impress the same principles or concepts upon one less active and alert. What the brilliant student needs to do is to progress as rapidly as he can from one level of abstraction to a higher level, from one difficult task to another more difficult. Far too many programs of "enrichment" propose to keep the mental activity of the able student down among the same relatively simple concepts as those with which his companions are struggling, while occupying his time with tasks that are simply more time-consuming than those assigned to the average child. This is precisely the reverse of what the situation calls for. The slow learners are the ones who ought to go through masses of material while concepts gradually take form in their minds. The brilliant student ought to take at once the next step up the ladder toward concepts more complex and mature.

What we need is not "enrichment" but a genuine program of education for the able child, constructed from the ground up, based upon the accumulated experience of all great schools of all countries. By facing this responsibility squarely and dealing with it in its own terms, we cut through at once much of the fog that envelops current pedagogical thinking. We are on high ground where much is known, not on the misty flats where there is little but conjecture to guide us. The fact is that we know vastly more about what brilliant students are able to achieve than we know about the potential capacities of average ones. We know it from experience. For centuries school systems throughout the world devoted their principal attention to the upper third, or the upper quarter, or the upper fifth of the population, measured in terms of intellectual ability. Many still do. We know very well what their students succeed in mastering. We know it from the syllabi they successfully follow, from the examinations they successfully pass, from the intellectual skills one can confidently expect them to put to use at the end of their secondary-school careers. A tremendous body of evidence thus exists as to what the able student can accomplish before the age of graduation from high school, if only he is given the education he is entitled to.

This is worth spelling out. We know from experience that the able student can master mathematics through plane geometry, trigonometry, and fairly advanced algebra so as to be ready to study the calculus at least by the age of 18. We know that he can acquire real mastery of two or three languages besides his own, for such a requirement is common in European school systems. We know that he can attain to high fluency and accuracy in the writing of his own language, and can have read and understood a substantial number of books of considerable difficulty, belonging to the classics of literature and thought. We know that he can obtain effective grasp upon the main features of world history and of the history of his own country. We know that he can acquire a substantial foundation of knowledge in such basic areas of science as biology, chemistry, and physics. We know that he can accomplish all these things simultaneously during the 12 years of schooling normally offered, and at the same time participate in the athletics that will keep his physical constitution sound. Finally, from the investigations of such American psychologists as Dr. Irving Lorge of Teachers College, Columbia University, we know that the gains achieved by the gifted child through accelerated academic programs geared to his abilities are "not at the expense of social or personal adjustment."

We know something else about the gifted child. We know that he will have real and pressing need for the kinds of knowledge and skill just specified. These are the intellectual tools that are required in the learned professions, in research, and in the conduct of public affairs at the highest levels. The right to equal opportunity means, for the child of high intellectual capacity, the right eventually to enter these professions and to compete for world honors in them, unhandicapped by deficiencies of training. He has a right to expect that the American public school will assist, not handicap, him in entering the professional and learned world, if he is willing to work toward this end. The school must not mislead the able student by suggesting that intellectual training is unimportant, and it must not slam the doors of opportunity shut in his face by denying him the chance to master the intellectual disciplines that are universally recognized as fundamental.

How is the American public school, especially the public high school, to fulfill its responsibility to the able student?

First of all, school authorities must accept the responsibility honestly, and not allow the discussion of it to be obscured by irrelevancies. In carrying out this particular task the question of the changed character of the school population is beside the point. The change has a bearing upon other policies of the school, not upon this. Children of high intellectual ability and interest may have constituted a larger proportion of the high-school population at the end of the 19th Century than now, but they are still present in our schools and their needs still have to be met. The gifted child is a gifted child whether he is enrolled in a selective school system like that of many European countries or in a system of universal education like ours. We have the same responsibility to such students as we had when our schools were less inclusive. Young men and women of brilliant intellect are enrolled in our schools in larger absolute numbers than ever before in history or than in any other nation. These students are entitled to as sound and thorough and advanced an education as they would have received in earlier days or as they would receive in foreign schools.

Given the present temper of those who call themselves professional educationists in the United States, it is exceedingly doubtful that programs suitable for gifted children will ever originate with them. Leadership must come, if it is to come at all, from scholars, scientists, and professional men. These are the men and women who are aware of the real requirements of the modern intellectual world. They know at first hand, as no person concerned solely with secondary education can possibly know, what is involved in the final stages of the education that the able student must receive on his way into his profession. Scholars and scientists, moreover, are not afraid of intellectual brilliance, as so many professional educationists appear to be, and they have never been tempted to treat it as a pathological condition, classifiable with blindness, epilepsy and mental deficiency. Accordingly I am hopeful that the learned societies of the nation will come together to work out the kind of program that students of high intellectual calibre ought to pursue in the public schools of the United States.

## WHAT SHOULD TWELVE YEARS TEACH?

The first task is to define the content that the able student should be expected to master by the end of the 12 years of secondary schooling ordinarily provided. Content, of course, is to be defined not only in terms of the range of knowledge that a student should acquire, but also, and especially, in terms of the level of difficulty of the concepts that he should be expected to handle with confidence in each of the basic fields. The standards for the various fields—specifically for English, for mathematics, for the sciences, for history and for foreign languages—ought to be based upon the known achievements of brilliant students in the best schools of the world. Our models should be drawn from the curricula of the schools that have consistently maintained the highest academic standards, whether in the United States or abroad, whether public or private. There should be consultation with the freshman and sophomore instructional staffs of the colleges and universities that insist upon the highest entrance requirements. The recommendations of educational commissions that were genuinely concerned with academic accomplishment must be resurrected and studied.

The final report of the scholarly and scientific commission charged with such a study ought first of all to state explicitly the standards of achievement to be expected of able high-school graduates in each of the various fields. Such a statement would be of immense value to the universities in revising their entrance requirements, and to state and local authorities in establishing standards for high-school courses and certificates. The commission ought to go further, by distributing these ultimate requirements among the appropriate grades of the 12-year American public-school system. At this stage the co-operation of educational psychologists, of persons experienced in the classrooms of public schools, and of teachers in the great independent (or private) schools of the country would be essential. Careful attention must obviously be given to the problem of equalizing and balancing the responsibilities assigned to different grades, and there must be provision for legitimate options and electives. The commission must also make sure that sufficient hours are reserved in each year for physical education and for moderate extra-curricular activities.

The final report should be submitted to the public in clear and understandable form, prefaced by a carefully reasoned argument respecting its desirability and feasibility. That such a program would be supported by many organizations of professional educationists is too much to hope. If, however, it were backed by leading scientific, scholarly, and professional societies, public opinion would, I feel sure, force educational administrators to take it seriously.

To bring into existence a well-reasoned alternative to the existing educational chaos is a first step to educational reform. Public opinion, now deeply alarmed about the quality of our schools, could make such a set of proposals a guide to action. The lines of action that ought to be followed may be briefly indicated.

## CONTROLLING THE CURRICULUM

No program for able students can exist in a school that does not actually offer the courses they must have if they are to obtain an adequate education. The first task, accordingly, is to make sure that every local high school offers the full complement of courses that are known to be needed. This is the duty, in the first instance, of local school boards and of the citizens of every community. Backing should be given by state and national agencies. At the very least, these should begin to obtain and to publish full reports showing which school systems and which schools are actually offering a complete roster of courses in the basic fields, and which are deficient. A local citizen is entitled to know how his school measures up, according to recognized, objective criteria like these.

State and federal agencies are justified, by logic and precedent, in going far beyond the mere compiling of statistics. They already do. Much of what is currently said about local control of the public schools is sheer myth. Very substantial control is—and for many decades has been—exercised from every state capital. Grants in aid constitute a large part of most school budgets, and these grants are conditioned upon maintenance of a wide variety of standards fixed by the state. Laws governing the certification of teachers compel a local community to choose its teachers from those who have pursued a particular course of study, heavily weighted with courses in pedagogy. The federal goverment, too, has played a far greater role in the determination of school policy than cliché-ridden discussions by educationists would indicate. For 40 years—since the Smith-Hughes Act of 1917—it has poured funds into vocational training, thus exerting (especially in smaller school districts) a tremendous pressure in a vocational direction upon the curriculum, regardless of the wishes and the needs of the local community. The Federal Office of Education has lent its prestige to such anti-intellectual programs as "Life Adjustment Education," and even its statistical publications reflect a definite bias in favor of "functional education," a concept which it blithely equates with declining emphasis on algebra, geometry, physics and Latin.

To say, in other words, that state and federal governments must come to the rescue of intellectual training in the schools is not to say that they must increase their influence in local affairs or invade a sphere hitherto untouched by them. The invasion has already taken place. The tragedy of the present situation is that the pressures placed upon local schools by state and federal agencies have had virtually nothing to do with the maintenance of *academic* standards. In many instances they have been highly inimical to such standards, forcing community schools into exaggerated vocationalism and obliging them to accept teachers with few intellectual qualifications but abundant pedagogical credits. The present need is not for an increase of state or federal control, but for a drastic reversal of policy in the use of powers already being exercised.

Many public-school policies ought certainly to be controlled locally. Whether vocational training should be offered, how much, and in what fields are questions so dependent on local conditions that they ought to be decided by the community without outside pressure. So too are such questions as the extent and character of extra-curricular activities and athletics. Local school boards, not state bureaus, should decide whether a potential teacher is qualified by personality and experience to handle the pedagogical problems arising in the classroom. Local citizens should decide upon the character of their school buildings and the luxuriousness of their equipment, in accordance with the standards of their other public buildings, and should, in general, meet the costs of construction and maintenance as for other tangible community assets. At present there is continual and unjustified interference by state and federal agencies with local control of these matters.

On other issues, the state and nation are so vitally concerned that their interference is justified. If a community fails to offer the fundamental courses needed by able students, the total intellectual resources of the nation are diminished. If it diverts funds from the educational program and from teachers' salaries to quasi-professional athletics and to the upkeep of over-lavish buildings, the same kind of harm is done. And if a community is too poor to support a full program of academic studies, then state and nation are justified in stepping in with subsidies for this particular purpose, in the interests of nationwide equality of opportunity.

No local prerogatives would be endangered if state and federal agencies were to undertake wholeheartedly to undergird the basic academic curriculum in the nation's schools. The fundamentals of learning do not vary community by community. Physics and mathematics are the same in Pasadena and Schenectady. English may be pronounced with a slightly different accent in Boston and Atlanta, but its grammar is the same and the classics of its literature are the heritage of all. Spanish may be the most important second language for a rancher in Texas, and German for an engineer in New York, but that foreign languages should be studied is a proposition independent of region. Some aspects of history, it is true, touch local sensibilities, but this very fact shows the universal relevance of history as such. To insure that these subjects are universally taught would involve no such invasion of local autonomy as occurs at present through state certification laws making course work in pedagogy an absolute prerequisite for teaching.

The first duty of a state in supervising the schools of its local communities is to make sure that students receive adequate educational opportunity in all of them. State aid to a given school should be made dependent upon its offering a complete roster of courses in the fundamental fields of learning. With respect to subjects deemed essential in the preparation of able students, small enrollments in a given class should not exempt a school from offering it.

If necessary, the federal government should take a hand. If all other agencies fail, it must be the one to sustain the fundamental disciplines, simply because the nation's strength and security depend upon these. It is especially disheartening that the recent proposals for expanding federal aid to education should have dealt solely with bricks and mortar. When the issue of federal aid comes up again, it is to be hoped that it will take the form of aid to *education,* not aid to building construction. The federal funds (whether old or new) that go into education ought to be concentrated upon a single great objective: making sure that the four-year high schools of even the poorest communities are offering four years of science, four years of mathematics, four years of at least two foreign languages, four years of substantial history, four years of effective training in the reading and writing of English. Then and only then will we have real equality of educational opportunity throughout the land.

To do justice to our able students we must have not only a sound curriculum but also instructors capable of inspiring students with first-rate minds. A teacher whose training has been mainly in methods of teaching will rarely, if ever, succeed. The dull student can be manipulated by experts in manipulation. But the respect of the student with intellectual interests will only be won by the teacher whose own intellectual interests are active and whose knowledge is broad and deep enough for him to lead his students on to further knowledge. The schools of the world that specialize in educating the ablest students rightly demand teachers whose training has been, first and foremost, in the basic intellectual disciplines. They rightly regard pedagogical training as a mere supplement to a thorough education in the liberal arts and sciences. They insist that their teachers return to the university for graduate work, not in pedagogy or education, but in their chosen fields of instruction. The concept of teacher-training fostered in the United States by professional educationists is the direct antithesis of this. A thoroughgoing reform of our system of teacher-training and of our certification requirements for teachers is a necessary part of the process of enlarging educational opportunity in America.

## RAISING THE AVERAGE LEVEL

To build an adequate program for the education of gifted children is actually the best way to go about creating an adequate program for those of average ability also. For one thing we need to stop treating the difference between pupils of varying ability as a difference in kind, and recognize it as a difference in degree. To offer intellectual training to one and vocational or "life-adjustment" training to another is not to create a classless education, even though all students may mingle in the same building. Programs that are inherently unequal in intellectual quality cannot furnish equal educational opportunity. Professional educationists are ready to assert the contrary and to quote with approval the dictum: "Equality does not mean identity." It is relevant to note that the phrase comes from the Supreme Court's decision in *Hall* v. *DeCuir* (95 US 485 at 503)—the decision of 1877 that legalized racial discrimination in the South.

If we genuinely believe in democracy in education, and if we accept the idea that democracy is a process of levelling up, then we come around to the position—in my judgment the only sound position—that the great function of the public schools is to narrow the educational gap between the gifted child and the child of average ability by offering to the latter the opportunity and the encouragement to obtain an intellectual training of the same high quality and seriousness, up to the very limit of whatever capacity he may possess. To raise the intellectual level of the nation means bringing the average student as far along the path of intellectual training as he is capable of going.

Beyond the problem of educating the gifted child looms the problem that should challenge the resources of a new generation of research workers in psychology and education—the problem of precisely how far up the ladder of intellectual training the students at each level of intellectual ability can be expected to climb. Once we have the facts, we will find, I suspect, that we can carry the intellectual training of the average child much farther than we have come to assume. In the meantime we have an obligation to act in accordance with our faith in the ability of the common man. If we do, we shall be preserving America's most valuable resource—intellectual talent—not merely at the highest level, but at every level of our educational system.

# Educating the Gifted Child *

### A Reply to Arthur Bestor by Nolan C. Kearney

Arthur Bestor's "Educating the Gifted Child" in *The New Republic* of March 4 needs supplementation and a bit of friendly criticism. It begins with some statements that most educators will accept, despite the implication that benighted schoolmen have failed to espouse them. Illustrative are the following quotes: "Children of average or less than average ability are not the only ones who deserve consideration in a democracy. The child of high intellectual capacity has his democratic rights, too." "The right to equal opportunity means, for the child of high intellectual capacity, the right eventually to enter these professions and to compete for world honors in them, unhandicapped by deficiencies of training." "What the brilliant student needs to do is to progress as rapidly as he can from one level of abstraction to a higher level, from one difficult task to another more difficult."

However, in charging that these truisms are disputed or ignored by professional educators, the following phrases and expressions are used: "worship of mediocrity," "fog that envelops current pedagogical thinking," "misty flats where there is little but conjecture to guide us," "school . . . must not slam the doors of educational opportunity shut in his face . . . ," "accept the responsibility honestly," "present temper of those who call themselves professional educationists," "concerned solely with secondary education," "afraid of intellectual brilliance," "sheer myth," "cliché-ridden

* Reprinted by permission from *The New Republic,* March 23, 1957. Nolan C. Kearney is Assistant Superintendent of Schools in St. Paul, Minnesota.

discussions," and "blithely equates." These are not the scholarly words or objective expressions of the careful student in either the physical or social sciences.

Further, educators as a profession are charged with incompetence and nefarious intent: "They somehow consider it undemocratic to honor and reward students for outstanding academic achievement. . . ." ". . . this denial of opportunity is being treated by countless professional educationists in this country not as an evil but as a positive good," ". . . it is exceedingly doubtful that programs suitable for gifted children will ever originate with them." These statements, unmodified, are of concern to more than one million professional educators.

A 60-word quotation, out of context, mentions 4 million children who deviate sufficiently from various norms to require special educational provisions and who are mentally, emotionally, or physically handicapped or are "extraordinarily gifted." The quotation is simple and statistical, but is presented as indicating that educators regard able students *"simply"* as deviates from the mental and behavioral norm. Actually, the statement goes back to discussion, at the White House Conference of 1930, of various types of special education. The author calls the statement a "peculiar, not to say demented definition" written by an official in the United States Office of Education. Actually, the statement favors special provisions for gifted children, which is precisely what the author advocates later in the article! Many other excellent things about gifted children have been written in the U. S. Office. For example a 44-page pamphlet in 1940 on gifted children discussed gifted pupils in terms of intelligence quotient, future potentiality, special talents, variations in capability, social development and health. It is one of literally thousands of publications on the subject.

Professor Bestor does not mention any of the careful programs in our schools that seek to meet the needs of talented children. There is no problem with which educators are more universally concerned. Havighurst and others in 1955 summarized programs from 63 schools selected from all parts of the United States. Passow and others reported in 1955 on The Talented Youth Project. Their bibliography contains 162 references. The Advanced Training Program under College Board auspices worked with 104 schools and 138 colleges in 1956. Beberman and others in Illinois, concerned with mathematics for engineers, were working with 18 secondary schools in that state in 1956. Connecticut outlines in Bulletin 77 a state-wide program for the education of the gifted through special classes, enrichment, acceleration, and special faculty and organization. Long Beach publishes detailed handbooks on gifted students for junior and senior high school teachers. The Colfax Plan in Pittsburgh provides for gifted children in the primary grades. There is an elementary school program at University City, Missouri. In 1953, Modesto, California, outlined in a 100-page booklet its *Instructional Program for Gifted Children*. The Major Work Program for gifted children in the Cleveland schools began more than 30 years ago and has gone forward with increasing success to the present time. In St. Paul, Minnesota, we have had double- and even triple-track plans for a generation, and yet we embarked in 1956 on a five-year program of further experimentation endowed by the Hill Family Foundation. There is no end to the list. Typical current programs combine selection with enrichment *and* some form of acceleration or advanced credit. In many current promotional systems, a 15-year-old child may actually be accelerated several years and still be classified as a tenth grader.

Professor Bestor's article contains but small reference to the tremendous amount of available research. Neglected are the classical studies of giftedness—Galton's *Hereditary Genius* in 1869, Alfred Binet in 1904, Whipple around 1920, Hollingsworth around 1930, and Terman's two-volume *Genetic Studies of Genius* in 1925. No reference is made to a score of current researches in the field, to articles in the scholarly *Encyclopedia of Educational Research* (1950), or to a variety of other summaries.

The article raises the old bugaboo of European superiority in manners, culture, art, music, letters (everything but morals), and now in education. The charge that American schools offer the gifted child less than other countries cannot be backed by objective evidence. In Europe children are classified early. Only the upper 10 or 15 percent who plan to go to college even enter the secondary schools. Approximately half of these are eliminated before college. It is extremely doubtful that these children achieve as well there as they would here, despite the fact that selection yields a very competent group to begin with. Tremendous social waste results from class distinctions, lack of guidance, an inflexible curriculum, and admittedly inadequate examinations. Foreign educators recognize the problem and are trying to modify their educational traditions. Even out here in the Midwest, each few weeks brings educators from foreign lands to visit our schools and study with the educators at our great universities. Their constant remark is that we achieve so much with so many!

What should 12 years teach, the article asks? Herbert Spencer, in 1859, asked "What knowledge is of most worth?" and the question has been asked frequently ever since. *Your* answer depends upon the age in which you live, your philosophy or value system, and your vocational and avocational goals. It is ridiculous to suggest, as this article does, that four years of each of two foreign languages and four years of mathematics be required of all American youth, in addition to four years each of English, history, and science. This would preclude any other high school subjects. American parents, laborers, farmers, businessmen, and industrialists would think poorly of any group (even scholars) who sought to deprive them of the business education, home economics, industrial arts, art, music, dramatics, athletics, on-the-job training, safety education, and other life adjustment courses they fought so hard to get.

Furthermore, it would take a generation to educate the necessary new teachers. Approximately 4 percent of all secondary-school pupils now study one or more years of French and less than 2 percent take one or more years of German. Suppose now that all 8 million children were required to take 4 years of both of these (or any other) languages! More than 600,000 classes, at 6 classes a day, 5 days a week (a very heavy teaching load) would require 100,000 additional language teachers and would increase more than sixfold the present number of French and German language teachers. We now employ 376,000 teachers in secondary schools (690,000 elementary)! We need 60,000 new teachers of all kinds now each year and can't get them. (And the number of college graduates who haven't had pedagogy are a drop in the bucket and can now teach in most places under provisional certificates.) What about the problems of the 100,000 teachers who are to be displaced by the new language teachers? It becomes clear that the proposals under discussion have ramifications!

Now note this charge: "They [the educators] are opposed to using public funds to maintain small classes in the specialized fields . . . that the ablest high-school students alone are likely to need. . . ." We now spend $9 billion annually to educate public-school children aged 5 to 17. The small classes referred to here would probably increase this cost by 22 percent or $2 billion. Unfortunately, the research is not clear that this is the best way to meet the needs of gifted youth, and what would happen when the parents of the children not classified as gifted began to elect new school boards pledged to give *their* children the small classes? Equality of treatment in our curriculum is there because the parents and other citizens want it there (and this is rightly so).

A serious problem, not mentioned, is that half of our gifted high-school graduates fail to go to college, and a considerable additional number drop out of college before graduation for economic reasons. Small schools are a problem, too. Remember, the average high school in America has 200 pupils, and the median size is 91. These facts suggest that the way to conserve human ability is to concentrate on some of the basic conditions.

Now, as to the proposed control of the curriculum. A "scholarly and scientific commission" (no educationists) would "come together" and lay out graded courses of study. Then, and not before, psychologists and teachers would be consulted about options and electives (what electives with everything prescribed?). The state and federal governments would then impose this program through support subsidies. According to the article, there is now much federal and state control. Educators who have urged federal aid without federal control will note the following quotation, "When the issue of federal aid comes up again, it is to be hoped that it will take the form of aid to *education,* not aid to building construction." Thus is proposed a rigid, universal, federally imposed educational program.

The author does not believe that courses in pedagogy (in colleges of education) contribute to educational efficiency. (Parents, boards of education, school administrators, and legislatures believe they do.) Study courses for teachers are, by law, he says, "heavily weighted with courses in pedagogy." Schools must hire teachers "with few intellectual qualifications but abundant pedagogical credits." These are strong words, but wait! "A teacher whose training has been mainly in methods of teaching will rarely, if ever, succeed." There is no possible evidence on this last statement because there is no such teacher, at least on the bachelor's level. The facts are that there are no 4-year graduates whose programs are "mainly" pedagogy. The "education courses" in the typical liberal arts college that educates secondary teachers account for about *18* semester credits out of 120, or *27* quarter credits out of 180. The universities will average less than *20* semester credits in pedagogy. The teachers colleges offer about *21* education credits to secondary teachers. These totals include practice teaching and psychology of education. So the "heavily weighted," the "abundant" and the "mainly" come to mean about 16 percent. How much better to say it that way. On the graduate level, students rightly concentrate on physics, business administration, statistics, hydrology, psychology, educational method, or other specialty. There's nothing to be made of that fact.

The final *faux pas* is the following quote, ". . . then we come around to the position—in my judgment the only sound position—that the great function of the public schools is to narrow the educational gap between the gifted child and the child of average ability. . . ." But this is the very crime which the article places on the doorstep of the educationists. There is preponderant and conclusive evidence that the more time and effort that is devoted to learning and the better the teaching and the more success there is in learning, the greater are the educational differences between the more gifted and the less gifted. This is true unless we neglect the gifted and set very limited goals that all or almost all may master. May I add that it is precisely because of facts such as this that people have to "work at democracy."

The conclusion seems inescapable that there is a jurisdictional dispute in some of the colleges and universities. However, the struggle will get out of hand if the capability and integrity of a whole education profession and the validity of an open approach to the solution of problems is brought into question. The great majority of scholars and educators are out in the schools. They will not allow the schools to be victimized in such a struggle.

## Democratic Provisions for the Gifted *

*Harold C. Hand*

Running through much of Professor Bestor's polemic is the idea that youngsters who lack the innate capacity to do rigorous work in advanced courses in science and mathematics, and in the other subjects of general education no less, should either be routed at an early age to what he called an "inferior" secondary school, or that they should be flunked out if such a second-class school is not established for them. This proposal

---

* Excerpt from Harold C. Hand, "A Scholar's Devil Theory," *The High School Journal,* April 1958. Reprinted by permission.

is antithetical to the educational requirements of a classless society. In our view, it has but three features that are desirable: it would assure that only the more capable students enroll in the advanced subjects required for successful college work; it would enable these courses to be made rigorous; and it would provide the more gifted pupils with competition suited to their high capabilities.

Scholars and professional educators alike are agreed that these are conditions which must be provided if our gifted youths are to be served as well as their needs and those of society require. But we believe that the scholars and professional educators who have joined forces in attacking this problem have a far better proposal, one that is fully consistent with the requirements of a classless society. Actually, this has gone well beyond the proposal stage in that many public schools have already traveled some distance down the road these scholars and professional educators would have them go.

The educators in charge of these schools believe with George Stoddard that the only sound answer to the Russian threat is "to push to the limit our own democratic ideal of developing the total resources of every person" and with William Benton that "A deep faith in man is the total opposite to the Soviet system which offers a vast technocratic Sparta. By our standards, their system is more like animal training than the education of human beings. . . . It is the state-take-all and let the individual take the hindmost." These American educators also believe that all kinds of giftedness, not just in science and mathematics alone, should be cultivated to the full. They know that youngsters gifted in one respect may be of but average or even mediocre capacity in other respects, hence that to set up superior schools relating to any given species of giftedness is to range the pupils in these schools from high to low as far as the other kinds of giftedness are concerned. Their belief, then, is in the comprehensive high school within which they arrange different tracks, as it were, for each subject area, with each pupil scheduled in terms of his best fit respecting each subject. A student properly scheduled in the classes for the gifted in science and mathematics might be scheduled with equal propriety in the classes for youngsters of average or less than average capacities in other subjects. And so it might be in respect to art, music, English, or any other subject.

Excellent descriptions of how this has been worked out in respect to science and mathematics, the subjects around which most of the Sputnik-induced fear centers, will be found in the accounts which have been published of the programs which were developed in the Forest Hills High School, New York, and the Evanston Township High School, Illinois, long before Sputnik was placed in orbit. The joint work of scholars and professional educators which is going on at Massachusetts Institute of Technology in the field of science and at the University High School of the University of Illinois in mathematics, both pre-Sputnik undertakings, is breaking new ground and gives every promise of revitalizing the teaching of these subjects in the high schools of this country.

# VI

## Are School Buildings too Fancy?

As the pressure mounts for more and more school buildings, a questioning attitude on the part of the public seems to increase. School building proposals are rejected and many schools are forced to operate double sessions. The situation warrants reflective study, for with the population curve pointing rather sharply upward, no end can be foreseen to the need for new buildings.

Sharp criticism of schools as "costly palaces" is followed in this chapter by general evidence that the charge is based on myths, and by strong support for good school buildings. The topic is technical, however, and each community that builds a school will have to determine for itself what constitutes a good investment.

### Do School Pupils Need Costly Palaces? *

*With underpaid teachers, overcrowded classrooms and burdensome school taxes at an all-time high, what can be done to bring down needless building expense?*

*Holman Harvey*

Not long ago, in a town in New York State, I saw a shining new public school, put up by the community to educate 350 grade-school children. Solidly built of masonry, simple and attractive, this school fulfilled all of the minimum standards laid down by the state's department of education. With 14 cheerful classrooms and all necessary facilities, it cost just under $400,000, or some $28,000 per classroom.

Several days later I visited a second school not far distant. It also had

---

* Reprinted by permission from *The Reader's Digest*, September 1957.

14 classrooms designed for 350 grade-school children. This school cost well over a million dollars, or around $80,000 per classroom.

One half of the entire space in the first school was devoted to actual teaching space—to classrooms. In school number two, less than 25 percent of the space was in its 14 classrooms.

Roughly, three schools like the first could be built for the price of school number two. In the near future, both communities will need additional new classrooms and will go to their taxpayers for still more money. How long will taxpayers stand for the excessive costs of building million-dollar establishments like school number two?

While school funds are lavished on facilities befitting an exclusive club, America is in a desperate plight for sheer lack of classrooms. As of this writing, the shortage is estimated at *200,000 classrooms.*

Millions of children can go to school only in the morning *or* in the afternoon—their schools are forced to doubled-up sessions. Or children are jammed, 40, 50 or more, into rooms designed for 25 or 30. Or they are being taught in school basements without sunlight, in converted libraries, in makeshift quarters tendered by churches and civic organizations. Room somehow must be found each year for 1,250,000 *more* pupils than attended school the year before. Within three years the overcrowding of classrooms can well blossom into a national scandal.

Meanwhile, school taxes are at the highest level in American history, and in thousands of communities are becoming an almost intolerable burden. To build their lavish schools, towns are being plunged into debt for a generation to come. In many places, school costs take up more of the community's total income than all other services combined.

Last year the American people spent, through their local school boards and with some assistance from their states, well over two billion dollars to build schoolhouses. Out of this immense taxation they wound up with only 60,000 or so new classrooms. At the same time, most of the schoolteachers of the nation—the very root and branch of the solid schooling our children need—are trying to live on salaries which no self-respecting bank would offer a junior clerk.

To find out why, after billions are spent on our schools, we still have underpaid teachers and overcrowded classrooms, this writer has criss-crossed the United States and consulted outstanding authorities in government, education and architecture.

"The waste of taxpayers' money in school building is fantastic," says one of America's foremost experts on schoolhouse construction, Dr. James MacConnell, director of the famed School Planning Laboratory at Stanford University. His organization is working with school boards in more than 100 towns and cities to eliminate waste and build schools which the community can afford.

A school board in the Far West recently put up a high school containing a $750,000 gymnasium with bleacher seats from which 3000 spectators might watch the basketball games. In the Middle West a $300,000 auditorium was built into a new high school. At the same time, and in both communities, grade-school children were limited to half-a-day schooling. Money spent on the splendid gym would have built some 30 new classrooms; that spent on the auditorium, 12 classrooms. America needs classrooms. But as one prominent educator says: "In many a U. S. community it is an open question whether the town builds a high school primarily for education or for the training of the basketball team."

Over one million dollars is being raised in one New England town to build, for children through 12 years of age, a school which will have only 14 classrooms—but will boast a large auditorium to which is attached a three-stage theater; a two-story-high gymnasium; a "meeting room"; two kitchens in stainless steel; a library with an open fireplace and "sprawl corner"; a teachers' smoking lounge; capacious quarters for the principal and his staff; a separate room for arts and crafts (which can be taught in any ordinary classroom); another for music instruction; a different one for piano alone.

The children in this school will travel through long, glass walled corridors and peer through colored panes so they may "see the world in many colors." Here they will find a school "home away from home" and can "curl up with a book" in the sprawl corner, at a cost to the taxpayers of over $3000 per child just to *build* the school. To maintain this palatial building will put a heavy burden on the taxpayers. There are a thousand or so windows to be washed, some 60,000 square feet of floors to be scrubbed and waxed. Yet soon these same taxpayers will be called upon to build another school —this one doesn't have enough classrooms.

Isn't it high time that school boards, parents and taxpayers wake up to such waste of public funds in building schools? A powerful group of educators, styled "liberal" or "modern," and including many school superintendents and school principals, is determined to build luxury schools, regardless both of the country's tragic classroom shortage and of often insufferable taxes. This group is flourishing on school-tax money in every region of the United States today and is preying on school boards in thousands of communities.

Fortunately, however, we have a distinguished society of educators who abhor the waste of school funds. It is the National Council on Schoolhouse Construction, and its scholarly studies of schoolhouse extravagance should be perused by school boards everywhere. Its headquarters are at George Peabody College for Teachers at Nashville, Tenn. Its secretary is Dr. William McClurkin.

I talked with a recent president of this group, Dr. William Flesher, professor of education at Ohio State University, who told me of a new school in suburban Buffalo with a clock tower costing enough to build many classrooms; of false chimneys 60 feet high. Many architects still perch parapets and cupolas on school roofs; they parade Grecian pillars at entrances; build flights of entrance steps (expensive both to build and to maintain); and pile on ornamental stone "trim." Professor Flesher points also to the needless expense of excavating for basements which burden the school with unsupervised space and serve no educational purpose.

At Stanford, Dr. MacConnell told me of an architect who recently put up on a school a decorative false chimney containing 128,000 bricks—enough to build 12 good-sized classrooms! Another architect, accustomed to building churches, designed a grade school with windows of 17 different sizes. They had to be cut to order, and cost three times as much as standard-sized windows.

The distinguished authority Dr. Walter D. Cocking, editor of *School Executive* magazine, and father of the noted Cocking Awards for architectural excellence in school design, said recently: "Too much building is being done on the basis of out-of-date know-how, hunches, prejudices and sheer lack of information." Other important authorities say that only one of every ten qualified architects in the country has made any serious study of schoolhouse construction. The rest know next to nothing of the economies possible.

But a small group of economy-minded specialists is pulling down costs while still using the best materials. Not long ago, in the village of Ardsley, in New York's Hudson Valley, a 14-classroom grade school was built on the relatively new principle of "unit construction." It won the highest award of the New York State Society of Architects. About one half of its area—an unusually high percentage—is devoted solely to classroom space. It is solidly built of well-set masonry, with all of its fittings of high-quality materials. The Ardsley school cost $13.70 per square foot, and $25,100 per classroom. Taxpayers in nearby communities, at the same time, are being required to spend $15,000 more *per classroom* for their schools. These, again, soon will be overcrowded.

Robert A. Green, of Tarrytown, N. Y., the architect of Ardsley, and of some 40 similar schools built in the past few years, explains that the plan means building a sound "core" school, to take care of immediate needs. Onto this core additional classrooms can be built at minimum expense. Ten new classrooms already have been added to the original 14 at the Ardsley school, with the core facilities amply serving all.

No interior walls in Green's schools are plastered, painted or otherwise "finished." They are built of a masonry block which is delivered "integrally tinted" in subdued but cheerful tones. One eight-inch wall separates two classrooms (or classrooms from corridors), provides colorful facing on both sides and insulates for both heat and sound. This solid-block construction does away with the original cost of lath and plaster, and with later re-plastering and repainting of walls.

Economy-minded school architects insist upon the imperative need to slash labor costs, which can run as high as 65 *percent* of the cost of the school. Labor costs can be cut one third to one half by using standard windows, doors, cabinets, fixtures (and often wall panels and other elements) which are made in factories to precise measurement, or "module," so that when delivered at the school site they fit accurately into the new building without further cutting or trimming. The Walt Whitman Elementary School, at Woodbury, L. I., another prize-winning school by architect Green, cost only around $13.50 per square foot, in a high-cost area—largely due to its "modular construction."

Untold waste of school-tax monies is going on everywhere in building schools whose expensive facilities lie idle much of the time. In a recently completed grade school for 350 children near White Plains, N. Y., I saw an immense two-story gymnasium large enough to accommodate three times that number; a spacious cafeteria used only at lunchtime; and three separate lounging rooms for fewer than 20 teachers, several of whom said they would rather have had a pay raise.

At Ohio State University, Professor Flesher said of such waste: "Here is a big auditorium, and you have an assembly maybe once every week or two, and then you hold commencement there in the spring. *The space is used only five or ten percent of the time.* I would rather see them take a gym and just put chairs in there. You can buy folding chairs for a lot less than you can build and maintain this auditorium with its overstuffed seats."

"Economy demands that all spaces be used as much of the time as possible," says the National Council on Schoolhouse Construction. "There should be multiple use of spaces which normally would be used only a few hours a day." And, says the American Association of School Administrators: "It is poor economy to build dining halls used only an hour or two a day."

Many school boards are finding an answer to economy in a "multipurpose room." There are many manageable combinations of the gym, the cafteria, the study hall, the auditorium, the library, the room for visual-auditory instruction, and other nonclassroom space, which can effect genuine savings. In some schools, serving carts and portable steam tables are rolled into a multi-purpose room, rendering a separate cafeteria entirely unnecessary. Sometimes there are "cafetoriums," or "cafenasiums."

Extravagant educators and architects, and duped school boards, however, go right ahead spending taxpayers' money, not for needed classrooms, but for excessively high ceilings, needlessly wide corridors, elaborate lobbies and so on.

The State of Washington has found one way to clamp a lid on this extravagance. Along with other states, in varying degree, Washington gives state aid to build school buildings. But Washington, as of this writing, aids a school only up to a cost of $13.62 per square foot. And Washington will not contribute a cent for: auditoriums, swimming pools, stadiums, fireplaces, spectator balconies, bleacher seats or other nonclassroom space. All these are agreeable luxuries, but America first of all needs more classrooms and better-paid teachers.

Some other encouraging examples of common-sense economy:

In Laredo, Texas, the school board cut down the traditional 12-foot ceiling of a new school to eight feet, ten inches, saving 27 percent of cubic space, and 27 percent of heating volume. Sikeston, Mo., saved money by building classrooms back to back, with one wall dividing two classrooms. This construction avoids separated wings which expensively increase the perimeter of the outer walls. Heating costs are materially lowered, and corridors can be reduced in length.

Architect Arsene Rousseau is producing schools in the Middle West at a square-foot cost of from $7 to $9. His recent Springfield Local High School, in rural Youngstown, Ohio, cost $7.24. It is built of face brick, glass block and heavy aluminum framing. In the St. Louis area, where current school-building costs are around $14 per square foot, architects Hellmuth, Obata and Kassabaum produced the award-winning design for the Riverview Gardens High School, the first completed unit of which has cost $11.82 per square foot.

By contrast, many lavish schools today are costing up to $25 or $30 per square foot.[1]

In Clearwater, Fla., architect K. Whitney Dalzell, Jr., has just completed an elementary school at a square-foot cost of $8.35. It cost $224,000. A school in the same area and being built at the same time, to the same requirements, cost $298,000—$74,000 more. Architect A. Blaine Imel has built the high school at Perkins, Okla., for $7.12, using a newly developed clay brick.

Available in most localities are prefabricated schools, or schools consisting mostly of prefabricated parts, in many materials—wood, laminated wood, aluminum, steel—and including portable classrooms to meet emergency school enrollments. Any economy-minded school board may make a choice of one of these when hard pressed by urgent classroom shortage.

And since school boards are ultimately responsible to the citizens, you, as a voter, can put a stop to the endlessly harassing increase of your school taxes if you'll act on the knowledge that pupils don't ask for or need the palaces that the architects dream up for them. Remember that our first need is for better-paid teachers—and for 200,000 new classrooms.

## Those Fairy Tales About "Palaces" *

Last year, over one-fourth of the dollar value of school-bond proposals was turned down at the polls.

There are many reasons for this unfortunate situation, but no doubt

---

[1] Since building costs vary greatly over the United States, cost comparisons can be valid only for their immediate area and for relatively recent construction.

* Reprinted by permission from *NEA Journal,* October 1958.

one of them is the peddling of the "palace" myth by a few national magazines. The "palace" jesters, through selection of examples from exceptionally wealthy school districts, through misrepresentation and partial presentation of facts, and through references based on superficial observations, have no doubt convinced some voters that schools are on the brink of such luxuries as Turkish baths and movie theaters for off-duty teachers.

Actually, in most communities, Americans get more for their school-building dollar than for almost any other construction dollar.

With many more bond elections now in the offing, it is important to look again at the facts—particularly since some the "low taxes regardless" groups are renewing the cry that modern school construction is extravagant.

Estimates indicate that during the past 20 years the average cost of construction has increased as follows:

- school building, 150%
- all buildings, 210%
- general construction, 275%
- medium-priced brick residences, 225%
- medium-priced frame residences, 228%
- highway construction, 200%.

Increases in these examples of construction are not surprising, as the cost of nearly everything that goes into construction has greatly increased.

How do we account for the economy in school construction? Much of it can be attributed to careful planning. School-board members, administrators, teachers, architects, and lay citizens—knowing that present and future school-building needs are staggering—have approached school-building planning by taking a good look at the kind of space and equipment teachers and pupils need and can use to best advantage in teaching and learning. They have designed buildings that will meet these essentials at minimum cost. For example:

- Gables, cupolas, parapets, decorative columns, and gingerbread in general have been eliminated. The long, straight lines that characterize the new school plants in crossroads neighborhoods, towns, and cities illustrate this streamlined, simplified school-building design.
- Expensive decorative materials have been replaced by attractive functional materials. Colorful tiles laid on concrete have replaced more expensive types of floors. Painted masonry classroom walls have replaced the more expensive plaster walls. Finished roof decks have been used in many cases to avoid costly ceilings.
- Classroom heights have been dropped from the traditional 12 feet to 9 or 10 feet, or in some instances even lower. The amount of corridor space has been reduced.
- Buildings have been made more usable by the inclusion of folding or movable partitions that permit rooms to be used for a variety of purposes.

– Wherever possible, plans have provided for the use of standard or stock materials.

Not only has this careful planning resulted in keeping school-building costs low, as compared with other construction costs, but it has added substantially to the quality of school plants. Classrooms are more attractive, better lighted, and better adapted to teaching and learning than ever before.

The real danger we face in hundreds of communities as the fall school-bond elections approach is not that we will build "palaces" but that we may not build at all, or that we will build too cheaply.

False economies forced upon some school systems in recent years have saddled these systems with future high maintenance and repair costs which may place downward pressures on teachers' salaries and other operating costs in years to come. Several sad illustrations of the results of "penny wise, pound foolish" approaches to school construction are pointed out in the October issues of *Coronet* and *Parents' Magazine*.

Each of us should make sure that the citizens in his community understand the facts and vote intelligently.

## "Bargain-Basement Education Is No Bargain" *

*In the guise of economy, misguided foes of new school construction are depriving children of a vital need in America today—better education.*

*Martin L. Gross*

Parents in the expanding suburbs of Colorado Springs, Colorado, went to the polls early this year and rejected a proposed new junior high school, amid heated charges that it was an "elaborate memorial" that was "too expensive to build."

"The truth," says a local physician who resigned from the school board over the controversy, "is that it was a modern building with labs and a gym—yet it would only cost $13 a square foot, which is average for our area. But opponents distorted the facts so much that we could never catch up with the real truth."

In prosperous, suburban Mount Vernon, New York, a proposal to replace two nearly half-century-old high schools was voted down amid charges that plans called for "plush Cadillac jobs."

In Phoenix, Arizona, a group of citizens defeated a school bond issue by charging that the proposed new $2,500,000 school for 2,000 students —a relatively inexpensive building that utilized the outdoors for an auditorium—was "too fancy." The defeat meant that students in two high

* Reprinted by permission from *Coronet*, October 1958. Copyright 1958 by Esquire, Inc.

schools will have to attend school on the stagger system from 7:30 A.M. until 5:00 P.M.

The startling fact that emerges from these instances is that while the American public has been fighting an eloquent verbal battle for better education in the post-Sputnik era, there has been a tremendous trend toward cut-rate education that is endangering the quality of our public school programs.

Throughout the nation, parents have been duped by a strong anti-tax, anti-public-education group who have deceptively, but effectively, been attacking badly needed new schools and modern educational facilities— from auditoriums to audio-visual aids—as "frills" that are "squandering" the taxpayer's money on "elaborate educational castles."

In fact, school communities have defeated more bonds for new schools this year than ever before in recent history. In school elections last May, parents rejected 33 percent of new school proposals—twice as many as in 1957. In the first five months of this year, $173,000,000 for needed schools was defeated at the polls.

"There have been charges of extravagance, but actually economy in school building is unmatched," says C. C. Trillingham of Los Angeles, president of the American Association of School Administrators. "While general construction costs have increased 275 percent during the past 20 years, school buildings have gone up only 150 percent.

"Expensive decorations have been replaced by modern buildings and functional materials. Classroom ceilings have been lowered and corridor space reduced. If there were 'frills,' they were in older buildings with their towers, gables, and parapets."

The new "economy" drive has hit hardest in areas where new schools are needed most. In Mechanicville, an upstate New York industrial town, sorely needed schools were blocked recently by a specious "economy" argument circulated in a last-minute anonymous letter.

Two of Mechanicville's elementary schools are antiquated Victorian buildings dating back to the 1890s. They are fire hazards, whose roofs often leak. Squinting children study by dull, dim lighting—less than one-third normal. There are no auditoriums, books are stacked in the hallway as a makeshift "library." Children must walk down to the basement to reach student toilets. The "gyms" are a converted classroom in one school and a make-do cellar space in another.

"We can't have a proper program in these buildings," says School Superintendent Michael T. Griffin. "We proposed a new 21-room school with average facilities including a library and a combined cafeteria-auditorium. It wasn't a fancy building but some critics called it a 'palace.' One man even said: 'Why do they need a kitchen? When I went to school there, we carried our lunches in paper bags.' "

Many communities, torn between growing taxes and the hope of buying a good education for their children, are asking: How can we separate good judgment from false economy? How should we spend our education dollar? What actually are "frills" and what should every good school contain?

"In education, like everything else, you get pretty much what you pay for," says Dr. A. J. Foy Cross, a National Education Association building specialist. "Our biggest danger is false economy. Many communities are building new but already obsolete buildings in a crash program—as if the crisis were temporary."

South Carolina embarked on a frantic crash program a few years ago to build "economy" schools without libraries, auditoriums or sufficient science labs. Students were cramped into 640-square-foot classrooms, three-quarters the normal size. Today, they realize that the small savings did not balance the damage to their educational program, and communities like Columbia are building excellent schools that cost just a little more.

A false economy in schools, heavily scored by architects, is the use of "cheap" building materials with high maintenance and hidden costs. "Bargain-basement education is no bargain," says Dr. Jordan L. Larson, president of the School Facilities Council, a nationwide group of architects, educators and industrialists. "Things like painted window frames, cheap roofing materials, and inferior plumbing will eat up more school dollars than are saved."

A sturdy '20-year' roof, for example, costs 35¢ a square foot installed in the New York area—approximately twice as much as a thinner '10-year' roof. "A cheap roof may seem like an economy at first," says a local architect, "but when it starts to leak, you have to pay to rip it out before it is replaced. This can actually double its cost."

Architect Larry Perkins of Perkins and Will, Chicago, points out that districts seldom want to repeat "economics" they insisted on the first time. "In one New York community," he recalls, "we cut $6,000 off the initial price by using an inexpensive fiber ceiling tile instead of gypsum, and $15 per classroom door by using hollow instead of solid doors.

"The cheap tile soon absorbed moisture and warped badly. The veneer of the doors took a tremendous beating from students and the doors will probably have to be replaced. Overall, the attempt to save money was costly."

The hallmark of economy-conscious school districts is often the stark cinder-block school. Building experts, however, consider it a prime example of misbalanced school budgeting.

"A brick-faced, 12-inch wall costs $2.60 a square foot today in the Midwest," says a prominent architect. "A 12-inch cinder block costs only $1.55 initially, but you have to add 75¢ for painting and water-proofing over 25 years. If you plaster the blocks, the savings disappear altogether. The brick is attractive and lasts the life of the building. The cinder block has a deadly garage-like appearance, it cracks and disintegrates, and leaks moisture which can ruin the inside walls."

Ceramic tile in student bathrooms is often omitted because of the initial cost—approximately $1,200 more for a 20' x 30' room. However, experts point out that there are few other materials that are so economical in the long run—both from a maintenance and health point of view. Many penny-wise schools have found it necessary to completely rip out fouled asphalt-tile floors and to refinish marked bathroom walls.

Glenview, Illinois, a mushrooming Chicago suburb, is an unfortunate case history involving a compendium of false economies. Fifteen years ago the town decided to build a school "cheaply," with inexpensive materials, including some salvage. The plumbing and the brick were reused, the floors were asphalt tile over wood—often green. When completed, the school seemed a miracle of economy. It cost only $11,000 a classroom, about one-third the national average.

"But it didn't prove cheap in the long run," says the school architect frankly. "Maintenance on that building has been shockingly high. Paint didn't stay on the raw wood, the transom-type windows leaked water, the asphalt-tile floor cracked, and the cheap plumbing had to be ripped out and replaced. Including wrecking, it cost twice what good plumbing would have originally. Glenview is not happy about its bargain."

Temporary frame schools are another case of expensive "savings." "I saw a lot of them in industrial areas in the Northwest," says one educator. "They were built a half-dozen years ago, supposedly until things got better. But they are still there eating up a fortune in maintenance—and a generation of children have been robbed of good schools in the towns that chose this answer to their building problem."

Hard-pressed Hicksville, New York, recently constructed eight of these temporary structures. "We did what the client requested," says Henry Johnson of Knappe and Johnson, the architects. "But they are not economical. They cost $15.00 a square foot instead of $18.00 for permanent buildings. Because they are not fire-resistant, the fire-insurance rates on some of them are eight times more than permanent buildings. The most economical thing about temporaries is that they can be demolished easily."

Under-building in the ostrich-like hope that rising enrollments will disappear is another false economy that is wasting precious tax dollars. Additions invariably cost 10 to 25 percent more.

"If you are going to add, do it while the building is still under construction," says architect Larry Perkins. "Otherwise you have new overhead and various connections such as plumbing and heating."

In Guilderland, New York, six extra classrooms were put on a high school while under construction for a phenomenally low $12,000 a room. In the same town, four classrooms added to an elementary school *after* completion cost $30,000 each!

Hedging against time is another false hope practiced by some school communities. Since 1949, school building costs have gone up an average of 6 percent a year. In 1952, Evanston, Illinois, defeated a $1,950,000 expansion plan. The bond was finally approved last year—but costs hit $2,600,000. "We wasted five years and $650,000 making up our mind," says a taxpayer.

Delaying can also mean less school for more money. A 1,000-student $2,597,000 high school for the upstate New York suburban school district of Scotia-Glenville was rejected twice by parents in 1953 as "too expensive." In desperation, the size of the school was cut—classrooms were made smaller, a science lab eliminated—and the price lowered to $2,266,000. However, when the bids were finally let in 1956, they came in 17 percent higher than even this last price.

Although attacks against new schools are often clouded with such vague epithets as "elaborate," the true target is usually the space allotted to students—at anywhere from $10 a square foot in the South to $18 average in New York State. Cutting this space down by eliminating education facilities—what school-bond opponents call "frills"—is the root of the cut-rate education argument.

"They would have people believe," says Dr. Walter Cocking, editor of *The School Executive,* "that auditoriums, lunchrooms, libraries, health rooms, teachers' offices and workrooms, and guidance rooms are not only unnecessary but actually nefarious."

Because of its size, the staid old auditorium has suddenly become controversial—and has evolved as everything from a combined "gymnatorium" to a luncheon-theater "cafetorium."

"Every elementary school needs a multi-purpose room as a minimum," says Dr. Henry Linn, prominent Columbia University school building consultant. "But in high schools these combinations create too many conflicts that hurt the program. When figuring the cost of a separate high school auditorium, parents should keep in mind that it is usually used as an adult community center."

One of the weakest—but most emotional—arguments of the cut-rate education group is their attack on "comprehensive" high schools. These schools are spacious, well-equipped structures that combine the traditional vocational and academic high schools, and prepare students for careers ranging from beauty parlor technicians to nuclear physicists.

Of the nation's 23,000 high schools, only 2,000 are considered truly "comprehensive." They have been singled out in Dr. James Conant's recent survey for the Carnegie Corporation as one of our best hopes in the educational sweepstakes with the Soviets.

Ann Arbor High School in Michigan, a 2,600-student-capacity school, is one of the nation's best equipped, yet it was built at the reasonable cost of $17.71 per square foot. It boasts everything from a student planetarium, a swimming pool, a community-sized 1,700-seat auditorium to a complete shop wing with a union apprentice program.

"We're sometimes called a 'palace,' " says School Superintendent Jack Elzay. "But all we have to do is show how well our students are doing.

We're the only school in Michigan that teaches Russian and has an Advanced Placement Program for gifted seniors. One hundred and thirty of our boys and girls are getting college credit for advanced work."

Instead of stampeding into "economy" programs, better schools are devising new, inexpensive facilities such as better audio-visual aids. Four Detroit high schools, for example, are teaching beginning French entirely with slides and tape recordings. "The entire kit costs only $850 and can be used by many classes," says Dr. J. J. McPherson of Wayne State University, where the technique was developed. "We found that students using the new course spoke French 50 percent better after one year than those who learned by traditional methods."

The battle against good schools has had a strange side effect. It has made beauty a suspect item, confused with plushiness. "Good design doesn't cost a penny," points out Dr. Cocking. "You can hire the nation's best creative architects for the same price it costs for a man who normally builds garages."

The situation has become so acute that a New England architect recently commented: "I not only have to build cheap schools—they have to look cheap." In Syosset, Long Island, a number of citizens complained that the beautiful, laminated wooden trusses in the high school were "plush." "They actually cost us less than steel," says a school official. "Because they aren't ugly, some people are convinced they are frill."

A similar incident took place in Minnesota where the supposed "marble" facing on a new school was roundly criticized. It actually proved to be local, and relatively inexpensive, granite.

Can dollars-and-cents economies be made, then, that will *not* jeopardize a school? Definitely, yes.

One of the most important is the consolidation of school districts to eliminate overhead waste and uneconomical small schools. In 1953, there were 77,000 school districts, which have been consolidated to 50,000. However, 25,000 would be even more economical.

Borrowing schoolhouse construction money at good rates can save more than cut-back in facilities. In 1957, the average school-bond interest rate was 4 percent, double that of 1950. In many cases this increased building costs by 30 percent.

A possible solution is State Bonding Authorities such as one proposed by New York. However, one administrator, Howard McEachen of Merriam, Kansas, took matters into his own hands recently. He traveled to Wall Street and successfully convinced financiers that his district's financial record had earned it a lower interest rate. "He saved the taxpayers more money with that one trip than I have in years," says the district's architect.

The economy of entirely prefabricated schools is debated, but experts agree on the value of "modular" or stock parts. In Liberty, Texas, architect Bill Caudill designed a ten-room elementary school with beams of two sizes instead of the usual dozens, and one stock column instead of a half dozen. The school's steel costs were almost 40 percent less, and the school won nationwide recognition, architecturally and educationally.

The intelligent *early* purchase of land for schools is a vital economy. Two towns, one that planned and one that waited, had exactly opposite experiences. Charlotte, North Carolina, started buying land before World War II and recently sold a parcel they could not use at a 300 percent profit. Woodbridge, New Jersey, a rapidly expanding suburb, sold town-owned land to developers ten years ago and is now buying it back for school sites at ten times the price. "And we're taking what's left over," says a disgruntled citizen.

Intelligent economies will undoubtedly help pay our education bill. Meanwhile, it is vital to understand the difference between a supposed "plush palace" and an efficient, attractive school properly equipped to teach our children. It may help defeat the dangerous fallacy of bargain-basement education—as it did in Schenectady, New York.

Four years ago, Schenectady erupted in a bitter fight over a new "dream" school, the $5,500,000 Linton High School planned to replace an overcrowded turn-of-the-century school in the noisy heart of town. The fourth floor of the building had been condemned and boarded up, and students had to fight two blocks of city traffic to reach their athletic field.

"We thought they deserved more," says F. Morley Roberts, a business executive who helped lead the Citizens Committee for Public Schools fight. "The opposition attacked it as a palace, but we brought our story to the people through newspapers, radio and a door-to-door campaign."

The new school won by a bare 684 votes in this city of almost 100,000. "The fight was well worth it," says Roberts. "Linton High opened this spring and is already the center of our community. We have 1,700 youngsters in a summer recreation program, the Schenectady Symphony uses the auditorium, and the Boys Club has an after-school program here.

"Ten thousand people came to our open house this May, and almost everyone was happy with it—including many former skeptics. We just made our first annual payment on it—$192,000, or about $8 extra taxes for a family with a $15,000 house. We think it's well worth the price."

But the fight against bargain-basement education has yet to be won in many other American towns. "There is a climate of opinion in thousands of American communities that is impeding the construction of superior school buildings able to provide a superior education," warns Dr. Cocking. "If we don't stop it, today's children and tomorrow's are the ones who will suffer."

# VII

## Can Teacher Training
## and Certification Practices
## Be Justified?

Teacher training practices and state teacher certification requirements to which they are closely related have, in recent years, been the subject of strong attack. In the main, teacher training has been criticized for emphasizing method to the neglect of solid subject matter, and teacher certification regulations have been characterized as having a stranglehold on teacher education.

Albert Lynd's *Quackery in the Public Schools,* reviewed on pages 29-34 of this book, contains one of the most devastating criticisms that have appeared. Another is the negative phase of the opening debate on teacher education in this chapter. The debate is followed by an item that epitomizes criticism of certification requirements; a defense of certification practices; and two statements of cold, hard facts, as seen by lay reporters, about the teacher crisis. These will suffice to underscore the fact that teacher education is not a simple problem.

## How Well Are Our Teachers Being Taught? *

### NEVER WORSE!

*. . . says John Keats, author of "Schools Without Scholars" and father of three school children.*

If your Johnny can't read, write, or do arithmetic, it may be due to the fact that his teacher can't do these things well herself. And the

### NEVER BETTER

*. . . says Robert H. Beck, Professor of History and Philosophy of Education, University of Minnesota.*

Contrary to a highly vocal segment of public opinion, teachers colleges are not a waste of time for

* Reprinted by permission from *Better Homes & Gardens,* May 1958. Copyright 1958 by Meredith Publishing Company, Des Moines, Iowa.

reason *she* can't do them is that *her* instructors in teachers college were told she should be taught other things instead.

In teachers college, they told her that all children should not be expected to read, write, or do arithmetic, anyway. She heard it was more important for Johnny to be well adjusted and happy than it was for him to be asked to use his head. In teachers college, she spent far more time learning to ventilate a classroom than she spent learning anything she might be asked to teach. Then she was told she could teach students a foreign language without being able to read, write, or pronounce it herself. Finally, she was warned that if she made a brilliant record in what formal studies there were in her teachers college, she might not be allowed to teach at all.

Therefore, we must not blame teachers for the ever-growing criticism that our public schools fail to make the best use of our children's abilities and fail to teach things worth learning. Our schools' failure may be traced to the zany educational philosophy dispensed at our leading teachers colleges—both independent teachers colleges and those that are part of a university. Let's visit a sample teachers college to discover what goes on at the source.

The school I will call Fairly Normal is a part of New York State's university system and it trains teachers for New York public schools. It is well-regarded by other teachers

the men and women enrolled in them, nor do they stand in the way of your Johnny's learning to read, write, or do arithmetic. There is, in fact, good reason to believe that today's professionally trained teachers are the best teachers our schools have ever had, and not only can Johnny learn from them, but he can learn faster and better.

Proof of this is found in a study by Professor Benjamin S. Bloom of the University of Chicago. He compared sample scores of the millions of high-school seniors taking the General Education Development tests in 1943 with those taking them in 1955. The GED has five sections —English composition, social studies, natural science, literature, and mathematics. Professor Bloom found that in all five areas the students' knowledge of the subject was greater than it had been 12 years earlier. "These consistent results," he said, "give evidence that today's students are achieving to a greater extent the objectives measured by this battery of tests than were students of 1943."

Results from other studies similarly favor the elementary school of 1958. Today's students do better work in mental arithmetic and in written arithmetic. Only in certain aspects of geography and in spelling do they fall behind.

Anyone who is surprised by these findings has probably fallen victim to rumors that today's teachers can't teach—that the education courses they take in teachers colleges are totally useless, and that these courses monopolize their time and

*[Never Worse!*

*[Never Better!*

colleges, and New York schools are far from the nation's worst.

"Good teachers," Fairly Normal's Dean of Education says, "are produced solely by scientific teaching methods. We say 'We teach children, not subjects,' and we say, 'A good teacher can teach anything.' "

Hence, Fairly Normal's undergraduates spend one-third of their time in "education," learning teaching techniques and manipulation of "teaching aids," such as movie projectors. The rest of their time, including training, is devoted to the subjects they may be called upon to teach.

A future English teacher may spend one-third of his time learning How to Teach, and as little as one-seventh of his time studying English. For this reason, the English courses are hasty surveys with no emphasis on mastery of any particular phase of the material. I plucked a paper at random from a pile of Fairly Normal freshman essays. It was eight paragraphs long, entitled "How To Shot A Bow." Unfortunately, the author will not have an opportunity to increase his proficiency, because Fairly Normal requires only one semester in English composition. Four years from now, he may be teaching composition to your child. Or perhaps he may be teaching French, which he did not study in either high school *or* at Fairly Normal, because teachers colleges believe good teachers can teach literally anything.

The real meat of Fairly Normal's "education" course is a collection

prevent them from learning anything worth teaching. It isn't so.

First of all, prospective teachers don't spend all their hours learning How To Teach. The National Education Association's Manual on Certification Requirements shows that high-school instructors in most states need no more than 16 or 18 semester hours of education courses. This is roughly one-seventh of a normal four-year college education. In contrast, the average requirement for state certification as a high-school teacher is 24 semester hours in English, modern foreign languages, or social studies for anyone who is to teach those subjects. And these minimum requirements are actually exceeded by most students. Future elementary school teachers ordinarily take about a fourth of their college study in education courses —considerably more than do budding high-school instructors. But this increased emphasis isn't strange, considering the difficulty of imparting basic concepts to very young children.

Nor are these education courses either useless or divorced from subject matter. A course in children's literature, for example, both familiarizes the future teacher with available material and gives her methods of selecting books for youngsters who vary in reading ability, in interests, in background. No college course in American literature can quite do that.

As an example of a methods course that has come under some ridicule, let's take the teaching of of classroom How To's which liberal arts schools offer as a one-year minor elective. At Fairly Normal, however, "education" is not only the undergraduate's major field but the school's sole reason for existence. In order to convert the essentially minor matter of pedagogy into a major course of study, Fairly Normal and other teachers colleges have magnified it beyond all belief to include such "learnings" as "the *need* for democracy in the classroom," and "meaningful student participation in the use of audiovisual aids." One teachers college text devotes 42 pages to how to get along with the school janitor.

There is no apparent limit to the lengths to which this mindlessness may be carried. A lesson on "proper classroom ventilation," for instance, is not just a five-minute lecture, but a separate course, the gist of which is that classroom air should be kept fresh and at a constant temperature. I regret having to say I am serious.

Not only are such purely mechanical matters as window-raising blown up into semesters of study, but there is a similar belaboring of the obvious in what passes for the intellectual aspects of Fairly Normal's scientific pedagogy. I sat in one sophomore class learning the necessity for "democratic group behavior in the classroom."

"How can we tell whether a man is a good democratic group leader?" the professor asked.

There was a silence, during which the young people stared at one another. The silence grew embar-

reading. Should an elementary school teacher take such a course? Surely she can read; why can't she teach reading? If you try this with your own six-year-old, you'll soon see the difficulty. The sound of the letter "a" will be the first thing to throw you. Which of the eight sounds listed in the pronunciation key of a dictionary should be taught first? "A is for apple," true. But "a" is also for "ace" and for "axe," not to mention "alphabet," which has two "a's," each sounded differently. Even at this first stage of instruction, you may give up, wondering how teachers ever do it.

Well, they do it because they've had a course teaching them when to introduce phonics and how to teach them—and when and how to teach blends, digraphs, variant endings, root words, compounds, prefixes, suffixes, and syllabification. All these things, they have learned, enter into effective word recognition.

It is significant, too, that a third of the future teacher's time in education courses is spent in practice teaching, where she can try out what she has learned on a sort of internship, under the direction of already qualified teachers. The potential teacher learns her methods in both the classroom and the "lab"— the secondary or elementary schoolroom where she tests the theory she has studied. The candidate thus not only adapts theory to practice but also learns whether she *can* teach or is suited to teaching. Without this trial period, a teacher would have to dive blindly into a profession for

[*Never Worse!*

rassing. I began to time it, and when nearly seven minutes had passed, the professor said; "Well, can we tell by looking at him? By what color tie he wears?"

One student took a deep breath and plunged in. "By what he does?" he wondered.

"Exactly!" the professor said. "We can tell by what he does!"

Everyone seemed startled by this revelation. The young lady next to me muttered, "Ask a silly question and get a silly answer," and wrote something in her notebook. I was reminded of another young woman at another teachers college who said, "If I hear one more dean tell me the school is important to the child, I'll scream."

In places like Fairly Normal, masters and doctors degrees are granted for deep research into such matters as the timed, observed use of the boys' toilet in an elementary school of 345 pupils. One thesis, hardly atypical, was entitled "Your Present Classroom Pencil Sharpener, Its Care, Location, and Use."

In my two years' research, I found that Fairly Normal believes in the following concepts:

1. An educated man is one who "is socially well adjusted and helpful in his community." By this standard, Fairly Normal's president says, a man could be considered educated even if he could not write his name or count to 10.

2. Johnny's mind cannot be trained by rigorous studies. "We know," the dean of education says, "that learning algebra leads only to

[*Never Better!*

which she might have neither aptitude nor zeal, in which case Johnny's classroom would reflect frustration and confusion.

Recent experience in Minnesota further illuminates this point. In 1949 and 1950, when Minneapolis was faced with a shortage of elementary school teachers, emergency certificates were granted to 54 recent college graduates who wanted to become teachers. All of them were given a six-week preparatory teaching course, but none of them had had a systematic college course in child growth and development or in the teaching of reading or arithmetic. During this same period, 183 teachers holding regular certificates were appointed.

Today—largely because of marriage, inadequate salaries, and the inferior social status too often accorded teachers—just 43 percent of the fully qualified instructors are still teaching. But only 22 percent of the "emergency" teachers are left! Why did nearly twice the percentage of trained instructors remain at their profession? Mostly because the untrained teachers were overwhelmed by an experience for which they had too little preparation.

Of the 12 provisionally certified teachers who have stayed on, some have become proficient through the process of trial and error. "But at what cost!" as one of them has said. A major share of that cost, of course, was borne by the children who missed out on their education while their teachers were making experiments—and mistakes—that could

[*Never Worse!*

knowledge of algebra. The mind cannot be trained like a muscle."

3. Not all children should be asked to master reading, writing, arithmetic, or any other formal study. "The sooner we realize this," the dean says, "the sooner we can build a better curriculum."

4. There are no objective standards in learning. "We no longer try to stuff the same diet down every child's throat," the dean says. "We try to set before each child a cafeteria of learnings, so that each child may choose what he wants, and needs, and would like to study."

5. A brilliant student is a poor risk as a teacher. "The more a student is enamored of his subjects, the more apt he is to be a scholar and the less likely to be a good teacher," the dean claims.

This philosophy has weakened our public school curriculum so that the only "subject matter" to which all our children are exposed during their 12 years is simple work in word and number. By no means all high schools require chemistry, physics, biology, languages dead or living, mathematics, history, geography, or English composition beyond the sentence and the paragraph. One Virginia high school recently dropped European history because too few students elected to study it. A Maryland high school offers training in beauty-shop operation, and spends more time on this course than it spends on Latin, French, mathematics, history, science, and English, or any combination of two. Our public school curriculum has so de-

[*Never Better!*

have been better handled in teachers colleges.

Other members of this untrained group took courses in child growth and development when they found time, and they immediately felt more at ease and more competent in their jobs. One woman in this group, still teaching, has written that her first problem was "lack of knowledge and understanding of the child." Another problem concerned teaching methods. She said of teaching reading, for instance, that learning by the phonics method is certainly no guarantee that you can teach by that method, unless you have studied it for that purpose.

What happened in Minneapolis was evidence of the value of professional preparation. Teachers with regular certificates, more prepared for the problems they would encounter, enabled their students to learn more easily than provisional teachers did. This fact was borne out not only by testimony from the teachers, but also by results of achievement tests of the pupils.

Why, then, are so many people so critical of teachers colleges? Probably because they misuse the term "teachers colleges," grouping under it a variety of schools that have nothing in common but this vague and misleading name. They don't know about the different schools in which teachers are trained or how many teachers come from each.

Historically, the first schools devoted to preparing teachers were normal schools, but by 1900 most of these had been absorbed into

112    TEACHER TRAINING AND CERTIFICATION PRACTICE

*[Never Worse!*

Education has compared it unfavorably with Russia's, particularly in
mathematics, languages, and the sciences, and cited the elective "cafeteria" and the shortage of qualified
teachers as major reasons.

The shortage of teachers is both
quantitative and qualitative, and the
teachers college is partly responsible
in both instances. The bulk of teachers college training is sheer piffle,
and this in itself is one reason why
schools like Fairly Normal fail to
attract either a good faculty or an
able student body. Fairly Normal
pays its associate professors more
than Ivy League colleges offer theirs,
but the last liberal arts doctor to
appear on campus took a $975 sal-
ary cut to escape to a tiny liberal
arts college where his chances of
promotion were nil, but where he
could find nourishment for his mind.

Sadly enough, another result of
the teachers college influence has
been to keep well-qualified teachers
out of our classrooms. Many states
require teachers to show credits in
"education." Thus, New Jersey children recently lost the opportunity
to learn from one of the world's
best biochemists. This man, full professor at an Eastern college, will
reach the mandatory retirement age
of 65 next year. Thinking to help
ease his state's shortage of science
teachers, he applied for a high-school
job, effective on his retirement from
college. His age was no barrier. His
international reputation was not sufficient recommendation, however,

*[Never Better*

teachers colleges. The teachers colleges then grew into four-year in
stitutions with departments of edu
cation, arts, and sciences. Moder
American colleges and universitie
include departments of general an
professional education—the latte
embracing engineering and, occa
sionally, other professional trainin
—as well as teacher education.

Of the 1,886 institutions of highe
learning in the United States today
at least 1,091 prepare future teach
ers, but only 126 are listed unde
the category of "primarily teache
preparatory" in the *Education Directory,* the authoritative source for
information on institutions of higher
learning. Most teachers do not come
from schools specializing in teacher
training, but from first-rate colleges
and universities where departments
of education work hand-in-hand with
departments of science and the liberal arts. There are, among the 126
"primarily teacher preparatory"
schools, perhaps 31 old-type normal-
school teachers colleges. These
schools—mostly two-year institutions that do not grant degrees—are
possibly guilty of the charges brought
against "teachers colleges." But to
condemn modern training in education because of a few relics is ridiculous.

There is overwhelming evidence
that teachers with professional training and a liberal arts education are
teaching effectively. And three recent
developments indicate that Johnny
will get even better instruction in the
future:

[*Never Worse!*

or was his 35 years of classroom xperience. Without credits in "eduation," he was told, he could not each in New Jersey's high schools.

There is no reason to prolong a ecital of dreary wrong-headness, scinating as it may be. If we are oing to make genuine contributions o public education, I would suggest e start at the source. We must raise ne standards of the teaching proession, beginning with teacher eduation, and we must diminish the ole our deans of "education" curently play.

Serious men have proposed abolion of our teachers colleges. I vould say it would be better simply o ignore our Fairly Normals, and o build our own teacher certificaion requirements in our school listricts. If enough of us do this, our eachers colleges will be forced to change their ways or close their loors, and in any event, we will have uilt real value into the school for ohnny in our town.

[*Never Better!*

1. Colleges and universities have taken steps to better their practices of selecting teaching candidates. More and more, teacher education is being reserved for men and women of high academic promise who also possess personalities and attitudes found in outstanding teachers.

2. Certification requirements are being raised by many states. In 1951, only 20 states demanded that an elementary school teacher hold a bachelor's degree. Today, 37 states call for one. The elementary school teacher of 1958 has had about one full year of college more than the teacher of 1947.

The requirements for high-school teachers are becoming even more strict. A master's degree, including advanced study in the subject the teacher is to instruct, is often required.

3. To improve teacher training, educators have created two accrediting organizations—the American Association of Colleges for Teacher Education, and the National Council for Accreditation of Teacher Education. With regional support, both the AACTE and the NCATE will investigate all phases of the college education of future teachers, and will exert every effort to assure correction of any shortcomings they might find.

Our teaching is good, but not perfect, and anyone who can improve it is encouraged. Those who find faults where none exist, though, are working against progress, not for it.

## KEATS ANSWERS BECK

Doctor Beck says high-school students scored higher on GED tests in 1955 than in 1943, citing this as proof of better teaching methods and standards.

*Criticism of these tests also increased during the same years. What do the tests test? A child's knowledge of* Moby Dick, *or of* The Three Little Pigs? *Solid geometry, or arithmetic? Isn't it more nearly accurate to say children are making higher scores in lesser subjects as more schools adapt themselves to "educators" tests and adopt "education's" watered curriculum?*

Doctor Beck says the N.E.A. Manual on Certification Requirements shows that "most" states demand no more than 16 or 18 semester hours in "education" courses.

*True, the N.E.A. Manual shows 32 of the 50 states and territories asking no more than 18 hours, but 21 of those 32 ask the full 18; only 11 ask less. The remaining states demand from 20 to 27 hours. Moreover, the Manual shows a further requirement: additional hours in "directed teacher training." This is part of the teachers college curriculum, but Doctor Beck forgot to include it in his calculations.*

Doctor Beck tries to show that English teachers must have 24 semester hours in English, which he then compares with "16 or 18" hours in "education."

*The* Journal of Teacher Education, *in a survey of 68 teachers colleges, shows that an average of*

## BECK ANSWERS KEATS

*Mr. Keats says there are teacher who spend far more time learnin to ventilate a classroom than the spend learning anything they migh be asked to teach.*

This statement is false. I canno conceive of any college—not eve the most dismal two-year norma school—where this claim would hol true.

*Mr. Keats assumes that the course he disdainfully groups under th term "scientific pedagogy" ar taught to all prospective teachers*

This, of course, is not true. Man of the courses at which Mr. Keat scoffs are intended not for teacher at all, but for students training to b school superintendents. And no community would employ as a superintendent of schools a man ignorant o the matters of taxation, school law schoolhouse construction, and maintenance of a budget.

*Mr. Keats says Johnny may b learning French from a teacher wh did not study French herself in eithe high school or college.*

I doubt whether there is an institution in the United States tha will recommend for certification, a a teacher of French, a student wh has not had at least six or seve courses in college French. The larg majority of colleges preparing teachers require a major in French (or whatever the subject for which the student is to be certified). This college major almost always exceeds the minimum requirements for state certification. A teacher teaching a subject she has not studied in col-

[*Keats Answers Beck*

*4.18 semester hours are spent on education"; an average of 15.6 ours are spent on English. The verage number of hours spent on 1athematics, by the way, is 2.84, pproximately 1/15th the time de- oted to "education."*

Doctor Beck says no American terature course can "familiarize" 1e teacher with children's books nd give her "methods" of selecting 1em, while an "education" course an, and does.

*I have watched grown men and 'omen fall asleep in a teachers col- 2ge while their professor read aloud o them from* The Little Engine That :ould *in order to "familiarize" them 'ith children's literature. A proper 1nglish literature course gives the tudent a sense of literary values and 'f our cultural heritage and prepares 1er to select children's books on the 'asis of the cultural and literary 'alues they contain—not from an 'educator's" reading list.*

Doctor Beck says only 126 "in- titutions of higher learning" are isted by the *Education Directory* as 'primarily teacher preparatory."

*The reason is that many schools 1re changing their names; few want o be known as "primarily teacher 1reparatory." Normal schools began he trend by calling themselves 'teachers colleges." Now, teachers :olleges have been calling them- 1elves "colleges," much as an un- 1ertaker might want to call himself 1 mortician for social reasons. It is 1 change in name only, made under he duress of increasing criticism. 'n a similar fashion, and for the*

[*Beck Answers Keats*

lege is being victimized—along with her students—by an irresponsible principal, superintendent, or school board.

*Mr. Keats says one high school offers training in beauty-shop opera- tion, and spends more time on this course than it spends on Latin, French, mathematics, history, sci- ence, and English, or any combina- tion of two.*

I wish he had mentioned the en- rollment in the beauticians course; I doubt that it was very large. For that matter, very few high schools other than vocational schools offer more than a few vocational courses.

*Mr. Keats says that by no means all high schools require chemistry, physics, biology, languages dead or living, mathematics, history, geog- raphy, or English composition be- yond the sentence and the paragraph.*

It is true that 25 percent of our high schools offer no physics or chemistry, but these high schools are the small, rural schools in which *only 2 percent* of our students are enrolled. Most high-school students *do* study the subjects Mr. Keats mentions. A survey of a recent freshman class at the University of Minnesota showed that only 9.5 per- cent of the students had had no science courses in high school.

*Mr. Keats says Johnny's teacher heard it was more important for Johnny to be well adjusted than it was for him to be asked to use his head.*

A teacher who helps the personal adjustment of a student is not

[*Keats Answers Beck*

same reasons, "progressive education" is now called simply "education" by its practitioners, who are apparently trying to fool the public.

Doctor Beck says at least 1,091 of 1,886 institutions "prepare" teachers.

*Many schools offer "education" courses as minor electives; fewer grant degrees in "education." If, however, Doctor Beck wishes to consider a minor elective in "education" an adequate preparation for teaching, I'll be the first to agree— as long as the applicant also holds a Bachelor of Arts degree granted by a genuine liberal arts college.*

Doctor Beck says to "improve teacher training" "educators" have set up two new organizations for "teacher education."

*It is refreshing to learn that our "educators" are at last suspicious, that they are finally willing to admit that something might be done to improve the sorry state of both our teacher education and our teacher training.*

[*Beck Answers Kea*

thereby preventing him from usin his head. Mr. Keats accepts the mi taken notion that knowledge mu: be boring (or teaching methoc harsh) in order to be intellectuall nourishing. Quite the contrar There is good reason to believe tha a pupil is free to use his head whe he is not distracted by persisten anxiety or angry rebelliousness Rather than resisting his teache and his studies, a happy, adjuste student has energy to use in learning

*Mr. Keats says that Johnny' teacher has been told not to expec all children to read, write, or d arithmetic.*

And it is a fact that some chil dren *can't* learn to read, write, o do arithmetic. Johnny's teacher wa: told that *most* children, however can learn the three R's, and she ha been taught how to assist that learn ing. High marks made by her stu dents in dozens of achievement test: prove that she has learned well, too

# They Wouldn't Let Beethover Teach Music in Indiana! *

One would have to look to our more bureaucratic trade-unions, with rigorous rules governing such endeavors as which painter can paint or wood and which can paint on iron, to find a comparison to the regulations under which teachers in many American communities are supposed to operate.

We have immediately in mind the case of Dr. Otto Miessner, former head of the music department at the University of Kansas, former professor of music at Northwestern University, founder of the State Teachers

* Reprinted by special permission from *The Saturday Evening Post*, July 19, 1958. Copyright 1958 by The Curtis Publishing Company.

College of Music at Milwaukee, former head of a music publishing house, and inventor of a spinet-type piano.

Doctor Miessner retired from the University of Kansas position in 1945, but soon tired of retirement and took a job teaching music in the Fairview Township School at Connersville, Indiana. He took the job on a permit. Being "on a permit" is what makes Doctor Miessner a case. The Indiana State Board of Education has ruled that Doctor Miessner's permit to teach in the Connersville school cannot be renewed unless he takes five more hours of courses on education! Doctor Miessner says he won't take the five hours because "it's silly." But Robert L. Pabst, director of teacher training and licensing of the State Board of Education, is adamant. "There are college teachers and there are school teachers," he said. "After all, you wouldn't let an architect pull your teeth."

That is the classic "educationist," trade-union-type argument. It is easily disposed of by asking: Would you have your plans for a house drawn by a man who had taken endless courses in How to Get Along With the Folks Upstairs, but was weak on design, strains and stresses and cost estimating?

The Connersville school board, teachers and pupils want Doctor Miessner to go on teaching, according to the Indianapolis Star, and, by the time this gets into print, they may have prevailed on the shop stewards in the State Board of Education to "evaluate" Doctor Miessner's record and give him another chance. In the meantime, it looks as if the Star said a mouthful when it blamed the people of Indiana for "permitting a bunch of doctrinaire educationists to make and enforce their self-serving rules."

## The Case for Certification*

*Daniel Tanner*

Among the many attacks levied at American public education in recent months, perhaps none has been more vociferous than those which strike at teacher preparation and certification practices. Spokesmen who condemn the current practices in professional teacher education point out that programs for preparing teachers are top-heavy with how-to courses which emphasize theory or method as opposed to subject-matter content. Also deprecated by these spokesmen is the practice of granting salary increments for teachers who pursue graduate study and degree programs. It is contended that the teacher has little choice but to take his advanced work in pedagogy. It is argued, moreover, that the teacher shortage is to be blamed on the closed shop operated under the control of the colleges of education in cooperation with the teacher certification offices in the state departments of education.

* Excerpt from "The Certification Racket: The Case for Certification," *The Atlantic Monthly,* July 1958. Reprinted by permission. Daniel Tanner is an Assistant Professor of Education, San Francisco State College.

While any professional group must welcome constructive criticism, these pernicious attacks can do only harm to our teachers, schools, and national welfare. In these critical times it is important that our society demand the establishment and enforcement of the highest possible standards for the governing of teacher education and certification. Our teachers must be rewarded with prestige and status commensurate with the great magnitude of their task. For many years, the individual states have recognized the need for accrediting professional programs and certifying professional personnel in veterinary medicine, chiropody, dentistry, library science and many other fields. Can we honestly say that the man who treats our dumb animals must undergo a more careful program of preparation and certification than the man who is responsible for educating our children.

The answer is obvious. If anything, the current requirements in professional teacher preparation and certification are far too weak. Every one of our states authorizes emergency or provisional credentials for thousands of unqualified teachers each year. A good portion of our teaching force is comprised of married women who are working to supplement their family income. Teaching, to them, is not a professional career. The high school English teacher whose daily schedule consists of six classes, each with thirty-five pupils, works with more than two hundred individual pupils each day. A single daily written assignment means correcting more than a thousand papers each week. Youngsters need and crave individual attention and guidance. Indeed, these demands on the teacher are far more taxing than those made on members of other professions.

The critics of professional education programs for teachers allege that the emphasis is on theory or method as opposed to content. A critical examination of the facts does not support their view. At the secondary school level, the trend is for certification programs based upon five years of preparation. In California, for example, high school teachers must have a bachelor's degree before they are admitted to the professional teacher education program.

The post-baccalaureate program in teacher education is concise and functional. At San Francisco State College, for example, the so-called fifth year of professional teacher education covers the equivalent of one and a half semesters of work. The candidate, during his junior or senior year, takes a course in educational psychology and sociology, combined with active participation in various community youth groups and agencies. During the first semester of the fifth year, the candidate devotes half of his academic load to the professional sequence. The other half of his program is kept open for the purpose of enabling the candidate to develop greater depth and breadth in his subject specialties. The teacher candidate must observe and assist master teachers in the public schools. During this semester, in addition to the observation-participation program and advanced graduate study in the candidate's chosen subject areas, the student enrolls in a special methods course in each of his major and minor areas.

the special methods work is under the jurisdiction of the various subject departments at the college. Concurrently, the student is given experience in the preparation and use of audio-visual aids.

The second semester is devoted to a student teaching internship in two subject specialties under the supervision of public school teachers and college instructors. Upon the satisfactory completion of the student teaching internship, the candidate is granted his certificate. Thus, with the equivalent of only one and a half semesters of professional preparation, built on a solid foundation of liberal arts courses, the candidate earns full certification as a teacher in our secondary schools. No one can accuse us of operating a teacher education program that is top-heavy in pedagogical courses. We are interested only in the development of the most effective program for creating the highest caliber teacher in the shortest possible time.

When a candidate does receive his teaching credential, his preparation does not come to an end but, rather, enters a new phase. The many school districts in our state, as in most other states, provide extra salary increments for teachers who pursue graduate courses and degrees. No pressure or inducement is applied to attract these teachers to education courses. A high school teacher can qualify for such salary raises by securing his master's degree in chemistry, physics, zoology, history, mathematics, English, or in any subject field which has a bearing on the subject areas taught in the schools. The teacher who wants to become a school psychologist may take his graduate degree in psychology, rather than in his subject area.

Every reputable organization for the preparation and certification of teachers is fighting for higher standards of subject preparation and general education for teacher candidates. The literature of the American Association of Colleges for Teacher Education, along with that of the National Commission on Teacher Education and Professional Standards, constantly stresses the importance of building the professional teacher education work on a solid foundation of liberal education and subject specialization.

As in the case of other professional groups, each state assumes the legal responsibility for the certification of its teachers. Since the standards for each state differ, a teacher from a state that has comparatively low licensing requirements cannot expect automatic certification for teaching in a state with stringent requirements. There is a need for more uniform accreditation and certification standards. The American Association of Colleges for Teacher Education and the National Commission on Teacher Education and Professional Standards of the NEA are now in the process of sharing this responsibility. Where standards in teacher education and certification are uniformly high among several states, teacher certification reciprocity is functioning.

Teacher educators are the first to recognize that it would be a naïve and serious mistake to conceive of teaching methods as being opposed to teaching content. Yet, many persons who attack our programs in professional teacher preparation tend to view content and method as antithetical. Does the nuclear physicist ignore the scientific method in his researc work? Of course not. Teaching is a science and an art. It must be far mor than drillwork in facts and skills. The teacher must be concerned wit both content and process.

It would be dangerous for society to license a medical doctor as a brai surgeon simply because he gave evidence of knowing the theory of brai surgery, without any preparation and demonstrated proficiency in actua surgery practice. Yet some people advocate that any person who manage to secure a bachelor's degree be given the privilege of walking into th classrooms of our nation and taking control of the minds of our childrer

Admiral Hyman G. Rickover has attacked the teacher certification regu lations of the state departments of education. Admiral Rickover maintain that Albert Einstein could not have been certified for teaching in our publi schools without first having completed a battery of courses in pedagogy Obviously, Admiral Rickover has not examined carefully the teache certification codes of the various states. The truth of the matter is tha any superintendent of schools in any state could have hired Dr. Einstei immediately under the provisional certification structure of that state.

Our society must see to it that the rewards of teaching are such that th teaching profession will attract the best minds in the nation. Teachers mus work together for higher salaries, more reasonable teaching loads, bette facilities and equipment, improved tenure conditions, and other benefit which they rightfully deserve. Teachers must see to it that only the highes caliber young men and women be permitted to join their ranks. If we ar satisfied with less, then our society will have to be satisfied with a lowe caliber of performance in the education of its future generations.

# Teaching Attitude and Training in Methods*

*Irving Adler*

Some observers express a more pessimistic view of the quality of the young people who are becoming teachers. William H. Whyte, Jr., for example, in *The Organization Man,* complains that prospective teachers are at the bottom of the heap in I.Q. and in academic achievement. "It is now well evident," he says, "that a large proportion of the younger people who will one day be in charge of our secondary-school system are precisely those *with the least aptitude for education of all Americans attending college."* However, I see no grounds for alarm here. Let us admit that the best mathematicians do not become mathematics teachers, and the best writers do not become English teachers. This is as it should be. The most competent

---

* Excerpt from Irving Adler, "Teacher Shortage: Cause and Cure," *The Nation,* May 10, 1958. Reprinted by permission.

mathematicians should go into mathematical research and the best writers should write. Any other employment for them would be a shameful waste of their talents. Besides, all of us who have gone to college know that the best scholars are not necessarily the best teachers, and vice versa. Granting that the people who prepare for teaching are not all sparkling intellects, this fact does not prove that they will be poor teachers. We have no more right to expect every teacher to be a creative thinker than we have to expect every automobile mechanic to be an inventor. The moderately capable college graduate may not become an educational innovator, but, with proper training and good supervision, he can become a competent craftsman.

This brings us to the third aspect of the problem of teacher supply: the kind of training a teacher should get.

In recent discussions about teacher training, critics like Arthur Bestor have charged that schools of education pay too much attention to methods of teaching and too little to the content that should be taught. As a result, he says, they turn out teachers who know how to teach, but who do not know their subjects. Schools of education have countered by asserting that all the knowledge in the world is useless if it is not communicated. To people who observe this dispute from the sidelines, it may seem pointless; surely a teacher's preparation should include instruction in *both* content and methods. However, there is a real point at issue, and that is the question of choosing the best *time* for stressing one or the other aspect of teacher preparation. On this question, we may well be guided by the teachers' own judgment of the value of the preparation they have received. Most teachers feel that, except for practice teaching, the courses that they took in methods of teaching were of little help. Either the courses were too vague to have any bearing on real classroom problems, or too specific to mean anything to someone who isn't actually teaching. The best time to learn methods is while you are teaching, when the problems of teaching are real and immediate. It would be more appropriate, therefore, to put more stress on content during the period of pre-service training, and rely more on in-service training for mastery of methods.

## The Truth About the Teacher Crisis*

*Setting the record straight on education's most confused decade.*

George B. Leonard, Jr.

You are a parent, one of the 30 million who have 32 million children in America's public schools. If you're typical, you are 35 years old. You

* Reprinted by permission from *Look*, February 21, 1956. Copyright 1956 by Cowles Magazine, Inc.

think you've done pretty well in life, but you expect your children to do even better.

For the last few years, you've been bombarded with information that is disturbing, confusing and often contradictory. You have been told that Johnny can't (can) read; that schools are worse (better) than in the Good Old Days; that classes are too large (too small); that teachers should (shouldn't) have aides; that it is statistically impossible (possible) to get enough teachers. Crisis, crisis, crisis!

As one of you, as a parent with daughters in the second and third grades, I went out in search of reasonable answers to the questions that have vexed the 1950's. As a parent as well as a reporter, I talked with scores of teachers, visited their classrooms, went to their meetings. I interviewed principals, superintendents and education experts, attended workshops and conferences. I talked with hundreds of children and parents. In my search, I came upon no ready-made solutions; nor did I find justification for the sharply angled criticisms directed at the public schools. The teachers I met weren't dolts, nor were they geniuses; they were hard-working, dedicated people with a remarkable faith in the future. The answers to the questions you hear—as you will see on the following pages—should set the record straight and bring you not despair, but hope.

*Is the quality of teaching higher now than it was in the Good Old Days?* In the Good Old Days (say, the late 1800's), you walked to school (through the snow, no doubt) and took your seat on a hard, backless bench. The "scholars" seated around you ranged in age from five to 18. Your schoolmarm was the proud possessor of a high-school diploma and had had one year in a normal school. She had few textbooks to help her, perhaps a reader and a speller. She taught only the three R's and maybe a little geography. She knew only one method of teaching—drill. Again and again, you repeated sums, tables, spellings. You weren't allowed to speak out or ask questions. And the schoolmarm spent a lot of her time keeping order—which meant absolute silence—with the flat of a ruler.

If you got as far as high school (which probably was in the same one room), you were a member of the elite. In 1890, less than 10 per cent of the nation's 14- to 17-year-olds were in school. Most of the dullards, most of the juvenile delinquents, most of the potential remedial-reading cases had long since dropped out.

Today, close to 90 per cent of the 14- to 17-year-olds are in school; and they are learning a lot more than the three R's. Every time a researcher finds a way to compare the elite corps of the Good Old Days with the Johnnys and Janeys of today's mass education, the results come out generally in favor of modern youth—*even in the basic subjects.*

Perhaps progressive education did go too far. (It reached its peak in the mid '30's, when, in some schools, drill was completely discarded.) But the pendulum has now swung nearer the center. And the demands of modern education couldn't have been met without the progressive movement away from the dreary, hard-bench Good Old Days.

Teaching today is not as good as it should be or could be, but it is definitely better than ever before. The phrase "the Good Old Days" is a nostalgic hoax.

*Is there any truth in Rudolf Flesch's book,* Why Johnny Can't Read? There is a little truth in it, but not much. Flesch charges that American teachers teach reading by word recognition or "guessing," completely ignoring phonics or "sounding out"—which he claims is the only effective method. In the more than 50 classrooms I visited, I didn't find a teacher who was neglecting phonics. Among the dozens of educators I interviewed, there wasn't one who considered word recognition the *only* method for teaching a child to read.

For the most part, teachers use word recognition, context and phonics in skillful combination. A topnotch elementary teacher with her reading group is like a practiced surgeon wielding several instruments to perform a single operation. Today's children understand what they read; they don't merely drone out sounds. And if the trend away from phonics went too far in the '30's, it has been swinging back rather quickly in the last decade.

Flesch was tilting at windmills, but his book undoubtedly lit a fire under teachers who weren't getting the most out of the phonics method. He also made teachers very angry; I've seen them turn white with rage at the very mention of his name. Even the children get in the act. At a Midwestern grade school, a first grader told his teacher that his "mommy" had a book that said "you don't teach reading right." When the teacher explained Flesch's basic charge to the class, one of the children said:

"Maybe Mr. Flesch didn't go to school."

"He went to school," the teacher said, "but it was in Austria."

"Well, he should come to *our* school."

"I'm afraid that won't be possible."

"He's for the birds," another child piped up, ending this discussion to the teacher's obvious satisfaction.

*Do teachers let children get away with murder?* In rare and isolated cases, they almost literally do. But even in the most "progressive" schools, experiments in extreme permissiveness don't last long. Children expect and want limits on their behavior. On the other hand, a teacher who makes himself a cop soon finds he has little time to teach. Abolishing the hickory stick was more a practical act than a humane one.

Good discipline, I found, is mainly a matter of good teaching. Today, only poor teachers enforce absolute silence and rigid attention—and this is one reason modern teaching can accomplish so much more than that of the Good Old Days.

Vocational and high schools bear the brunt of behavior problems. "A neurotic kid can simmer through elementary school," a high-school principal told me. "But when we get him, he's ready to explode—no matter what method of discipline is used. The big postwar population bulge hasn't hit the secondary schools yet. When it does, our problems will get tougher, and we'll need parents' cooperation more than ever."

There is not much teachers can do with the neurotic or psychotic child. But with normal children, they are generally doing a good job, even in big-city vocational schools. Michael Katzoff, principal of Bronx Vocational ("the *Blackboard Jungle* school"), has a favorite story. A new student there came up to a teacher and said he had just seen a movie called *Blackboard Jungle*. "It was awful," the boy said with feeling. "I'm glad I'm not in that school."

~ *Is getting enough teachers "statistically impossible"?* The figures are frightening. According to the U. S. Office of Education, we are already short about 130,000 teachers for our 32 million public-school students. By 1965, this enrollment will have swelled to over 42 million. To get enough teachers for this tidal wave of young humanity will take nearly half of all expected college graduates for the next ten years. Now we are getting one fifth of them. It looks bad.

~ "We can't ask people to stop having babies," a school superintendent of a small Texas town told me. "But it sure complicates things. Take a nice young male elementary teacher I had. Liked his job. Didn't make enough to live on, so his wife worked. She got pregnant, had to quit work. So he had to get a better-paying job, quit teaching. What happened? I lost a teacher and got myself another pupil to educate."

~ But wait. Don't ask people to stop having babies. There is a joker in those statistics. They are based on the *present* rate of teacher loss. Each year, we lose 85,000 teachers. Another 30,000 are trained as teachers but don't go into teaching upon graduating. If teaching as a career can be made more attractive, many of these 115,000 can be saved, and the statistics will no longer be so frightening.

Other sources, too, can be tapped (for example, liberal-arts graduates after a special postgraduate course in teaching). And teacher recruitment can be stepped up. The great fear among educators is that the public will panic and accept lower standards or jerry-built gimmicks that will permanently scar the quality of teaching.

*Can we get more teachers by lowering standards?* This should work, but it just doesn't. Where standards are lowest, the shortage is at its worst. T. M. Stinnett, the National Education Association's specialist on professional standards, told me: "The better and more intensive a man's training, the more likely he is to stay with the profession he's trained for. If a young man has invested a lot of time and effort to get a highly prized and respected certificate, he's not likely to chuck it all and go into other work."

*Should teachers, like nurses, have aides?* In a widely publicized experiment designed to ease the teacher shortage, Bay City, Mich., hired teachers' aides at $45 a week and placed them in classrooms containing anywhere from 45 to 52 children. The aides took over such jobs as dusting, typing reports, erasing the boards, correcting papers, collecting for charities and bandaging skinned knees—leaving the teacher free to teach. Bay City officials claimed impressive results. Teachers spent twice as much time on lesson plans. Recitation time increased 57 per cent; pupil counseling, 80 per cent. Bay City teachers, aides and parents expressed approval.

In spite of the claims, many educators think the plan—if used eventually just to increase class load—is extremely dangerous. And the White House Conference on Education didn't endorse it.

Why? In Bay City, I think I found out. Fifty children inside four walls are too many, no matter how many adults are present. The perfectly natural hums and squeaks and rustles of first graders become a dull roar and must be hushed. In one room, I watched an aide spend an entire 20-minute period walking up and down the aisles, motioning children to be quiet and listen to the teacher.

Aides don't stop overcrowding, nor do they cure bad teaching. Then, too, the experiment lumped together "nonteaching chores" in a highly arbitrary manner. Children can dust the room and water the plants, while teachers may learn as much about a child while bandaging skinned knees as in a week of normal teaching. Where overcrowding can't be avoided, the teacher-aide plan may be of value as an *emergency* measure. But educators fear it may become permanent. The recommended maximum in grade-school rooms is still 30.

In happy, inspired classrooms, there is a certain sparkle in the children's eyes, an indefinable but unmistakable spirit that you can practically reach out and touch. This sparkle, this magic spirit can never be analyzed in a time study or reduced to a statistic. In Bay City's crowded classrooms, it was not to be found.

*Should there be a national minimum salary for teachers?* A San Francisco school administrator was apologetic because his city had a salary of $3,720 for starting teachers with bachelor degrees, while Los Angeles started them at $4,000. At the other end of the scale, Mrs. Anne Campbell, superintendent of Madison County schools in Nebraska, faces a situation reminiscent of the Good Old Days.

"I don't have any elementary teachers with degrees," she told me. "In my 75 school districts, I have 60 one-room rural schools that take children from kindergarten through the eighth grade. The teachers there have an average of 36 hours of college preparation. Generally, we get new teachers by taking June high-school graduates, giving them 12 hours of training in the summer and starting them as teachers in September. Often, they're only 16, and since we have a compulsory attendance requirement, the students are sometimes as old as the teacher. There's no set salary schedule. Our rural teachers often start at $1,800 a year. Each school board is autonomous, and they shop for teachers as they would for a bargain in a store. They'll say, 'I prefer a young teacher. You can get her for less.' But there's really not much money in Madison County. The lack of education holds the earning power of the county down, and the lack of earning power holds the level of education down. We hope by 1958 to have a requirement of one year of college for rural teachers."

Obviously, it is impossible to set a national minimum. Then, too, education is traditionally a state and local matter. I was told by a top educator that state-wide minimums are good for laggard communities. "The money for good schools is available," he said. "The question is how and where we'll get it."

The average salary for the city grade-school teacher, with his years of training, his arduous and responsible job, is $4,570. The average auto worker makes $5,065. We spent $8½ billion in a year on public education and over $10 billion on personal automobiles. Only we can decide how important is the education of our children.

*Are teachers really people?* Sometimes they wonder. For years, they have been made the butts of cruel jokes. Some have been forbidden to smoke cigarets. They've been forced (in some states) to sign special loyalty oaths not required of other public employees. They've been entrusted with the minds and hearts of our most precious possessions, then pushed around, vilified and laughed at.

We fail to appreciate teachers. We are an impatient nation and education's results take a lifetime. We are materialistic and teachers bring us no immediate profit. And we are adults and teachers don't enter our day-to-day existence.

But there is a deep current in America running against the tide of materialism. There are many among us parents (and nonparents, too) who see, with Dr. Samuel M. Brownell, U. S. Commissioner of Education, that: "The most dramatic fact about education is the gradual transfer of character and competence to the child through his contacts with many teachers. This is not an explosion—it is an evolutionary process. . . . And yet, I insist, it is just as dramatic, and just as important, as the surgeon operating, or as trial by jury."

Everywhere I went, I found parents and other citizens honoring teachers, helping them with their chores. (Vice-President Nixon told me he was inviting the principal of his children's school to a formal presidential dinner.) At the same time, teachers' colleges are raising standards of teacher training and balancing curricula; while states are making certificates harder to get—and more valuable. Thus, teachers are winning prestige by deserving it more. In West Hartford, Conn., I talked with a superintendent who is on his way toward paying teachers up to $8,000 by a system of merit increases.

Still, teachers won't really be people, won't attain the prestige they deserve, until they're *all* paid enough to live in dignity in their communities. People always will look askance at professionals who must turn milkman in the summer (as in a suburb of Chicago) to buy food for their children.

*Why should anyone want to teach?* As in any other type of work, teachers come into their jobs in many a strange and devious way. A sincere, dedicated and highly able administrator in Michigan told me he started teaching during the depression because it was the only type of work he could get. Many teachers told me they *always* wanted to teach ("I taught my dolls when I was six"). Others were inspired by some particular teacher ("My first-grade teacher was so wonderful I knew I'd just *have* to teach"). Good teachers want to teach because they love children and are up-lifted by magic moments of learning and inspiration. They also teach (and this is important to remember) for the money they receive. This paradox is illustrated in a letter I received from an Atlanta school administrator who has given her life to teaching.

"The money has been to me—regardless of my need—never the primary incentive," she wrote. "And yet I have always taught because I needed the money which I have earned. That doesn't make sense, does it? Maybe I can make it a little clearer by a sharply etched memory experience. On October 1, 1919, I was paid my first check for my first month of teaching—a fourth grade in Union Springs, Ala. The check was for $70.

"My reaction was a very emotional one—really quite silly—I loved my 36 children, their parents, the teachers, my principal, the whole town. So I wasn't unhappy. But I came home, and with my check in hand, I threw myself on my bed and cried like an idiot. Papa and Mama were distressed. They said, 'Why, what is the matter?' I said, 'Take this old $70. I don't want it. Who thinks they can pay me that or anything else for what I've done this month? My heart, life, strength, love lavished on those sweet children! They not only can't pay me for that, but I don't want money for it!' Of course, I eventually used the money—and all I've ever earned. But that incident might have meaning. I believe many teachers feel that way."

*What can you do to help?* Visit your child's school. That is the first step. Teachers and educators will welcome you. Their earlier fear of citizens' committees and other lay groups has all but disappeared. They have learned that where parents are most interested and most deeply involved, schools are best. And parents and other citizens seem to be reawakening to a fact that is so simple it is easily forgotten: The primary responsibility for public schools lies not with any level of government or any body of officials, but with the individual citizens of each community. If your child's school is bad, it's your fault. The growth of citizens' organizations for the public schools is actually the biggest news in education's most confused decade.

When you have seen your child's school, visited his class and met his teacher—perhaps his principal, too—you will have a good start in under-standing the teachers' problems. But don't stop there. Join the PTA. Join or co-operate wtih the local citizens' committee, or form one. Go to meetings which concern the schools. Keep informed about your teachers' problems. From this, good schools will follow: It is that simple. "When the people are well informed and know what has to be done," Vernon Nickell, state superintendent of Illinois, said, "they'll come through. You can depend on it."

# chapter VIII

# Decision of the Judges

"Let's take a look at the record." This reaction was made famous by Alfred E. Smith, candidate for the Presidency of the United States in 1928. It applies as aptly to matters educational as to political records.

In this chapter, two professors of education report that schools are much more open to criticism for being traditional than for following modern practices; two other professors of education present research evidence that schools are doing a good job; and an educational research organization summarizes public opinion on the schools. The chapter closes with a comparison of European and American education, and a clear-cut exposition of the point of view that the schools are what the public makes them.

## They've Been Criticizing the Wrong Things! *

C. M. Lindvall
C. P. Hooker

*A study of current classroom practices reveals an irony—the ills of education are being attributed to methods we've hardly begun to apply. But herein lies a warning . . .*

Each fall we read a lot about education in the consumer magazines. Much of what we read is sharply critical. This could be helpful if it were not that

---

* Reprinted by permission from *The School Executive*, November 1957. Dr. Lindvall and Dr. Hooker are associate professors in the School of Education, University of Pittsburgh.

the more sniping attacks present a distorted picture of current school practices.

Most teachers and other informed persons wonder what schools are being described in these attacks. There is little resemblance between these "typical" classrooms and those with which most school personnel are familiar. Of course this is not strange when these critics base their descriptions on accounts given them by one or two disgruntled parents, or on practices proposed by an educator trying to give some newer procedures a fair trial.

But what would these attackers find if they actually took the time to visit a large number of schools and classrooms? If these persons feel that today's pupils are not receiving a solid, "old-fashioned" education, what current practices are causing this?

Most persons associated with the public schools, while understandably indignant over uninformed attacks on the schools, are never fully satisfied with the educational product and welcome constructive criticism of their work. However, if such criticism is to help improve present practices, it must be based on an evaluation of these practices. Confusion, not help, comes when the critic places blame on procedures that are largely nonexistent.

To provide some idea of what is actually being done in public school classrooms, an analysis was made of subject matter sources, degree of pupil freedom and provision for individual differences. These practices were studied in the classrooms of 318 teachers in 14 school systems, ranging in size from 1,000 to 10,500 students, in a rather widespread geographic area in western Pennsylvania.

To gather this information, trained observers actually sat in the classrooms for approximately 600 clock hours and kept a record of what took place using a modification of an observation form developed at the University of Illinois.

The results obtained can shed some light on certain charges made against the present-day public schools.

## ARE THEY TEACHING SUBJECTS OR CHILDREN?

One charge leveled against the schools is that they are ignoring subjects and subject matter and are "teaching children." In this study the observers kept a continuous record of the source of the subject matter being studied in the classrooms and categorized it in one of the five categories listed in Table I. This Table shows the percent of total time spent in the classrooms during which various sources of content were being used.

It shows that during 84 percent of the time the learning content was definitely subject-matter centered. There is little here to suggest that the schools are ignoring subject matter and concentrating on the interests of the children. Rather, these pupils are spending the majority of their time in

TABLE I

PERCENT OF OBSERVED TIME DURING WHICH VARIOUS SOURCES
OF SUBJECT MATTER WERE BEING USED

| Sources of Subject Matter | Percent of Time Used |
|---|---|
| One textbook or one workbook | 64 |
| Several texts or reference books | 5 |
| Traditional subject matter being taught but being obtained from non-book sources such as demonstrations, movies, and field trips | 15 |
| Projects or broad problems designed by teacher on basis of pupil needs and interests | 12 |
| Individual projects and problems selected by pupils on the basis of their own needs and interests | 4 |

the classroom being taught material from the rather traditional and conventional textbook sources.

Certainly any criticism of the product of these schools cannot be leveled against a departure from traditional practices. On the contrary, these results might suggest to the person acquainted with educational and psychological theory that any of the shortcomings in these schools may be due to the *failure to adopt* the newer recommended procedures in presenting learning content.

## TOO MUCH FREEDOM IN THE CLASSROOM?

Another criticism of the teacher is that he has abdicated his real responsibility in the classroom and given the pupil too much freedom in controlling the learning situation. This conception may be based on the fact that many educators feel that a certain amount of pupil participation in the planning of the learning activities can aid pupil motivation and also provide valuable training in self-education that will be valuable in out-of-school life.

Table II provides a picture of what the observers actually found with respect to this aspect of classroom procedure.

In this Table the first two categories describe situations in which the teacher dominates activities—she tells the pupils what should be done in each phase of the classwork, occasionally permitting pupils' questions and comments to play some part. The third category applies to such activities as when the teacher assigns a report or project and permits the pupils some freedom in planning and selecting specific materials to be used.

In all three of these categories, totaling 95 percent of the time that observers spent in the classrooms, the teacher is definitely controlling the

TABLE II

PERCENT OF OBSERVED TIME DURING WHICH VARYING DEGREES
OF PUPIL FREEDOM WERE NOTED

| Degree of Pupil Control | Percent of Time Occurring |
|---|---|
| Teacher domination: All activities and actions dictated by teacher | 43 |
| Teacher domination with minor provision for pupil suggestions and questions | 36 |
| Teacher control of activities with pupil suggestions, questions, and planning permitted to determine specific activities and procedures | 16 |
| Pupil initiative permitted to control choice of activities and procedures with teacher providing overall guidance, as in activity program or pupil controlled class project | 5 |

situation and determining what types of things the pupils should be studying. This can hardly be described as an abdication of control.

## TOO MUCH ATTENTION TO INDIVIDUAL DIFFERENCES?

Some critics of present-day education contend that our schools are wasting their efforts in trying to provide for individual differences among students in aptitudes and abilities. Schools, they say, must realize that it is impossible to provide for all such differences. They contend that the efforts of the schools in this direction are another example of widespread waste and inefficiency.

But the data presented in Table III shows what the schools are actually doing with respect to this problem.

TABLE III

PERCENT OF OBSERVED TIME DURING WHICH VARIOUS PROVISIONS
WERE MADE FOR INDIVIDUAL DIFFERENCES

| Type of Provision | Percent of Time Occurring |
|---|---|
| Identical work for all pupils— no individual teacher assistance | 34 |
| Identical work for all pupils— teachers giving individual assistance | 55 |
| Work differentiated by grouping | 7 |
| Work differentiated on individual basis | 4 |

Since the schools visited practice heterogeneous grouping, it is astonishing that during only 11 percent of the observed time was any provision made for individual differences among the learners. While this observation adds little comfort to sincere parents who want their children to experience challenging and satisfying learning situations, it again reveals the absurdity of the charge that too much is being done for individual learners. In fact, it would appear that the opposite charge, that schools are doing too little for exceptional children, has greater validity.

While the figures presented in this study are based on a rather restricted sample, it is doubtful if the situation is much different in a majority of our nation's schools. The critics of our educational system are placing the blame on practices which are largely non-existent.

However, school teachers and administrators can gain no consolation from this fact. Certainly being able to point out that classroom procedures are no different now from those found 30 or 40 years ago cannot be taken as a commendation of our schools. It would appear that now is the time for school personnel to take a careful look at the practices that are actually being used in their classrooms to see how far out of step they are with current psychological theory. The results of the present study seem to indicate that many of the more promising teaching techniques that have been developed during the last quarter of a century have never really been given a trial.

If attacks upon these procedures, by persons unacquainted with present classroom procedures, serve to further delay a fair trial of modern practices, then educational leaders will be guilty of abdicating their responsibility. They can then expect to be the recipients of justified criticism by truly informed and responsible critics.

# We Can Be Proud of the Facts*

*Harold G. Shane*

*Would you like to have some ammunition, and not be caught with that frustrated feeling, when next you hear that our children aren't learning the fundamentals? Are you interested in some evidence to explode the charge that the schools are breeding a nation of dim-wits and are brain wasting by neglecting our gifted children? Or that instead of teaching history and geography the schools teach children how to act when they go out on a date and call it social studies? If your answer is Yes, let's apply the rules of evidence to some of the recent derogatory statements directed at our elementary and secondary schools. Let us look at the record and substitute information for misinformation the next time a school patron says that he has read or heard that elementary schools are "too easy" on children or that our high schools have deteriorated.*

* Reprinted by permission from *The Nation's Schools*, September 1957. Harold G. Shane is a Professor of Education, Northwestern University.

During the last six or eight years, criticisms of education have become familiar to most school people and to seasoned members of boards of education. Also, since 1950, numerous professional and popular magazines have published a variety of "replies," "corrections," "denials" and rebuttals of all kinds whenever a critic has lambasted the schools.

In the heat of discussion, however, there rarely has been time for us to take a long, careful look at the last 50 years in order to locate the facts that contradict the vague claim that schools in the United States are cheating children out of a first-rate education. Here are some of the blunt questions raised about schools in America and some forthright factual answers. They suggest that public education is something of which to be proud rather than apologetic.

*Are elementary schools "too easy" on children?* First let's look at the field of elementary education. Is our average 6 to 12 year old youngster doing much more than merely earning an "A" for digging in sandpiles, a pat on the back for neat paper cutting, or a gold star for being a "good relaxer" during rest period?

Despite widespread opinion to the contrary, elementary school age children are learning the fundamentals, the 3 R's, more thoroughly than in 1900. Studies of test scores extending back to 1844 show that each successive generation is learning more subject matter than did past generations.[1] For instance, a top official in one of the largest companies publishing our public school reading and arithmetic tests recently reviewed the test scores made by 230,000 pupils. Even in so brief a period as the past decade there was indisputable evidence of the increased intellectual attainments of children. The average child's reading, mathematics and language usage scores *on the same tests* improved by 12 per cent over a 10 year period.[2] And this despite the fact that a study just completed in New York proved that the average child in a given grade today is *one full year younger* than was the average child of 35 years ago![3]

One research worker in a midwestern city gave third and fifth grade children the same tests used in 1934 and compared their arithmetic and spelling achievement with that of the past generation. What happened? Today's children made significantly higher scores than did mother or dad.[4] At least 16 similar investigations tell the same story about every one of the 3 R's.

Modern education, often given the vague label "progressive" education,

---

[1] Rock, B. R.: Children's Achievement: Today and Yesterday. Austin: The Texas Elementary Principals and Supervisors Association, 1952.

[2] Bulletin of the California Test Bureau: A Comparison of Pupil Achievement Before and After 1945. Los Angeles. Pp. 8.

[3] Wrightstone, J. Wayne: Class Organization for Instruction. Washington, D. C.: Department of Classroom Teachers and American Educational Research Association of N.E.A. 1957, p. 4.

[4] Lanton, Wendell C.: The Proof of the Pudding, The Phi Delta Kappan, *36*:136, December 1954.

has long been accused of debasing our schools academically. Actually, modern educational practices have been maligned by writers who have given any shoddy educational practice the name "progressive."

As schools interpret the term today, so-called "progressive" or modern educational methods are designed to help children learn more than they once did and to make learning have more meaning. For example, certain arithmetical processes today are commonly introduced about a year later than they were in the elementary school of the 1920's. This change was not made to soften the curriculum. Rather it was made in order to help children master content in a few weeks rather than wasting months trying to learn abstract number concepts before they were intellectually mature enough to grasp them.

Clearly, schools today are *not* trying to produce "—at great expense and with the most incongruous self-congratulation—a nation of Henry Aldriches." [5] After 25 years in the field of education I have yet to meet either a teacher or professor of education who believed that "it really isn't important what children learn, just so long as they're happy." (The cartoon about the second grade child who asked the teacher, "Do we *have* to do what we want to do today, Miss Jones?" was amusing but sadly misleading when it appeared in a popular magazine.) The improving levels of national standardized test scores clearly suggest that the fundamentals, far from being neglected, are now taught more thoroughly than ever. The scores also contradict the statement that "all children are promoted" regardless of whether they have learned the "essentials." Today's high standards of academic achievement patently were not reached by de-emphasizing the importance of study.

*What has happened to history and geography?* Nor does the evidence support the vague claim that social studies in the elementary school (and "life adjustment" courses in the secondary school) are reducing the teaching of history and geography to a heap of rubble. In the majority of schools the social studies period is one in which geography and history are taught as one subject in order to make clear to young children the way in which the two fields are related.

*Are we "brain wasting" gifted children?* Do elementary schools, or high schools for that matter, merit the charge that they are "brain wasting" by neglecting gifted children? A gifted child is one with an intelligence quotient or I.Q. of 140 or above. In an exhaustive study of such brilliant youngsters one of the country's top psychologists found that even some years ago nine-tenths of our gifted children were being identified by their teachers. Far from being neglected, the typical gifted children who were tested were achieving 44 per cent higher test scores than were their less able classmates. That is, gifted fourth grade children had learned approximately as much in four years as the average child learned in eight years of school.[6] All large

⁵ Bell, Bernard Iddings: Know How vs. Know Why, Life 29:89-98, Oct. 16, 1950.
⁶ Terman, Lewis M., et al.: Genetic Studies of Genius. Stanford University Press, p. 306.

school systems, and many small ones, have for years made special provision for the intellectually promising boy and girl. There is relatively little brain wasting here considering how limited school funds are.

Further evidence of the fact that mass education has *not* harmed quality education is afforded by a 20 year study of 1,470 young men and women of top intellectual promise. Nine out of 10 of this genius-level group went on to college, and two-thirds of the men and one-third of the women completed at least one postgraduate university degree.[7]

But at the same time we cannot afford to be complacent about the educational opportunities of our top-flight students! Rear Admiral H. G. Rickover, the gifted engineer-scientist who created the atomic submarine *Nautilus,* was completely correct when he stated earlier this year that ". . . our schools are not equipped to do justice to the special needs of such pupils." [8] *Truly, the accomplishments of our schools often have been made in spite of limited funds with which to nurture the truly gifted!* If we are not to waste "our most precious natural asset," as Admiral Rickover called the brain power of our genius, the schools must be given additional means to increase their underfinanced programs for the gifted. In view of what the schools have already done on shoestring budgets they will accomplish wonders when stimulated by an awakened public interest in and support for education which challenges our gifted youngsters. We have the wealth to do the job, but often have lacked the vision to invest sufficient capital in the "cold war of the classrooms" in an era when our national survival depends on the outcome.

*Are Europe's elementary schools better than ours?* Both prevalent and inaccurate is the view that the instructional programs in American elementary schools are markedly inferior to the European variety. The results of tests administered *in Europe by Europeans* indicate that the reverse may be true. One report published recently by the University of London Press revealed that children in the United Kingdom were below a comparable group of our children in reading ability.[9] This was despite the fact that the children overseas often began their reading instruction earlier than those in the United States. "Worriers" who are alarmed lest American reading is handled too lightheartedly in the primary grades will be pleased to know that a study (made by a Scot in the ruggedly academic schools of Scotland) showed that only about half as much time was spent on reading in these schools as in American ones at equivalent age levels.[10]

Speaking of European schools, the "childhood disease" of leisure time comic book reading proved to be roughly twice as widespread among 11 to

---

[7] Terman, Lewis M., and Oden, M. H.: Genetic Studies of Genius: The Gifted Child Grows Up (Vol. IV). Stanford University Press, 1947.

[8] Rickover, H. G.: Let's Stop Wasting Our Greatest Resource, The Saturday Evening Post, 229:108, March 2, 1957.

[9] Taylor, C. D.: The Effect of Training on Reading Readiness, Studies in Reading. University of London Press, 1950. Vol. II, pp. 63-80.

[10] Inglis, W. W.: The Early Stages of Reading. A Review of Recent Investigations, Studies in Reading. University of London Press, 1948. Vol. I, pp. 1-92.

15 year olds in England as in the U. S. Two recent British polls of comic book reading habits published in a European psychological journal pointed to this conclusion.[11,12]

Despite the reassuring evidence, we cannot be smugly satisfied. While our schools do at least a comparable and perhaps a better job of educating a large number of students than Europe's schools, we do our least effective work with our most able pupils.

*Have our high school programs deteriorated?* Since factual information supports a proud 50 year record in elementary education, what about the record of the American high school? It was stated recently that "the schools have retreated from modern life" because of the way they have de-emphasized science and mathematics. The speaker, an articulate and ardent proponent of a return to "basic education," contended that the percentage of high school students taking science and mathematics had declined from approximately 85 per cent to about 55 per cent since 1900.[13] These figures are a beautiful illustration of how information, taken out of context, can be used to support a faulty argument.

As I write, I have before me recent official records from the U. S. Department of Health, Education and Welfare.[14] These reports show, in round numbers, that 400,000 children were taking science and mathematics courses at the turn of the century out of a total population of 75,603,000. Fifty years later, while our population increased by some 100 per cent, the number of high school students enrolled in science had increased by 600 per cent and mathematics class enrollments have grown by 900 per cent.

Bear in mind that this tremendous gain was registered during a period in which nearly all our children had an opportunity to go into high school, not merely the children of the socially or economically privileged. The schools certainly have not "retreated" when today from six to nine times as many of our intellectually competent boys and girls are taking science and mathematics courses as were taking these courses at the century's turn.

*Are languages being ignored?* The status of foreign language teaching also has been viewed with alarm by the proponents of "fundamental" education. Here, again, the story is an interesting one. According to the careful records of the Modern Language Association, there was a 400 per cent increase at the elementary level in the teaching of a second language in

---

[11] Stewart, Mary: The Leisure Activities of Grammar School Pupils, British Journal of Educational Psychology, *20*:11-34, February 1950.

[12] Williams, A. R.: The Magazine Reading of Secondary School Children, British Journal of Educational Psychology, *21*:186-98, November 1951.

[13] Bestor, Arthur: We Are Less Educated Than 50 Years Ago, U. S. News and World Report, *41*:68-82, Nov. 30, 1956.

[14] U. S. Department of Health, Education, and Welfare: Offerings and Enrollments in Science and Mathematics in Public High Schools, Washington, D. C.; U. S. Govt. Printing Office, 1956. Pp. 24. Supplementary population figures cited are from the Biennial Survey of Education (1950-52) also issued by the Govt. Printing Office.

Grade 6 and below in a recent three-year (1951-54) period.[15] By 1957 the total number of young children engaged in foreign language study hovered near the 400,000 mark. At the high school level the number of pupils studying one of the four major languages most commonly offered (Spanish, Latin, French and German) has increased threefold while the U. S. population has merely doubled.[16] The number of children taking high school Spanish, for instance, was too small to be recorded by the Office of Education in 1900; about a half million students are now enrolled.

Latin class enrollments have proportionately kept pace with the national population increase, and 10 children take French today for every one who studied it in 1900.[17] Only German language teaching has shown a net decline, and this is traceable in part to an antipathy to all things Germanic during two World Wars. During these periods some schools dropped the language in response to public demand.

*How competent are our teachers?* In view of the academic record made by children and youth it seems self-evident that the vast majority of teachers know their subjects as well as their teaching methods. Nevertheless, it is reassuring once again to examine the evidence. In the first major survey of teacher status, made in 1911 by a gentleman who later became president of the University of Minnesota, the findings were sad indeed. The average teacher was young, poorly paid, and had begun teaching *without completing even one year of college study*.[18] Today it is the rule rather than the exception to find elementary schools hiring teachers with a B.A. degree, while secondary schools often require the M.A. degree. Also, particularly at the high school level, state requirements have been stiffened tremendously with respect to the subject matter courses teachers must complete in order to qualify for a license to teach.

Does job tenure protect teachers, as critics of the schools have claimed, if such instructors are inefficient in the classroom? This charge is only a half-truth at most, since states with tenure laws generally require that teachers prove their skill over a two or three year period before they go on tenure. Also, state laws permit teachers to be fired for incompetence.

Job protection legislation pertaining to teachers was enacted to protect them from peremptory dismissal but also allows school boards to shield children from those who might harm them intellectually or physically. It is true, however, that teachers are sometimes removed from the classroom only with much difficulty and red tape. Trouble is especially likely to arise when a dismissal becomes a *cause célèbre* and is fought by organized teachers'

---

[15] Mildenberger, K. W.: The Status of Foreign Language Teaching in American Elementary Schools. Washington, D. C., U. S. Dept. of Health, Education, and Welfare, 1955.

[16] U. S. Office of Education: Biennial Survey of Education (1948-50).

[17] *Ibid.*

[18] Coffman, L. D.: The Social Composition of the Teaching Profession. New York: Bureau of Publications, Teachers College, Columbia University, 1911.

groups. Also, in all fairness, it must be recognized that, with the present shortage of teachers, people of marginal ability are sometimes retained because no better qualified persons can be hired. The same generalization holds true, of course, for engineers, stenographers or ribbon clerks!

*Does public education cost too much?* One of the proudest achievements of our public schools is the way they have given the public its increasingly high level of pupil achievement *at increasingly lower cost!* A typical misrepresentation of the cost of education appeared in a recent article, circulated among businessmen. The writer pointed out that ". . . we are now spending three times as large a part of our national income, *after war costs,* on education than [sic] we did in 1900." [19] The catch is in the phrase "after war costs."

*Actually, the proportion of our national income spent on education has averaged approximately 3 per cent for many years and has shown little significant variation for decades. Yet the proportionate number of students has greatly increased. In 1900, there were 699,403 students in our high schools. In 1956 there were 8,472,478! We now educate 12 or 13 children at the high school level for every one enrolled in 1900, yet the percentage of income invested in their education remains identical.*

*What do report cards report?* The charge has often been made by critics that schools have disregarded parental opinion by dropping the ABC type of marking system on report cards. This point is cited as an example to prove that the public isn't getting what it wants from the schools. Let's explode this myth!

In the first place, most high schools and virtually all universities and colleges continue to use grades of the ABC type, a fact many critics ignore. Even at the elementary school level traditional report cards are the rule. A student in one of my classes polled the 15 largest cities in his midwestern state and found that all but one of these school systems still used ABC grades, even at the elementary level. As a further check I polled 35 suburban school systems noted for their distinguished educational programs. In Grade 6 and below a substantial majority of my replies stated that ABC grades (which are sometimes coupled with parent conferences) were currently in use!

In the second place, there is reason seriously to doubt that parents really want ABC type grades. Recently I asked 700 Chicago area parents what they most wanted to know about their child in elementary school. Most of them wanted to be assured that he is an effective human being and that he is getting along well with other children. Only about one parent in three was primarily interested in grades. In short, the hubbub raised about marks in school not only conceals the fact that most schools still have ABC grading systems, but ignores the fact that many parents probably want to know more about their children than a grade of "C" or "A" reveals.

---

[19] Freeman, Roger A.: Dollars and Sense in Education, The Civic Federation, Bulletin 498, November 1956, p. 3.

*Does education lack purpose?* It seems fitting to close this review of the reassuring achievements of our public schools with a passing glance at the fuzziest of the criticisms they have received. "The schools have lost their purpose," it has been alleged, because "unessential activities are squeezing out the basic subjects."

Enrollment trends and test scores, previously mentioned, clearly show that relatively more children are taking basic subjects today than in the past, and that the individual child (despite the one year decrease in his age in a given grade) is learning more subject matter than ever before. Obviously, the schools have not defaulted on their academic goals. But are the schools doing more than merely passing along the best in our cultural heritage? Are they preserving and extending moral values? The answer is a resounding Yes, and the evidence is abundant.

The products of our educational system are, with each passing decade, demonstrating our growing maturity as a nation. They are making real the American dream that human beings can live together with dignity and self-respect.

In 50 years the integrity of our country has stood firm through many harsh tests. In depression and war the graduates of our schools and colleges have proved that, while a few of us may be petty or mean, the average American is someone to be proud of. He has shown vision that lifts him above himself. He is friendly and basically respectful to others, but he has proved he can and will fight in every quarter of the globe for the things in which he believes. The typical product of our educational system may occasionally be misdirected or misinformed, but in the long run he stands for what proves to be right.

*These qualities are no happy accident. They have been fostered and strengthened by the objectives of our schools which, like home and church, are the repository of the ideals that make up the American dream of a better world. Truly, we have more often succeeded than failed as a people, and a substantial measure of credit for this success is due to the effectiveness of public education.*

# How Good Are Our High Schools? *

*Harold C. Hand*

There is precious little of this "then vs. now" statistical evidence, but all the studies involving objective measurement that have been reported disprove the thesis that the high schools are doing a poorer job than formerly.

---

* Excerpt from Harold C. Hand, "Black Horses Eat More Than White Horses," *AAUP Bulletin,* Summer 1957. Reprinted by permission.

In one such study, the Recorder at the University of Illinois compared the college marks made during their freshman year by (a) the combined entering classes of 1935-36-37 with (b) those made by the entering class of 1949 (in which only 83 of its 1,819 members were veterans). The 1949 freshmen made higher average college marks in every division of the University (see the October, 1951, issue of *College and University*).

The June, 1954, issue of *Changing Times, The Kiplinger Magazine,* reported two "then vs. now" investigations at the high-school level. One was a 1919 vs. 1941 study in Indiana; the other an 1848 vs. 1947 comparison in Cleveland, Ohio. The results favored the 1941 over the 1919 students; in the Cleveland study, the results were "a clean-cut victory for the modern-day student," the article stated. Further, the Kiplinger article just noted observed that the College Entrance Examination Board, whose activities range over the whole country, has found no decline in the quality of entering college freshmen today when compared with those of twenty-five years ago—this despite the fact that only the more academically able high-school graduates tended to go on to college then.

The most inclusive study of the "then vs. now" question yet reported is the one described by B. S. Bloom in the March, 1956 issue of *The School Review*. He renormed the high-school tests in the fields of English, social studies, science, and mathematics which are used by the United States Armed Forces Institute by giving them, in 1955, to the senior students in a representative 5 per cent sample of all the public high schools in this country—which is exactly the same thing that had been done with exactly the same tests in 1943. Bloom found that the 1955 seniors made higher average scores on each of these tests than the 1943 seniors had made, with the superiority of the 1955 students being greatest in the field of mathematics.

## Public Approves Public Education*

What do the American people really think about their schools? To answer this question, the NEA Research Division compiled reports of all major polls on the subject made since 1950.

The public opinion polls show five significant facets of opinion:

– A strong endorsement of the goals of American education; to create an enlightened electorate and to provide all children with an education appropriate to them as individuals.

– A general lack of agreement on what should be done to remedy curricular deficiencies.

– A conviction that the value of practical training is greater than liberal education.

---

* Excerpt from "Public Opinion on Education," *NEA Research Bulletin,* October, 1958, p. 74.

– Evidence that educators are more demanding of American education than is the general public.

– An overwhelming majority opinion in favor of federal financial support.

## Are European Schools Better Than Ours? *

Get to talking with your friends about American education and sooner or later someone will drag in European schools. The argument runs like this:

"The trouble with education in this country is that we make things too easy for our kids. What they need is the kind of intensive drilling that children in European countries are given. Over there standards are high and youngsters really have to toe the mark. When those kids go to college, they're well prepared."

It's an impressive argument, because European standards are indeed high and European university students do have good preparation. Nevertheless, that doesn't mean that their school systems are better than ours. See some of the crucial differences and decide for yourself.

*Numbers.* A far greater proportion of our kids go to school for a longer period.

– At 16, 70% of our youth are in school, compared with less than 20% of the 16-year-olds in Europe.

– At the college age, between 18 and 20, about a fourth of our boys and girls are in school, compared with fewer than a tenth of European kids in that age group.

*Selection.* Suppose your youngster gets average or slightly above average grades. If he likes, he can probably take an academic course in high school and then find a college to suit his abilities and interests. He may even begin to shine in college and go on to a successful career.

But see what happens to the European youth.

– At about age 10 or 11 he takes a tough national exam. If he does well—say in the top quarter or better—he's permitted to attend an academic high school where he prepares for the university. If he doesn't clear the high hurdles, he takes a general course, maybe a vocational course, and then drops out of school at about 15 or so.

– Youngsters who do get into the academic high schools and stay the full time receive the rough equivalent of an American high school academic course plus two years of college. But the going is pretty rocky, and a great many drop out—in England, some 80%.

– At the age of 17 or 18, those who have survived take another stiff na-

---

* Reprinted by permission from *Changing Times,* The Kiplinger Magazine, June, 1958.

tional exam. Anyone who fails cannot go to the university and is also shut off from the best government and executive jobs.

Last spring 60% of the French youths who took this test failed. The result was a parents' revolt that has caused French schools to begin loosening up. In fact, rumblings from discontented parents have been heard in England, Germany and other countries where tough screening programs tend to favor kids from upper social and economic classes—that is, kids whose parents can afford to hire tutors or pay for private schools.

*Standards.* Yes, European schools do work the kids hard. A French 10-year-old puts in about 45 hours a week on school and homework. Youngsters are drilled endlessly on the basic subjects. And students who go on to college do seem to have a better academic background than the average American undergraduate. But here are a few things to keep in mind:

– European secondary and university students are an intellectual elite. The only fair comparison is with our bright students, the ones, say, who attend our best colleges or make honor societies. In that case, our youngsters stack up pretty well.

– European students get stronger doses of traditional subjects—languages, literature, history, math. Ours get a better grounding in the social sciences —economics, political science, sociology, psychology. Probably we ought to put more stress on the traditional subjects and they ought to do more with the social sciences.

---

#### THOSE SOVIET SCHOOLS

You've heard how efficient Russian education is supposed to be. Here are some things to remember about it:

– All USSR students take rigid national exams in order to pass the fourth, seventh and tenth grades.

– Above the secondary level, the government fixes quotas for enrolment in various fields and assigns graduates to jobs in industry.

– Political supervision and indoctrination permeate all schooling.

– Boys get regular military instruction from the seventh through the tenth grades. Tenth graders have rifle and machine-gun practice with live ammunition. This was cut out of the ninth grade because there were too many accidents.

– School and home assignments are so heavy that several prominent physicians once complained publicly that students were suffering from "chronic overexhaustion, frequent headaches" and other ailments.

– A graduate from a higher institution doesn't get his own diploma. It's mailed instead to his future employer.

---

Relations between teacher and student are easier in this country. Our youth ask more questions, engage in freer discussions. European schools are more formal, and in the lower grades discipline is stiffer. Maybe many of our schools ought to get a bit tougher. But the open frankness of our young people is one of the American qualities most admired abroad.

– We train our kids more conscientiously than Europeans do in non-academic things—how to understand and get along with people, how to take an active part in the political and economic world in which they live. Our boys and girls get many more opportunities, too, to develop special talents through extracurricular activities such as student government, dramatics, publications, clubs, sports, music.

– At the professional level, training here is as good as it is abroad, often much better.

Without doubt, our schools need improvement and could pick up a few pointers from the Europeans. But don't be surprised if you hear more and more about changes in European educational systems. Quite a few people over there are dissatisfied with their schools and think they might pick up a few pointers from us.

## Schools Reflect the Public*

*George B. Leonard, Jr.*

\*        \*        \*

One thing about an American town is this: The residents get the kind of school program they want, including winning teams—if they want them badly enough.

Most of the critics of American education have chosen to ignore this fact. Instead, they blame every ill of the schools on the professional educators, to whom they apply the derogatory term "educationist."

According to the critics, the educationists, following the theories of philosopher John Dewey, created progressive education, then seduced the public into accepting it. Now they are riding high, say the critics, while blocking the tough academic schools the public *really* wants. All the nation has to do is repudiate the theories of John Dewey, knock the educationists off their thrones and—presto!—Johnny will read, spell, know calculus and build nonfizzle missiles.

The critics unhesitatingly blame the educationists for the features of modern education they do not like; among them, easy schooling, automatic promotions, nonacademic courses and so-called "life adjustment" or "practical" education. It is true that at various times professional educators have favored one or more of the above. But more significant are the following facts:

* Excerpt from George B. Leonard, Jr., "Who Runs Our Schools?" *Look,* June 10, 1958. Reprinted by permission. Copyright 1958 by Cowles Magazine, Inc.

*Parents, more than educators, prefer easy schooling.* What kind of courses do most parents ask for their children? Said a school-board member from Logan, Utah: "Courses they can pass—period." A recent Gallup Poll shows that 90 per cent of school principals and only 51 per cent of parents say the public schools today demand too little work from students.

*Parents insist upon automatic promotion.* "Some very brave superintendents hold back or refuse graduation to inferior students," says Dr. Garford Gordon, scholarly research director for the California Teachers Association. "But those superintendents keep moving from town to town —before they're pushed."

In today's America, the educator who holds back or refuses to graduate children is in trouble. In Russia, children who can't pass (at least two thirds of the total) are simply shunted off to vocational schools, to the factories or the military-training camps. In Russia, the people do not run the schools.

*Most pressures for nonacademic courses begin outside the schools.* "School boards have been victims of pressure groups," says Carl B. Munck, president of National School Boards Association. "In my 16 years as a school-board member in Oakland, California, as well as in my work with other school boards, I've seen that the public, not the professionals, puts on the pressure for extra courses. There are many sincere groups. The automobile associations want driver training, the lumbermen's group wants a forestry course, the Red Cross wants required swimming and safety education, industry and the labor unions want a shop apprenticeship program. The parents of the big middle group of average children are the quietest. Their children are getting a pretty good education. Parents of gifted children are just beginning to speak up. But in my 16 years, the greatest pressure has come from a sincere, dedicated group that wants education for the subnormal."

The schools are expected to do everything for everybody.

*Parents like "practical" courses and "practical" teaching.* Many critics have proceeded on the belief that most parents are weeping and wailing for a return to stern Three-R teaching. This is not true. Look's research has shown that, while parents *say* they do not approve of "progressive" education, a majority of them look with great approval at any course or way of teaching which relates learning to practical life experience.

"I think it's just common sense that a child shouldn't have to take Latin or higher mathematics," a Los Angeles mother told Look. "What my daughter needs to know is how to cook and how to figure up her bills after she gets married."

Parents who prefer traditional academic training are today in the minority, though their number is growing.

The above illustrations and many others show that the critics have selected the wrong target for their major attacks. If the schools are to upgrade their intellectual content (and educators and critics alike feel they hould), no superficial revamping of theory and method will do. Mainly what is needed is for parents and other voters to take a new look at their own attitudes toward intellectual and cultural activity.

To help in this painful task, LOOK has prepared a report card on the adult American, the man or woman who not only is a product of the schools, but who also runs the schools. The results of this special survey, prepared by Audience Research, Inc., are not encouraging.

According to the survey, barely half of the high school and college graduates could identify the Bill of Rights. Only 35 per cent could give a single advantage of our economic system over Russia's. Only 40 per cent could work the equation "6 is to 18 as 'x' is to 72" in their heads. Only 9 per cent could identify the philosopher Schopenhauer. Only 38 per cent knew the chief religion of Pakistan. And only a bare one fourth knew the chemical composition of table salt.

The survey shows how little the average American values cultural activity. Only one out of twenty was studying cultural subjects at the time questioned. Only one out of five was reading a book other than the Bible or a textbook. Only one out of four could name a book he would *like* to read. And 40 per cent could not recall when they had last read *any* book all the way through.

These results should not come as a shock. It has been possible in recent years to attain great success, prestige and wealth without identifying Schopenhauer or knowing the chief religion of Pakistan. On the other hand, a majority of Americans have found the ability to "sell yourself" and get along with others tremendously valuable in their drive to the top.

According to most experts, however, these conditions will not long prevail. The world is changing fast, and is requiring more and more of the human mind. If the schools are to meet the challenge, Americans must face up to their own deficiencies. They must change their attitude toward intellectual activity. They must value and reward scholarship. They must insist on winning academic programs as well as winning athletic teams. The schools are, and always will be, exactly what the people make them.

# IX

## Some Proposals for Action

What can and should the public do about the current crisis in public education? This is the 64 or 100 thousand dollar question. It is not answered conclusively by the materials in this chapter and no definitive answer is possible except as individuals and communities develop their own. The articles herein could help with this.

In brief, a controversial book on retooling our schools is reviewed both favorably and unfavorably; three historic proposals, which could change the form of public education considerably, and a significant conference on teacher education are summarized; a call is made for ingenuity in approaching educational problems; an educator's challenge to fellow educators that they provide leadership in the crisis is followed by a school board member's dictum that good schools require aggressive support; and, finally, some propositions concerning public education that the public should understand are succinctly stated. The whole chapter provides basis for hope that the outcome of the current great debate will be improvement of public education.

## How Should We Retool Our Schools? *

*Here are two opposing views of a controversial new book,* Education and Freedom *(Dutton), by Admiral H. G. Rickover, father of the Nautilus. Admiral Rickover's serious criticism of the American public-school system has the support of Arthur Bestor, Professor of History at the University of Illinois and author of* The Restoration of Learning *and other books. A dissenting view is taken by Theodore Brameld, Professor of Educational Philosophy at Boston University, whose most recent book is* Cultural Foundations of Education.

---

* Reprinted by permission from *The New York Times Book Review*, February 1, 1959.

# A HISTORIAN AGREES WITH ADMIRAL RICKOVER'S PROPOSALS

*Arthur Bestor*

The problems of the world—today, our problems—will tomorrow be our children's problems. Are we equipping the younger generation to deal effectively with them? This is the central question in education—a perennial question, which every adult generation must, in a sense, answer anew, taking into account the changes that may have occurred in the nature of the world's problems.

In the great debate now going on over the adequacy of American education, both sides take off from this same starting point. Defenders and critics unite in believing that the public schools should prepare young men and women for the world in which they are going to live. The debate is over the kind of education that will do the job. Parents and citizens should keep the central issue in mind, for efforts are frequently made to obscure it.

Professional educationists in the United States often claim to be the only group interested in preparing young people for contemporary life, and they accuse their scientific and academic critics of wishing to turn back the clock. This completely misrepresents the position of those who are anxious to re-emphasize intellectual discipline in the public schools. One of the most distinguished spokesmen for the latter point of view, Admiral Hyman G. Rickover, states the matter with complete clarity in his latest book, "Education and Freedom." Through "bitter disappointment," he writes, we have come "to the realization that America's predominant educational philosophy is as hopelessly outdated today as the horse and buggy."

The educational philosophy that Admiral Rickover considers outdated is the one that takes "life adjustment" for its central aim. The result, he charges, is "substitution of know-how subjects for solid learning" and "the widespread tendency of schools to instruct pupils in the minutiae of daily life." His own alternative is concisely stated: "English, foreign languages, mathematics, sciences, history, geography—these are the subjects which must be mastered. They are the intellectual tools that enable us * * * to understand the complexities of today's tense and uncertain world. Those who do not have the mentality to master all these subjects need the same kind of intellectual fare, only less of it."

The issue is squarely joined. How completely opposite the two positions are can be neatly shown by a single sentence that Admiral Rickover quotes from an educationist source. The sentence describes a situation that Admiral Rickover would obviously consider sound. In actual fact, the sentence appears in a pamphlet published by the Association for Supervision and Curriculum Development of the National Education Association as a description of the situation which that association prides itself on having helped to destroy: "Physicists wrote the text on physics; literature was

selected and interpreted for high-school pupils by college professors; mathematicians decided on the order and content of arithmetic texts; and so
the experts dominated the content of the curriculum."

The question, be it remembered, is which kind of education will best prepare young men and women for the task of the immediate, foreseeable future. Professional educationists argue that they alone are competent to
answer the question. They insist that no one but an expert in pedagogy
possesses the kind of information and experience necessary to reach a
sound judgment. The arrogance of this argument is bad enough, but what
destroys it utterly is its manifest illogicality.

Who, after all, is an expert on the nature of the intellectual problems that
are posed by the technological world of today and tomorrow? Is it the professor of education, employed to teach teachers how to teach, and perhaps
engaged in research on the ways of adolescents? Or is it the scientist, constantly engaged in solving the problems that arise along the advancing
frontiers of knowledge or the professional man, actively applying new ideas
to practical affairs? Merely to ask the question is to wipe out the educationist's claim to expertness on the question before us.

No one is better qualified than Admiral Rickover to assess the intellectual
demands that the future is certain to make, for his pioneer work on nuclear
power plants for the Navy has brought part of the future into actual being.
Generalizing from his experience in these development projects (including
that which produced the Nautilus), he writes: "Whatever the world of
tomorrow may turn out to be, one thing is certain. Greater mental effort will
be required of all mankind." Military considerations are not necessarily
uppermost in the author's mind. Some of his most telling passages picture
the need for a prompt and intensive technological effort to stave off the
collapse of civilization through exhaustion of fuels, metals and other natural
resources.

Given the intellectual needs of contemporary society, Admiral Rickover
reaches the conclusion (inescapable to this reviewer's way of thinking)
that the first duty of American schools is to "develop in all children—
talented, average, and below average—the highest level of intellectual
competence of which they are capable." The author intends every word
to be taken literally. He believes that even below-average students are
capable of far greater intellectual effort than American schools usually call
upon them to make, and he proves the point by citing the achievements of
pupils of like ability in Russia and other countries.

Though defenders of the educational status quo will no doubt call this
a book of "negative" criticism, it is, in fact, crowded with positive suggestions, attesting Admiral Rickover's sincere and intelligent concern with the
improvement of American schools. Almost the first of his specific suggestions, one should note, is phrased as follows: "An immediate step in solving
our educational problem is to increase [teachers'] salaries drastically."

Of most concern to him is the education of the talented, because the waste of their abilities exposes the nation to the most direct and immediate danger. A rigorous program in the basic intellectual disciplines, with a minimum of electives and a maximum of continuity, is his prescription for the top 15 or 20 per cent of the population in intellectual ability. Special accelerated "tracks" for these students in the high schools he considers indispensable. And in his most publicized proposal he urges the setting up of twenty-five demonstration high schools throughout the country to show the acceleration possible for talented students under subject-trained teachers in a strictly academic environment with a lengthened school year.

Such an experiment might well be a Nautilus for American education.

## An Educationist Opposes the Stand of the Admiral

*Theodore Brameld*

Because everyone except the most myopic apologist agrees that American schools suffer from grave deficiencies, and because many earnest citizens are groping for solutions, uncritical readers of Admiral H. G. Rickover's book are likely to applaud both its objections to and corrections for public education.

Viewed critically, however, "Education and Freedom" rests upon an array of dubious, indeed ominous, assumptions. The many facts it presents, only some of which are contradictory and unsubstantiated, lend themselves to more than one kind of evaluation. To be sure, the contention that we need "a thoroughly reorganized educational system with totally different aims"—a contention that, in another context, some of us might applaud—appears on the surface little more than a hackneyed proposal to return to "the traditional task of formal education in Western civilization." This task is to transmit "the social heritage" and to provide "rigorous training of young minds."

But consider more carefully the meaning of "rigorous training." Admiral Rickover insists that "the school's concern is with the intellect alone." The primary process of learning is "storing the mind with knowledge." It never occurs to him to ask whether the psychological principles that he takes for granted are defensible in the light of modern theory and research.

Had he done so, it is unlikely that he could have found a single contemporary authority recognized as such by peers in the behavioral sciences to support his proposals. On the contrary, these sciences are demonstrating that learning and teaching in the cultural as well as formal sense are vastly complicated phenomena involving not only mind-training but multiple emotional, biological, social and personality factors. Of course, a major purpose of good education is to develop knowledge and competence of the highest order. But the way to achieve it is certainly not to advocate a "revolutionary reversal" to so outmoded a psychological doctrine as the mental storehouse

—a doctrine more appropriate to the seventeenth-century psychology of John Locke than to the organismic psychologies of our day.

Or consider an assumption of quite a different order. Admiral Rickover is anxious about "freedom," and to his credit he pleads for the right to engage in intellectual discovery unhampered by bureaucratic red tape or social pressures. Yet, where in his liberal-arts curriculum does he explicitly provide for either experimental or philosophical grappling with the complexities of this supreme value? "English, foreign languages, mathematics, sciences, history, geography"—what assurance do we have that freedom will become integral to the lives of young people as they "master" these subjects? Admiral Rickover, after interpolating feeble reservations, holds up the class-structured European, even the Prussian and Soviet, systems of education as models for us to emulate. The fact that to a large extent the kind of mastery he lauds is at least as appropriate to nondemocratic as to democratic countries disturbs him very little. Rather, he is almost gleeful that Soviet education has largely repudiated experimental methods of learning and returned to the storehouse doctrine.

Quite consistently, then, the admiral sees no reason why children should learn the meaning of democratic freedom by participating, deciding and planning together. Such activities are considered merely a waste of time. Quite consistently, too, no place is provided for intensive study of the great controversial issues of our day—problems of race discrimination, say. Thus, though Virginia is praised as a "true pioneer for excellence in education" because it has lowered teacher-training requirements, no mention is made of the schools closed by its white-supremacy Governor and no question is raised as to whether this kind of contempt for the Supreme Court of the United States would be tolerated by a really well-educated people.

As has recently been fashionable among conservatives, the scapegoat is again John Dewey and "progressive education." Unlike some other critics, the author is honest enough, however, to make a devastating admission: "Fortunately, progressive educational methods have not found too wide application in our schools * * *." Well then, even going along with him for the sake of argument (though not agreeing that "the spirit of Dewey permeates our teachers' colleges and state boards of education"), how can we blame these methods for the present sorry plight of American education? It is truer to say that we cannot blame them because, except in distorted or superficial form, they have rarely been tried—certainly not as Dewey, a profound student of psychology and the philosophy of science, meant them to be tried.

Admiral Rickover simply caricatures progressive education when he identifies it with "life-adjustment education" that "aspires to adjust the child to life as it is." The intent of Dewey's philosophy is opposite—to develop a capacity in learners to engage in constant re-adjustment by the disciplined application of scientific methods to all important problems of human life.

A much stronger case could be made that American school programs are frequently dull or otherwise mediocre just because they continue to practice the author's own obsolete brand of learning and teaching.

The central issue remains unresolved; how shall America create a powerful program of education suitable to the age of space which Admiral Rickover himself has helped to accelerate? Despite some well-justified strictures, especially against an over-methodologized teacher education, he does not effectively answer this question. The best advice he can give to parents is that they read Albert Lynd or Arthur Bestor—authors whose familiarity with the frontiers of behavioral science is about on par with his own. Nowhere does he suggest that perhaps a fairer way for parents to weigh the issues involved would be to study sources on various sides of the question. But apparently such procedure is unnecessary, since "Bestor's book has never, to my knowledge, been refuted by the educationists in any point * * *." Let the Admiral then look only at the heavily documented rebuttal by Professor Bestor's own colleague at the University of Illinois, Prof. Harold C. Hand.

The tragedy is that, with all its deep concern, never once does this book ask whether we might cope with the current crisis not by rejecting or retreating but by correcting the weaknesses and advancing beyond the contributions of Dewey and other pioneers of modern education. The goal of a strong education, not only for America but for all parts of the earth, is the first imperative of the next half-century. Much better training for all professions, including teaching and technology, is crucial to this imperative. But we can no more afford to meet the competition of Russia by imitating its authoritarian policy and program in education than we can afford to meet the threat of any kind of totalitarianism by aping its disdain for civil liberties.

A rebuilt philosophy of education that can generate both the vigorous means and magnetic ends essential for our times is needed. It will not be found along the road that Admiral Rickover commands us to follow.

# The Pursuit of Excellence in Education*

*A free society, says this history-making report, cannot afford to argue over "quantity" and "quality" in education. Our job is to develop the individual potentialities of our youngsters to their maximum at all levels.*

* Reprinted by permission from *The Reader's Digest,* November 1958. Copyright 1958 by Rockefeller Brothers Fund, Inc., and published by Doubleday & Company. This material appeared in the *Ladies' Home Journal* for July 1958. This report has been called by *Ladies' Home Journal* "a document that will shape educational philosophies and practices for years to come." Prepared by the Special Studies Project of the Rockefeller Brothers Fund, Inc., it is one of a series which attempts to assess major problems and opportunities confronting the United States today. Participating in its preparation were 42 leading citizens and educators, headed by John W. Gardner, president of the Carnegie Foundation for the Advancement of Teaching.

There is no more difficult problem for a free people than to identify, nurture and use wisely its talents. Indeed, on its ability to solve this problem rests its fate as a free people. An undiscovered talent, a wasted skill, a mis-applied human ability is a threat to our capacity to survive—not just as a nation but as a nation of free individuals. Society as a whole must therefore come to the aid of the individual, finding ways to identify him as a unique person and to place him alongside his fellow men without inhibiting or destroying his individuality.

One still hears arguments over "quantity" versus "quality" education. Behind such arguments is the assumption that a society can choose to edu-cate a few people exceedingly well, *or* a great number of people somewhat less well—that it cannot do both. A society such as ours has no choice but to do both; it calls for the maximum development of individual poten-tialities *at all levels*.

The 18th-century philosophers who made equality a central term in our political vocabulary never meant to imply that men are equal in all respects. Men are unequal in their native capacities and therefore in their attainments. In elaborating our national views of equality, we have empha-sized *equality of opportunity*, a conception that candidly recognizes differ-ences in endowment and the certainty of differences in achievement. By allowing free play to these differences it preserves the freedom to excel which has produced so much human greatness.

In the pursuit of excellence several considerations must be kept firmly in mind. First, our conception of excellence must embrace many kinds of achievement at many levels—in abstract intellectual activity, art, music, managerial activities, craftsmanship, human relations, technical work. Sec-ond, we must recognize that excellence is a product not only of native ability but of motivation and character. The more one observes high per-formance in daily life, the more one is impressed with the contribution made by the latter two ingredients. Finally, we must recognize that judgments of differences in talent are not judgments of differences in human worth.

## OUR EDUCATIONAL SYSTEM

Our educational system has been our most basic instrument for realizing the ideal of equality of opportunity. But in many areas our educational facilities are poor, our educational effort slovenly. Our schools are over-crowded, understaffed and ill-equipped. In the fall of 1957 there were 1,937,000 pupils in excess of "normal classroom capacity." Some schools have found it impossible to hire well-qualified teachers in such basic sub-jects as English and social sciences; some have even had to drop chemistry, physics and mathematics from their curriculum for lack of teachers. And the population bulge of the future will press even more urgently on already overburdened facilities.

But our schools require more than financial support. They need an unsparing re-examination of current practices, patterns of organization and objectives.

One of our most pressing needs is a revision of the false emphasis which the American people place on the purely formal evidence of education. We have made receipt of a college degree an accolade of merit, not in terms of intellectual achievement but of prestige. A college degree is becoming an essential for entry into many careers, even though that career may not utilize the kind of education that has been received. It is not surprising, therefore, that some people insist that no one should be made "unequal" by a lack of higher education.

This dilemma is manifest in the entire educational spectrum. By insisting that "equality" means an exactly similar exposure to education, regardless of the student's variations in interest and capacity, we inflict a serious form of inequality upon our young people. We limit the development of individual excellence in exchange for a uniformity of external treatment. In too many of our school systems all young people from the age of six on, march forward in lock step, one grade per year. Because many educators reject the idea of grouping by ability, the ablest students are often exposed to educational programs whose content is too thin and whose pace is too slow to challenge their abilities. Yet to fall short of excellence is to deny our ideal of personal fulfillment.

## THE TEACHING PROFESSION

No educational system can be better than its teachers. But we face severe problems both in the supply of teachers and in their quality. The number of new schoolteachers needed in the next decade is equal to about 50 percent of all the four-year-college graduates of every kind expected during the same period—yet only about 20 percent of college graduates are entering teaching.

The danger of a decline in quality is equally obvious. As of 1956, approximately 21 percent of all public-school teachers had had less than four years of college. And the National Education Association reports that "since 1953-54 holders of the doctor's degree among the newly employed full-time college teachers have decreased 25.2 percent." Moreover, it is hard to attract the ablest people into academic life, for many of the qualities most necessary for effective teaching are in great demand in other fields—where the financial rewards are generally much higher.

Even with aggressive recruitment there is little likelihood that we can bring into teaching anything approaching the number of qualified people we need. Therefore we must utilize our superior teachers more effectively. One way is to eliminate many of the petty tasks which occupy a teacher's time. Less highly trained classroom assistants may accomplish much in the lightening of this burden. Another measure is to employ television and films to bring extraordinarily effective teachers into contact with larger numbers of students. Such innovations should not be thought of as stop-gap measures but as the beginnings of a long-overdue revolution in teaching techniques. A rigorous reappraisal of present patterns and courageous experimentation with new patterns is called for. This must include a candid weighing of essentials and nonessentials in the curriculum; more imaginative approaches to the problem of class size; and—at the level of higher education—the trying out of methods which place more responsibility on the student for his own education.

But the root problem of the teaching profession remains financial. Until we pay teachers at least as well as the middle echelon of executives we cannot expect the profession to attract its full share of talent. And almost as important as the level of pay is a reappraisal of the promotion policy which for most school systems depends more on seniority than on merit.

## SCIENCE EDUCATION

The dimensions of these problems can be illustrated by discussing one field in which our inadequacies have come to our attention most painfully: science education. The crisis here is not an invention of the newspapers, or of scientists, or of the Pentagon. Nor is the U.S.S.R. the "cause." The U.S.S.R. has merely served to awaken us. The heart of the matter is that we are moving with headlong speed into a new phase in man's long struggle to control his environment. Nuclear energy, exploration of outer space, revolutionary studies of brain functioning, important new work on the living cell—all point to changes in our lives so startling as to test to the utmost our adaptive capacities, our stability and our wisdom. Clearly we need an ample supply of high-caliber scientists, mathematicians and engineers.

There is a danger of training scientists so narrowly in their specialties, however, that they are unprepared to shoulder the moral and civic responsibilities which the modern world thrusts upon them. Still, just as we must insist that every scientist be broadly educated, so we must see to it that every educated person be literate in science. In the short run this may contribute to our survival. In the long run it is essential to our integrity as a society. We cannot afford having our most highly educated people live in intellectual isolation one from another.

## THE IDENTIFICATION OF TALENT AND THE USES OF DIVERSITY

Any educational system is, among other things, a great sorting-out process. But sometimes it seems that rather than take responsibility for assessing differences in talent we prefer to encourage mediocrity. Tests are most effective in measuring academic aptitude and achievement. But many kinds of talent must go unmeasured because no adequate measuring instruments exist. We cannot measure aspiration or purpose, courage or vitality or determination. No single test should therefore become a basis for important decisions. A series of scores obtained over years can enable teachers to achieve a reliable perspective on a young person's aptitudes and minimize the possibility of false diagnosis.

Our schools cannot do full justice to each youngster until they face frankly the need to provide different programs for different types and levels of ability. The academic capacity of students should be tentatively identified by the time eighth grade is reached. An adequate guidance system should then ensure that each student be exposed to the sort of program that will develop his gifts to the full. No effort should be spared to provide the top two percent with opportunities for challenging study. From this group will come many of the young men and women who will reach the pinnacles of intellectual achievement and creativity in the years ahead.

Some critics of our schools have advocated the European pattern of two separate systems after approximately the sixth grade: one college-preparatory, the other vocational. Such separation would be unpalatable to most Americans. In any case there is no reason why youngsters at all levels of scholastic ability should not sit in the same home room, play on the same team, attend the same dances and share the same student government.

The important thing is to rid ourselves of the notion that either a flexible promotion policy or a flexible curriculum is undemocratic in spirit. If we are to do justice to the individual, we must seek for him the kind of education which will open *his* eyes, stimulate *his* mind and unlock *his* potentialities. We should encourage all kinds of individuals to run on all kinds of tracks. In this way we can distribute widely the rewards of self-esteem and self-respect. Though the educational patterns may differ, the goals remain much the same for all: to enable each young person to go as far as his aptitude will permit in fundamental knowledge and skills, and to motivate him to continue his own self-development to the full.

# Reform Plan for Schools*

*Kindergarten-through-college revision, says expert, is only remedy for inefficient U. S. education system.*

*Paul Woodring*

John Dewey once observed that controversy over education was a healthy sign, demonstrating that people were interested in their schools. If this is

* Reprinted with the permission of the McGraw-Hill Book Company, Inc., from *A Fourth of a Nation* by Paul Woodring. Copyright © 1957 by the McGraw-Hill Book Company, Inc.

true, American education today must be in a state of robust health, for our schools have become the subject of a great national debate. Charges are made that they have become educational wastelands, that they offer little for the mind, that there is quackery in the schools and teachers colleges, that Johnny can't read, and that our high schools are blackboard jungles.

Even if we take the more extreme charges with a grain of salt, most of us are left with an uneasy feeling that something is seriously wrong with our vast educational structure.

The fact is that we Americans have never quite made up our minds just what we want the schools to accomplish. Because we are vague and confused about what we want, we disagree about what should be done. Despite this confusion, the areas of disagreement can be sharply defined in these questions:

– Should the school place its emphasis on teaching the younger children the three R's and teaching the older ones how to reason? Or should it give equal attention to social adjustment, mental health, recreation and vocational training? Put another way, should education stress the development of the mind or the total growth of the whole child?

– Should the brighter child be (a) moved ahead in school, or (b) placed in a special class with other bright children, or (c) kept with those his own age? And should the slow learner be held back, or put in a special class of slow learners, or should he too remain with his age group even though the work is too difficult for him?

– Should grades reported to parents be based on the child's academic achievement or on the effort he has expended—or should the teacher try to judge the child's social competence and emotional adjustment by making marks on a check sheet? Or, as another alternative, should we abandon report cards altogether and substitute conferences between parents and teachers?

– Should a high school diploma be given to a student for (a) scholarly achievement, or (b) hard work regardless of achievement, or (c) merely years of attendance?

These questions all involve conflicts stemming from the basic disagreement between two divergent views of education. The first, the classic thesis, holds that the most important fact about man is that he is a thinking being and that the aim of education is to improve his ability to reason. The schools, the classicists say, must stress intellectual excellence and require their students to hold to high standards.

The newer view of education, the progressive approach which has become popular in the 20th Century, holds that thinking is only one of many functions the human being must perform and that the mind therefore cannot be educated separately from the rest. To the progressive educator, education is the total development of the whole child.

If we accept the classic view, the schools will emphasize knowledge and clear thinking beyond all else. Children will be grouped in classrooms on the basis of their intellectual maturity and academic achievement and regardless of their age, physical size or social maturity. Grades will represent academic achievement and a diploma will be evidence of substantial knowledge and of ability to think clearly.

If we accept the newer view, the school must expand its curriculum to include not only academic subjects but every aspect of the child's life. Grouping becomes much more difficult, for no group of children can be alike in all aspects—intelligence, age, social maturity, physical size and so on. We are forced to use the easy way of grouping—by chronological age, promoting each child a grade each year. A high school diploma then represents little more than 12 years of attendance.

Progressive methods have been in wide vogue in American schools for 30 years or more. As a result this approach has been the target of most of the criticism of recent years. Much of the criticism has been well-founded. Progressivism started as a reform movement at a time when reforms were badly needed in American education. The classical educators dominated American schools and many of their methods were old-fashioned and badly in need of overhauling. In its early years the progressive movement played a valuable part in developing new ways of teaching, in adapting education to a wider range of individual differences, in encouraging more freedom and spontaneity and in making the classroom a happier place for children to live. All this was good. But the progressive movement did not stop here.

## THE FRINGES OF PROGRESSIVISM

One of the great dangers of any reform movement is that militant extremists tend to become the movement's best-known spokesmen. Through exaggerated emphasis the extremists unwittingly make any good idea appear ridiculous. This happened to the progressives. As the progressives gained confidence, they became more outspoken in their attacks upon traditional education. It appeared to many people that they stood in sharp opposition to academic scholarship, to intellectual discipline, to clear and consistent standards of achievement, to rationalism and intellectualism, and to civilized standards of behavior for children and adolescents. Because its adherents were uncritically tolerant of their movement's lunatic fringes, progressivism came to be identified in the public mind solely with the excesses of those fringes.

This was unfortunate because many of its doctrines were—and are—sound. In the current debate between the progressives and classicists most people on the sidelines find themselves torn between the two points of view. We would educate for excellence and hold to high standards—and yet we know that many children cannot meet such standards and we are reluctant to let the slow learner suffer the consequences of repeated failure. We would stress knowledge and clear thinking—yet we are not at all sure that we want the school to neglect the child's health, his social and emotional adjustment, or even his recreation. We want each child to move through the school at his own best rate—yet we are reluctant to remove him from his social group.

A solution is possible but it cannot be a mere compromise. It must represent a logical meeting of the two points of view.

To begin with, the traditional organization of our school system, with its eight-year elementary school, four-year high school and four-year college, should be sharply revised. There is nothing magical about figures. Elementary education does not require eight years for every child. A prepared student can start high school as easily at 12 as at 14. At 16 the adolescent is fully capable of coping with the demands of higher education.

The existing 8-4-4 division of school years is arbitrary and accidental. The eight-year elementary school was developed in the mid-19th Century not as a high school preparatory course but to offer a complete education for the average citizen. When, in the late 1880s, the public high school began to spread across the nation, it required eighth-grade graduation for admission simply because the eighth grade already existed as a standard stopping point.

Many of the early high schools were two- or three-year institutions. But their standards varied widely. When the nation's colleges were called upon to accept graduation from high school as evidence of preparation for higher education, a four-year high school curriculum was imposed, simply to achieve standardization at a reasonably high level.

So 12 years were required to get a high school diploma. Since most children started school at 6, 18 thereby became the standard age for college entrance.

Postponement of higher education until the student is 18 is wasteful and unnecessary. It has caused the colleges to compress liberal education into two years, devoting the remaining years largely to specialized work which logically does not belong in the liberal arts college at all. It forces the brighter students to remain in high school long past the time when they are ready to move on. Indeed, experiments made in the past few years demonstrate that the last two years of high school may be all but a total waste of time for superior students.

## An End to Patchwork Remedies

The problems of the present educational system are so complicated and so serious that nothing short of a radical reorganization of our entire grade structure will solve them. Merely patching and cobbling will not do. The system needs to be replanned as a whole. What follows is a detailed proposal for such a major revision in U. S. education, from kindergarten through college.

Under the reorganization I am proposing, children will start primary school in an ungraded class which combines kindergarten with the present first and second grades. Admission may be at any age from 5 to 7, but it is probable that most parents will want their children to enter as early as possible. Because this primary room will be ungraded, it will be possible to make provision for individual differences if classes are not too large. For each teacher or teacher's aide, there should be at most 25 children.

At first, many of the activities in this room will be similar to those in a good kindergarten, but as soon as any child is ready, a part of his school day will be devoted to reading. Other academic skills will receive little stress.

The child will remain in the primary room for an indefinite period, although normally for two or three years rather than one. His next step upward into the elementary school will be decided on by the teacher after conferences with the parents and the school psychologist. The decision will be made on the basis of readiness for the third grade rather than on either age or length of time in the primary room. Readiness will be judged in terms of physical, emotional and social maturity plus capacity for learning. One evidence of progress will be the child's ability to read at some predetermined level.

A few children will move into the elementary school at the age of 7 or 7½. Most probably will be ready at 8 or 8½, but some will not be moved up until they are 9. An effort will be made to keep either children or parents from assuming that any given age is the "normal" or expected age for beginning elementary school. At this age the concept of "failure" should be avoided, and because the primary room is ungraded, it can be avoided more easily than under the present system.

Some children who are still unable to read at the age of 9 and are becoming too large for the primary room will probably need to be given special attention in a room set aside for that purpose. If it is found that they are greatly retarded and unable to enter the third grade, it may be necessary to keep them in the special room. But their number should be small.

In the graded elementary school which follows the primary school, the child will lead a rich and varied life with a wide range of experiences. Major stress will be placed on writing, spelling and arithmetic, and there will be a continued effort to improve his skill in reading. Regular reports will be made to parents of the child's success in learning these skills, and separate reports will be made of his social adjustment.

Because entrance to the elementary school will be made on the basis of total maturity and readiness for learning rather than age, nearly all children should proceed through the four-year elementary school at about the same pace—that is, in four years. Here again there will be little if any "failure."

The average child will enter high school at about the time he now enters junior high school, when he is about 12 or 13. There will be some variation in age, but all students will have in common their readiness for high school, which is not always true under a system which promotes on the basis of age alone.

## ADAPTING FOR DIFFERENCES

However distinct differences in learning capacity will be apparent by now and the high school will be prepared to meet these differences by making a second major departure from present practice.

High school students will be specially grouped on the basis of demonstrated ability in each subject. For example, in ninth- and tenth-grade mathematics there will be three groups of students. Group C (you may call it Group A if you like, but no one will be fooled) will include those who find mathematics difficult. They will try to master elementary arithmetic and work on improving their ability to calculate accurately. Group B, consisting of those who have learned the principles and can calculate accurately, will study practical mathematics: the applications of arithmetic, elementary algebra and geometry to problems of life. They will learn, among other things, to calculate an income tax in half the time required by their fathers, and with much less fretting about its complexity. They will learn to interpret statistical tables accurately and to decide whether an instalment loan which purports to be based on 6% interest is really 6% or 12%, regardless of what the salesman says. Group A will undertake a rigorous study of algebra and geometry in preparation for their use in higher education and in those professions which require such knowledge.

No one will be required to join Group A. To enter it the student will have to demonstrate both ability and willingness. If after joining the group he decides that he does not want to work as hard as the group's work requires, he will not be coaxed, chided, wheedled or cajoled. He will simply be moved over into Group B. He is a big boy now and is no longer to be treated as an irresponsible child. He will be guided only in the sense that an effort will be made to insure that he understands the full, long-range consequences of his decision.

I have no fear that such a procedure will cause many able students to chose the easier course. Rigorous standards do not keep able athletes from trying to make the first team, even though life might be easier on the third. Adolescents are not afraid of hard work, they resent only useless or unrewarded work. They choose the easier road in high school only when all roads lead to the same honor roll, the same diploma and the same colleges. At present the easy way to make the honor roll in most high schools is to elect the easiest courses, and every student knows it even if his parents do not. Under the new plan honor rolls should not be necessary. If they are retained they should not be available to those who reject the more difficult classes.

A student in Group A in mathematics may or may not be in Group A in literature, for in each subject students will be regrouped according to interest and ability. If he does join Group A in literature, he will spend his time in reading, discussing and interpreting serious books picked for their intellectual content. The teacher will be aware that the student is not yet an adult and that he will prefer *Romeo and Juliet* to *King Lear,* Shelley to Browning, and Millay's early sonnets to her later poems, but there will be no effort to substitute easy trivia for more serious works.

The student who, because of lesser motivation or ability, is not found suitable for Group A will study in Group B, where the pace will be slower and the most difficult forms of literature will be avoided, though the emphasis here, too, will be upon serious literature with important intellectual content.

If all serious literature confuses him, the student can be moved over into Group C, where he will at least learn to read the newspapers and other current publications with understanding.

Although the teachers of all three groups should be professionally competent and should be able to work sympathetically with their groups, it will be essential that the teachers of Group A be selected for their superior scholarship and intelligence. This is the most controversial part of my proposal, for it has become standard practice in the schools to ignore individual differences among teachers even while stressing the difference among pupils. But in every high school the brightest students are superior in intelligence to some of the teachers and have very frustrating experiences in the classroom unless they can be assigned to teachers who think as well as they.

For the average student, graduation from high school will occur at about 16. Three courses are now open to him. He may go to work immediately; or he may enroll in a trade school or junior college, which will be open to all high school graduates; or, if he can meet the requirements, he may go to a liberal arts college.

For those who choose unskilled or semiskilled occupations (and despite the increasing complexity of modern industry, there are still a great many such jobs) no further formal education is necessary. There is no harm in going to work at 16 or 17. Many boys and girls will even prefer to do so. Once such employment would have been condemned, but we must remember that agitation against child labor goes back to a time when much younger children were put to work for 12 or more hours a day in mines or dangerous and unsanitary factories; such conditions were obviously bad for a worker of any age. The healthy adolescent will not be harmed by working 30 or 40 hours a week in a clean, well-lighted, modern factory, where his work on the assembly line will be far less tiring and dangerous than trying out for football on the high school team. Many a slow learner who never succeeded in really adjusting to school becomes a responsible and satisfactory unskilled worker, happier than he ever was in school.

The second group, that of intermediate learning capacity, will presumably choose to attend a trade school or junior college for a year or two before going to work. The junior college will be an all-purpose institution. Although it will include general subjects like English, mathematics, history and the sciences, the emphasis will be on more practical trade and commercial courses. The junior college will not offer preparation for professional study or for graduate work in the universities.

All students who plan professional careers will first attend a liberal arts college. It will differ from the average college of today in that truly liberal education will be emphasized. There will be less specialization, less emphasis on specific preparation for professional courses or departmentalized graduate education. Each student will take courses in all the major areas of knowledge: the humanities, the social studies, the sciences, mathematics and philosophy. Vocational or professional preparation will come later.

Liberal arts colleges will be both public and private, as they are now. The present private and parochial colleges will probably change comparatively little except for the elimination of vocational courses. Students will enter and will leave a year or two earlier than is now the case, but because entrance examinations will be required and because secondary education will be more rigorous for this group, there will be no need to lower standards. In all probability standards will be raised.

State or municipal liberal arts colleges will be available in all cities of any size so that parents who are reluctant to allow their sons or daughters to go away to school at 16 may send them to a commuters' college which offers the same curriculum.

Because the liberal arts college will not try to prepare students for a vocation, most of its graduates probably will go on to universities or to separate professional schools. Since most students will enter the liberal arts college at 16 and graduate at 20, they will be able to complete professional education with no greater delay than now occurs. In universities or professional schools the student will go directly into a course that will prepare him for law, medicine, commerce, engineering, the ministry, teaching or graduate study looking toward a career in scholarship. Because college graduation will be earlier and because the college will be less specialized, the university courses will be a little longer than at present in order to include some of the specialized work now a part of undergraduate education.

The bachelor's degree will signify graduation from the liberal arts college and nothing else. There will be no more baccalaureate degrees in specialized subjects or professional fields. University or professional schools will grant master's and doctor's degrees only. Instead of a bachelor's degree in law, there will be a master's or, more probably, a doctor's degree in law. The underlying assumption is that every lawyer should have a liberal education and that any education coming after the bachelor's degree should lead to a master's or doctor's degree.

Master's degrees will require a minimum of two years beyond the baccalaureate, and the doctorate will require approximately five years of graduate work, so that most doctor's degrees will be received at the age of 25. This is not far from the present age of those who go straight through without interruption.

## EDUCATING OUR SCHOOLTEACHERS

Teachers for the primary, elementary and high schools will take a Master of Arts degree in teaching. This degree will require two years of professional work following the liberal arts degree. The teacher will thus begin his career at about the same age he now does, but every teacher will be educated both professionally and in the liberal arts—which unfortunately is not always the case at present. The two years of professional education will include both advanced work in the field to be taught and professional courses in such subjects as educational philosophy, educational psychology, and an introduction to the methods and materials of instruction.

This approach guarantees that secondary teachers will be well-grounded in their major fields as well as in the philosophy and techniques of education. For example, a history teacher will study American, European and world history as a part of his liberal education and will probably elect at least two or three additional history courses as well. As a graduate student he will take at least one additional year of more advanced history.

Primary and elementary teachers will study less specialized subject matter but will spend more time on child psychology and methods of instruction, with particular attention to methods of teaching reading.

Any plan such as the one I propose is necessarily utopian by nature, however sound it may be. There are many vested interests which are opposed to change. Graduate schools suggesting changes always meet resistance from the individual departments. Changes in the college and high school are often resisted by the college-accrediting agencies, and the elementary school which changes its organization or its program always meets resistance from some parents as well as from teachers and administrators. Yet the schools have changed more rapidly over the years than most other institutions and, at least in the levels below the graduate school, some degree of change is accepted by many people as desirable.

Much of the objection to recent changes has been entirely sound, for the changes have come about without an over-all plan and without any underlying philosophy. But if the public philosophy of education can be clearly stated, and if it can be shown that the present organization of the schools departs from that philosophy, much of the objection will disappear.

Many of the elements of the plan I am proposing have been tried at various times and places. Where they have been found unworkable, it is only because a single element of one educational system cannot be changed without reorganization of the whole. Several colleges, for example, have recently experimented with admitting superior students at 16, accepting them on the basis of an entrance examination instead of a high school diploma. Opposition to these experiments from accrediting agencies and other colleges is not based on any evidence that the plan would be unworkable if all colleges accepted it. The ungraded primary school is now being tried in several schools, and tentative results seem to be uniformly good.

If the various parts of the new plan were put together in a logical pattern I feel most of the objections to them would disappear. The plan would not in itself overtax the public schools or colleges. To see how it would work let us take a brief statistical look at a typical city of 100,000 population. In such a city there would be about 7,500 youngsters attending the ungraded primary school and 10,000 in elementary school. These 17,500 children would fill 35 buildings, each designed for 500 pupils. Assuming no one drops out, there will also be about 10,000 high school students who would occupy 10 schools of 1,000 each. Forty-five public schools is a reasonable total for a city with a school population that size.

Of the 2,500 high school graduates each year about 750 will go to work immediately and 1,000 will enroll in vocational courses in the junior college. The remaining 750 will attend liberal arts colleges. Of this number perhaps 250 will go away to private or state residential colleges. The remaining 500 will study at a municipal or community college, so that in its four-year course this college will have 2,000 students, a workable enrollment.

Finally, about 250 college graduates may be expected to go on to universities, teachers colleges or other professional schools. Presumably only the larger cities will maintain universities; cities with less than half a million population will not be able to afford them.

In the past, professional educators have often led those opposing any suggestions for radical changes in the schools. But just as war is too important to be left to the generals, education is too important to be left to the educators.

There is growing recognition in the U. S. that just as a good education can be a great boon a bad education can be a great evil, allowing the child to confuse propaganda with truth, to value the trivial, to follow the crowd wherever it may lead him. Today we are giving our children more and more education, but that is not enough. Only by taking drastic steps can we make sure that it is better education as well.

# A Hard Look at Our High Schools*

*Dr. Conant, whose study was financed by the Carnegie Corporation, is an educator, statesman and scientist. He was president of Harvard University, ambassador to West Germany and a renowed chemist, and played a key administrative role in developing the atomic bomb.*

*Dr. James Bryant Conant*

There is only one way of appraising American public secondary education, and that is by an examination of each school, bearing in mind the type of community it serves. There is no such thing as the "typical" American high school. Such a school is a myth.

During the past school year, I have traveled throughout the country visiting public high schools. I have spent a day in each of 55 schools in 18 states. I have talked with administrators and small groups of teachers, visited classes and met with schoolboard members and student leaders. In all, I must have questioned at least 2,000 teachers and discussed school problems with many hundreds of high-school students. My overwhelming impression is of the great variety of American high schools.

As a result of my study, I am about to make recommendations directed to school-board members, superintendents and high-school principals. I hope in this article to acquaint a wider audience with the basis for my findings. All my recommendations stem from practices and procedures which I have seen in operation and which seem to me worthy of imitation. In short, they are based on fact, not theory.

My recommendations can be understood only if one examines the nature of the American educational system.

Our free society is unlike that of any other country. Therefore, it is not strange that our educational system—and its problems—should also be unique.

First, our educational ideals reflect the history of our nation; unlike European countries, we have never been divided by a class system based on conqueror and conquered. We believe, uniquely, in equality of opportunity for all youth, irrespective of the economic status of the family. Our system of education must provide for a wide diversity of talents and of vocational goals.

Geographic diversity is another unique characteristic of our educational pattern. Our democratic tradition demands local control of schools, and this has meant the development of high schools specially geared to the

* Reprinted by permission from *Look,* February 3, 1959. Copyright 1959 by Cowles Magazines, Inc.

needs of the thousands of diversified communities they serve. In America, there are about 21,000 public high schools. Some 17,000 are so small that they are totally inadequate. I hope that, by district reorganization, most of these can be replaced by schools large enough to offer satisfactory programs. Two thirds of the nation's youth in high school, however, attend the 4,000 public high schools which are large enough. I know from experience how great the differences are even among those 4,000 schools.

A third distinctive aspect of our educational system is the peculiar nature of our universities and colleges.

In Europe, where I have had the opportunity of examining schools in both the Federal Republic of Germany and in Switzerland, one looks in vain for a four-year liberal-arts college or its equivalent in a university. The European university is essentially a collection of professional faculties —theology, law, medicine, science and engineering. As compared with American institutions, these universities are few in number and enroll not more than six to eight per cent of the young men who are of university age. Passing a state examination entitles a youth to enter any university. The standards for degrees are uniform throughout each nation, and migration from one institution to another is quite frequent. The contrast with the United States needs no underlining.

In our country, there are well over a thousand colleges and universities that award bachelors' degrees. Something like a third of our youth enter these institutions. There is a wide variety of standards for admission and no uniform standards for degrees. The courses of study open to the American college or university student cover an enormous range.

Some colleges are highly selective, and only those students can hope to enter whose academic abilities place them in the top five to ten per cent of the population. Other institutions, both private and public, offer an opportunity to anyone who holds a high-school diploma, no matter how little is his or her talent for academic work. Under such conditions, it is obviously impossible to specify a satisfactory preparatory course for colleges in general. One can talk about entrance requirements for *specific* institutions only.

The fourth unique aspect of American education results from the fact that the ambitions of parents for their children are by no means uniform throughout the United States.

In small industrial cities some distance from a metropolitan area, one can usually find a widely comprehensive high school from which less than half the boys and girls proceed to a college or university. In such schools, a majority of the students in the 11th and 12th grades are enrolled in courses designed to develop a skill marketable on graduation—stenography for girls, for example, carpentry or auto mechanics in the case of boys. The pull of the local industries offering employment for high-school graduates is strong.

The minority who plan to go to college from such a school are rarely interested in attending those private colleges that are nationally noted for their selective policy of admission. Indeed, the attitude of many families in the community is likely to be neutral or negative as regards the advantages of a college education. The counselors in such a high school often are concerned because some bright boys who ought to be taking advanced mathematics and science, and who ought to enter an engineering school or university, are not interested in further education.

In contrast to the school I have just described is one in a typical suburban area. In many suburbs, parental attitudes are just the opposite of what one often finds in an industrial city. All or almost all the families want their children to go to college. Some desire the school counselors to "get" their boys into particular colleges that have a highly selective admission policy. And the parents often refuse to allow their children to take vocational courses.

The counselors, instead of being concerned with the bright boy whose family is not interested in his going to college, are more often worried by families in which the talents of the offspring do not measure up to the collegiate ambitions of the parents. Every year, some mothers or fathers must be persuaded that it is worse than useless for a child with little ability for handling mathematics or foreign languages to attempt the courses that certain colleges recommend to prospective candidates for admission.

Each of the two schools I have described corresponds to schools with which I am familiar. Each type may be doing a good job within the limits set by the attitude of the parents. Yet the schools are obviously quite different. If the suburban high school could be transplanted to the small industrial city, and vice versa, two highly unsatisfactory high schools would result. This one example may serve to emphasize how varied are the problems one encounters when one sets out to get the facts about American secondary education.

In Europe, little effort is made to direct toward a university the able children of families who have no interest in having them become lawyers or doctors, scientists or engineers. The selection of those who are to go to a university is made at about 11 years of age; those who do not apply or who are not selected for admission to a preuniversity school finish their formal full-time education at 14. Much potential talent is lost.

European families who wish to have their children go to a university do their best to have the boy or girl in question admitted to one of the tax-supported preuniversity schools. Since the selection is made on the basis of ability, some parents are certain to be disappointed. Others will suffer a similar disappointment when a child flunks out of the preuniversity schools. These failures run as high as one half to two thirds of the student body during the eight- or nine-year course.

The curriculums of these preuniversity schools are of three slightly different types, but are identical from one community to another, because neither local pressures nor parental desires play a part in determining school policy. The tax-supported school in Europe is a state school. There is no local control even over the appointment of teachers, and all matters of curriculum and organization are settled in the capital of each individual state. One looks in vain for a local board of education. Again, the contrast between the United States and Europe is quite clear.

The fifth and final distinctive aspect of our educational system is the employment situation in the United States, which differs so radically from the practice of employing youth in other lands.

I have said that those who do not enter the European preuniversity schools at about the age of 11 finish their full-time education at 14. Such is the case for the vast majority, who proceed at once to get a job; only a small fraction may continue in an intermediate school for another two years. The fact that so many of the young people of a nation enter full-time employment at 14 obviously affects the educational picture.

Perhaps in no other respect is the contrast between Europe and the United States more marked than in this matter of the employment of youth. During the two decades from 1910 to 1930, the American scene changed drastically as regards child labor. In 1910, about 30 per cent of the children of 14 and 15 were gainfully employed; in 1930, only nine per cent were employed. Today, it is difficult for a youth under 16 to get a job because of laws governing employment and because of the established practices of management and labor.

Therefore, even in those communities where, unlike the suburbs, there is relatively little pressure for *all* the youth to go to college, nearly all the youth are enrolled at least in the first high-school years. Clearly, unlike any other nation, we in the United States are committed to a system of education that, at both the high-school and college levels, must provide for a wide variety of abilities and vocational aims.

In spite of the complexities of the problems, there are a few simple guides for citizens who are concerned with their local high school. First of all, a good school board is essential. A school board should be composed of honest, devoted, intelligent citizens who realize the difference between policy-making and administration, and who resist all temptations to become involved in matters that should be left to the superintendent and principal —particularly the employment of teachers. Once petty politics enters the picture, the morale of the teaching staff goes to pieces and hopes for a good school disappear. A good school board will find a good superintendent and a good principal, and these two administrators will recruit and lead a fine teaching staff. It goes without saying that, in the last analysis, on the quality of the teachers all depends.

A fine school board, good administrative officers, a first-rate teaching staff and a high school of considerable size are essential. But many problems may still remain; a citizen may need to ask questions of his school board, and a school board may need to direct many questions to the superintendent. What I wish to suggest in this article are certain broad considerations that will help a citizen analyze the complexities of a given school and direct significant questions to his school board.

I would recommend that a citizen think of the program of instruction in the American high school in three categories. First, there are the courses that should be *required* of *all* students, irrespective of their academic ability or their vocational goals. Then, there are two types of elective programs—the nonacademic and the academic.

The required program should occupy about half of every student's time. It should include four years of English, three or four years of social studies including two of history, at least one year of mathematics and one year of science. These courses are intended to provide the groundwork for citizenship in a democracy.

The program in English deserves a special comment. Half of the time assigned to the study of English should be devoted to composition, and students should prepare an average of one theme per week. To make correction and discussion of these themes possible, English teachers should be responsible for no more than 100 students.

In the eighth grade, the counselor must advise each student about the elective programs, which would start in the ninth grade. Depending on the student's school record, the opinions of teachers and the results of aptitude tests, a good counselor will try to steer a student into the particular elective program—academic or nonacademic—that best corresponds to his or her interest and potential ability. And here parental ambition often becomes all-important.

The nature of the non-academic elective program will depend almost entirely on the community. There may be a considerable number of parents who are interested in having their children, whose talents are nonacademic, take vocational courses geared to employment opportunities in the community. In that case, such courses should be offered. I have seen excellent work in such programs. What is more important is the fact that the students enrolled in those meaningful programs have an attitude toward their vocational work that carries over to their work in those academic courses required of all. These pupils know why they are in school: they are *committed* students. I strongly suspect that few committed students turn up as juvenile delinquents.

Moving now to the academic elective program, I am convinced from my many talks with teachers and students that, on a national basis, something like 15 per cent of the youth of high-school age have the ability to study effectively and rewardingly advanced mathematics, science and a foreign language. And I think those academically talented students should be urged by the counselors to elect a minimum academic elective program that includes four years of mathematics, four years of *one* foreign language and three years of science. Such a wide program, including the students' required courses, will demand 15 to 20 hours of homework a week.

Two techniques will encourage students to elect the harder and more challenging academic courses. One is to stop the practice of designating rank in class by an average of all marks received. The other is to inaugurate an academic honors list for graduates who have made an honors average in courses for the academically talented. I also recommend that each graduate be given a durable record of all courses and grades, so that a prospective employer can see a detailed record rather than only a simple diploma.

I do not think it is a good idea to have fixed programs bearing labels such as "academic" or "college preparatory," while others are "vocational" or "general." To my mind, every student should have an individualized program. The counselor must follow each student's record as he or she progresses from grade to grade, and if it becomes evident that a student does not have the ability to handle the wide program I am recommending, then some other arrangement should be made. Individualized programs permit flexibility, and exceptional cases can be easily accommodated. The elective programs of all or almost all students should include art and music. This should be the case in every high school, irrespective of the community it serves. The intensity of the interest in art and music, I found, varies from place to place.

I should like to comment on one of my recommendations for the academically talented—that a student study four years of *one* foreign language. This recommendation is based on what I have seen in only a few schools. One current criticism of American public high schools that is well founded is the criticism of the foreign-language courses. In school after school, I found that not more than two years of any foreign language were offered. And these were all schools with a good reputation. Ambitious students were studying two foreign languages for two years each. Such programs are very nearly a waste of time. The purpose of studying a language is to master it. Those who have ability can acquire something approaching mastery in a four-year high-school course.

I conclude my discussion of the problems facing our high schools by reminding the reader that the American public high school has been under heavy fire for many months. Some of the criticism has been based on solid fact and is therefore constructive; much of it, however, is irrelevant and even dangerously misleading, because the critics start from oversimplified assumptions. Radical changes are being suggested that are quite unrealistic; the proponents completely ignore the complex problems facing the administrators of our tax-supported schools.

Many of us rejoice that there exist many, many high schools throughout the land where the future mechanic, the future electronics specialist and the future lawyer can come to understand one another by sharing experiences in the classroom. In these widely comprehensive high schools, adequate education can be provided for boys and girls whose abilities cover a wide spectrum of academic talent and whose ambitions are directed to a variety of goals. I say it can be done because I have visited a few schools where it is being done.

I see no reason why all schools cannot be made as satisfactory as the best I have seen, if citizens in each locality elect a good school board, demand improvements and are prepared to support the required changes. In short, our high schools can be made adequate if the citizens demand it.

DR. CONANT'S RECOMMENDATIONS *to the nation's school boards and school administrators will be detailed and precise. Their substance is also of vital interest to every parent and community-minded citizen. Here is a summary of Dr. Conant's major points, as he has touched upon them before audiences in various localities.*

1. Eliminate small high schools with fewer than 100 in the graduating class and develop comprehensive high schools which can meet students' varied abilities and interests. Do not create separate academic and vocational high schools.

2. Counsel students to plan their high-school programs on an individual basis. Do not fit students into rigid curriculums.

3. Require all students to take certain courses as general education for citizenship. These should include four years of English, three or four years of social studies including two of history, one year of mathematics and one year of science.

4. Place all students in their required courses in class sections according to their ability, subject by subject. The same pupil may be in a fast English section but in a middle section in history. Such divisions should be flexible and individual.

5. Enable students not going on to college to elect vocational courses of direct use in their communities. Do not separate these students from others taking academic courses.

6. Encourage the top 15 per cent of students to take more challenging academic courses, including four years of mathematics, four years of one foreign language and three years of science, in addition to the English and social studies required of all.

7. Give special attention to the highly gifted three per cent of the school population and to pupils whose reading ability is particularly low.

# Education in Review*

*Scholars and teachers find a common ground in a debate on training.*

*Loren B. Pope*

The goals outlined for American education in the ninety-sixth annual convention of the National Education Association at Cleveland last week

---

* *The New York Times,* Sunday, July 6, 1958. Reprinted by permission.

reflect the spirit of an historic meeting on teacher education that preceded it at Bowling Green State University, Ohio.

The N.E.A. platform, putting a priority on quality of public school teacher preparation, urges at least four years of college education, plus a successful internship for every teacher. It advocates both general and professional education, and professional recognition only for those beginning teachers who graduate from institutions accredited by the profession. More uniformity in teacher certification among the states, based on standards developed by the profession, also is suggested.

These declarations take on more than usual significance because they largely parallel proposals for improvement of American public school teaching made at Bowling Green in five days of give and take between a thousand representatives of the public school teachers and their most vocal critics— the liberal arts professors and scholars. The Bowling Green meeting was sponsored by the N.E.A.'s Commission on Teacher Education and Standards, in co-operation with seven other educational, scientific and learned societies. In all, delegates from sixty organizations attended.

## BASIC AGREEMENT

The leaders of a divided educational world went to Bowling Green expecting a battle of the decades on the issue of subject matter versus professional training in the preparation of public school teachers. Instead, both sides were pleased to discover they were fighting on the same side. Both want the school teacher to be well educated as well as technically trained.

The discovery produced such a strong, new sense of co-operation that both professional educators and scholars in the sciences and humanities have pronounced the week's reconciliation and collaboration a more important event than the 1955 White House Conference on Education.

This meeting was the first time in half a century of feuding and epithets that the school teachers and teacher-education officials had met on a grand scale with the liberal arts people for a common discussion of teacher-education needs.

It grew out of a desire of a few persons on both sides of a divided educational world to talk things out. . . . The professional societies in the sciences and the humanities agreed to be cosponsors, and a hundred of the nation's leading universities sent representatives. . . .

The liberal arts professors, arriving at Bowling Green, edgily expected a fight on the issue described in the old story that the professional educator argues that a teacher doesn't teach math; she teaches Mary. The liberal arts man replies: Why not teach Mary math? . . .

Instead, the liberal arts people found the teacher-education officials do want to teach Mary math. Neither side, however, expects agreement now on specific teacher-education programs to do this. For one thing, they don't anticipate resolving overnight a debate of decades. For another, the great diversity of American educational institutions is a barrier.

The one really important thing to them is the fact that both sides have found they want to, and can, work together. This apparent willingness and ability of the two long-divided parts of the education world to collaborate, the conference participants said, is a development of central importance to the American school system.

## CO-OPERATIVE MOOD

The mood for co-operation was set at the conference's start. Dr. T. M. Stinnett, executive secretary of the sponsoring N.E.A. Commission on Teacher Education, made it clear the teachers were interested in the scholars' ideas. . . .

Each side made some mutually reassuring commitments on matters of principle. The teacher-education group, for its part, declared in favor of a well-rounded education, plus depth of learning in their specialties for all school teachers, and higher standards for the colleges that train them. . . .

Many of the state teacher groups also voted at Bowling Green to ask the liberal arts professors to help plan both the teacher-education curricula and state certification requirements. This is something the liberal arts camp has long declared must be done if teacher education is to be improved.

## COLLABORATION EASED

In return, the science professors gave their tacit blessing to curricula for high school science teachers that "recognize" and favor good professional education courses.

The liberal arts professors, to meet the teachers halfway, must now convert their colleagues at home to co-operation with "those teacher-education people." The Bowling Green meeting, with the prestige lent by participation of the learned societies and the name universities, is expected to help make that collaboration a professionally respectable activity for the scholars, and therefore easier.

Over all, both sides at the Bowling Green conference confessed a sense of guilt for the neglect that has divided and hurt the education world. Both demonstrated a lively conviction that the education of teachers is too important to the nation to be left to the sole jurisdiction of either the liberal arts or the teacher-education group by itself. There was a sense of need for the strength of union—to achieve the teacher-education goals which the liberal arts group has not been able to force by itself, and to win the public support for education which the organized school teachers have not been able to do even in these times. . . .

# Is Money Enough? *

*Alvin C. Eurich*

The current emphasis upon "doing something about education" often leaves the impression that if only more money were available our educational problems would be solved. This approach is understandable in a country such as ours, where more people live comfortably and have more money to spend on luxuries than in any other nation of the world. More people have cars, refrigerators, radios and television sets; more people can also read and write than in any other major nation.

Actually, however, we *have* spent more money on education in recent years, yet the general situation has deteriorated. Between 1950 and 1957, school expenditures have risen 60 per cent and teachers' salaries 50 per cent. Despite this, our 1957 teacher shortage is 50 per cent greater than in 1950 and, although total enrollment is up only 30 per cent, we have 110 per cent more pupils on double shifts. Clearly we are confronted with problems in education that money alone cannot solve.

\*          \*          \*

The major question confronting the nation in regard to education is simply this: will we try to solve our educational problems by appropriating more money to do more of the same things in the same ways we have been doing them in the past in our schools and colleges, or will we try to find more effective, more efficient and more economical procedures?

First and above all else, we need the approach that brings continuing progress in other areas of American life, where if we fail to find solutions by traditional methods, we question the procedures and devise new and more effective ones. We need to act on a basis of belief that education can be constantly improved; we must abandon our current passive attitude, which seems to assume that if a given educational practice has been used over a period of many years, it must therefore be the best possible. Had we adopted such an attitude in our industrial development, where would we be today?

At the present time anyone advocating a new teaching procedure is immediately put on the defensive by our educators, who demand proof

* Excerpt from: Alvin C. Eurich, "Schools Need More Than Money," *The Nation*, May 10, 1958, pp. 145, 404, 405-06. Reprinted by permission. Alvin C. Eurich, director and vice-president of the Ford Fund for the Advancement of Education, served as the first president of the State University of New York and as a member of President Truman's Commission on Higher Education. He is the author of *The Reading Abilities of College Students* and co-author of several other books on educational problems.

that the new practice is as good or better than the old, traditional one. And yet at no time has proof been demanded or given that the older procedures are really effective, or even the most effective.

Take, for example, the question of class size. There are probably no more rigid notions in education than those regarding the number of students one teacher can handle effectively. We assume this number to be one teacher for every thirty pupils at the elementary school level, and one for every twenty-five in the secondary school grades. The unquestioning acceptance of these ratios represents the keystone of our entire educational system. Because of them, new school buildings are constructed with classrooms designed for twenty-five or thirty students. This, in turn, determines the number of teachers we need; and the design of buildings and number of teachers determine capital, operating and maintenance costs.

Yet we have no evidence that these ratios provide optimum conditions for learning. On the contrary, fifty years of research on this problem is summarized in the *Encyclopaedia of Educational Research* with the following conclusion:

> Mere size of class has little significant influence on educational efficiency as measured by achievement in the academic subjects. Although experimental evidence does not provide a clear-cut answer to the class size issue, the general trend of the evidence places the burden of proof squarely upon the proponents of *small* classes.

Why, then, should we continue to place the burden of proof solely upon anyone who proposes *larger* classes? Would it not be more constructive if this line of reasoning were followed to another conclusion, namely, that what we need more than anything else in education is the application of ingenuity to the solution of our problems? The following questions challenge our imaginations and suggest areas in which new answers might be devised.

1. *Class Size.* Suppose that instead of inflexible adherence to old formulas we begin to apply our inventiveness to define and then provide the optimum conditions for learning for each student. We might then utilize some of our very best teachers on television and film to make them available to many more students than is now possible. This would mean that we must recognize that teachers, like people in other professions, differ considerably in their skills. Some would be found to be most effective with relatively large classes, and some with smaller groups. Some would have great talent for teaching on television, others would be much better in directing small group discussions. If we then set up schools to utilize this variation in human abilities to the greatest possible extent, what would this do to our rigid ideas of class size?

2. *Teacher Incentives.* Suppose, further, we begin to provide greater incentives both in prestige and income for teachers to improve. At the college and university levels we have done this to some extent by setting

up a system of rank, ranging from assistant and instructor up to professor and distinguished service professor. But below the college level we label a person who is teaching in the classroom for the first day "a teacher," just as we call the most gifted and competent person with twenty-five years of experience "a teacher." We could, instead, set up a system of rank in the pre-college grades running somewhat as follows: assistant, tutor, instructor, teacher, television teacher—and pay each accordingly. Such a system, with salary gradations at each level, would offer constant incentives to teachers to improve and extend their effectiveness.

3. *Curriculum.* The late Ray Lyman Wilbur, while president of Stanford University, said that it is as difficult to change the curriculum of a college as it is to move a cemetery. We should ask ourselves why we teach the courses that we offer at every level of education, and whether our reasons for these offerings are valid in terms of what should be our prime concern, educating students. If every school in the country seriously asked itself which of its courses are absolutely *essential* for the education of students, it is likely that only a very small percentage of the courses now offered would remain.

All too often curriculum changes occur as a result of internal and external pressures unrelated to the learning process. Faculty members are frequently allowed to introduce courses which may or may not contribute to the students' education. When the teacher moves to another institution, the course continues to be offered. A short time ago I heard the end result of such thoughtless proliferation in the boast of a college president that it would take a student more than forty years, attending full-time, to complete all the courses offered in his college. Rather than something to be proud of, this seems to me a devastating indictment of his curriculum.

Course additions motivated by pressures from non-educational special interests also help to clutter up our curriculum. Recently, for example, a Mr. Reginald Johnson received the President's Award of the Salesmen's Association of the Paper Industry "for outstanding contribution in furthering educational programs for the industry." If you wonder how he advanced education, it was by attaining an increase in college courses devoted to the paper industry, with emphasis on sales.

Supposing we used an entirely new approach, and asked whether the curriculum could be worked out in relation to the *ideas* that have been important to the growth of civilization, rather than around subject-matter areas. We could begin by considering basic concepts essential to our democratic way of life, such as freedom and liberty, and teach them from one grade level to the next, to extend the pupil's maturity. We could go on to basic ideas in the physical sciences such as measurement, energy, momentum, stability. We would soon find that basic ideas overlap subject-matter fields. Would not a curriculum developed around such ideas and basic skills be more meaningful than scattered and elected subjects?

I hold no special brief for these specific examples or procedures. Some will work, others will not. But one thing is certain: unless we apply the same kind of ingenuity to educational problems that we have applied to other areas of American life, we will find no adequate solutions. Money is clearly not enough.

# An Educator's Open Letter to U. S. Educators*

*The following open letter by Dr. Paul Woodring was inspired in part by* Life's *series. Dr. Woodring, a former teachers college professor, is one of the country's most articulate educators, author of an analysis of U. S. education,* A Fourth of a Nation (Life, *Sept. 2), and currently consultant to the Ford Foundation's Fund for the Advancement of Education.*

Sirs:

The leadership of American education is rapidly passing out of the hands of professional educators. The crescendo of criticism that has assailed the schools for the past 10 years has, since the launching of Sputnik, become a deafening roar. It is obvious that our schools from kindergarten through college must make dramatic changes and equally obvious that the present tremendous public interest in education offers an unparalleled opportunity for us to make some long-overdue improvements.

But instead of leading the way, instead of planning new programs to meet the exciting demands of the last half of the 20th Century, most of us are fighting a futile delaying action. We are resisting the attacks, fending off the flying brickbats, offering evidence that our schools are just as good as they were in 1900, denying the charges, and advising our cohorts to cancel subscriptions to any magazine that dares to challenge current educational practices.

This is not leadership—leadership is not possible from a defensive position. If the control of the schools is not to pass entirely out of our hands we must again take the offensive. We must ourselves identify the weakness and shortcomings of our schools and offer bold and imaginative solutions.

It is futile to waste our time pointing out that much of the criticism misses its proper target and that some of the critics are confused by the enormous complexity of American education. The important fact is that, while educational spokesmen resist change and feebly defend the status quo, the critics offer strong and positive suggestions for the improvement of our schools. They are urging that we raise our sights, that we establish priorities based on a clear sense of purpose, that we resist, instead of going along with, the anti-intellectual trends of our culture, that we find ways of challenging the greatest potential efforts of bright and gifted students

---

without neglecting the less able, and that we find better ways of educating teachers and of making their job more attractive to men and women of high intelligence.

There is growing evidence that this is what a great many of the American people want. There is evidence, too, that many educators want the same things. A recent Gallup Poll found that 79% of high school principals think the schools demand too little work of their students, 63% are convinced that students do not read enough books, and 61% think athletics is over-emphasized. But the voices that speak for professional educators have failed to make this plain, have failed to offer solutions, have failed to lead the way or even to point out the weaknesses.

The critics themselves—those outside the schools—cannot rebuild the American educational system. All they can do is illuminate the errors. The rebuilding must be done by professional educators working with the support of lay groups.

The American people are ready to move. If we will show the needed courage, enthusiasm, perception and intellectual vigor, we can now build a system of education far superior to any that our nation or any nation has ever had. But first we must get out of this ridiculous defensive position and start acting like leaders again.

*Paul Woodring*

New York, N. Y.

# You Have to Fight for Good Schools*

*Edward L. Butterworth*

I'll tell you one thing—serving as a school board member is like going over Niagara Falls in a barrel—stirring, instructive, and bumpy. Those who live through it are never the same afterward.

*I'm not!* In a spirited community campaign several years ago, I won election to the Arcadia, California, school board and the right to devote most of my leisure time to the governing of a school district of 8,000 children. Within 30 days after election my character was brought into question because I didn't know the make and model of the sewing machine used in the home-economics classes; my ancestry was challenged because I couldn't discuss the contents of the third-year Latin textbook; I'd got used to calls like the one from a fellow citizen who rang up at midnight with the emergency intelligence that Fire-Prevention-Week-fell-at-the-same-time-as-Constitution-Week-and-what-did-I-propose-to-do-about-it?

* Reprinted by permission from *The Education Digest,* December 1958. This material originally appeared in *Parents' Magazine,* October 1958. Edward L. Butterworth is President of the Arcadia, California, School Board.

Within the same 30 days I came to realize that no member of any of the 70,000-odd boards of education in the United States lacks for advice, since all of his acquaintances have either been to school or know someone who went to school.

I've learned many other things, too. When I first went on the school board I had heard (so often that it sounded convincing) that modern public schools taught folderol instead of fundamentals; children ran wild; buildings were like country clubs. I had a lurking suspicion of educators. I was going to *stop* the waste of school money.

So I poked and pried and studied—and slowly came to the conclusion that 99 percent of the attacks I heard had no connection whatsoever with fact. American schools are being flayed by critics who in large part are uninformed—who somehow make schools responsible for bad manners, juvenile delinquency, the high divorce rate, and the popularity of the TV horse opera.

Money our willingness or unwillingness to dig down and pay for what we want—that's what a lot of the noise is really about. And the public-school systems in America must periodically stake their survival on the willingness of citizens to vote for school bonds or tax increases.

Take Arcadia. At a time when a school revenue election was desperately needed, an increase in assessed valuation in Los Angeles County, with widely publicized "tax revolts" of small groups, created an unfavorable climate. About the same time a national radio-television network released a somewhat slanted program on the educational system of a sister school district with a so-called "exposé" of coeducational cooking—with a palpable effect on many school districts in Los Angeles County.

## A LOT OF ARGUMENTS

When you set out to fight for the public schools, as we in Arcadia did on this occasion, you hear a lot of arguments. Business men kept telling me, when I went about speaking in behalf of our needs for the public schools, "Ed, we've gotta' stop babying these school people. Look at the soft touch they have—short hours, easy work, job security, a day off whenever they want it, long vacations—and anyway, the school budget is altogether too big. We just can't afford it."

Sometimes people point to school buildings and grumble, "Look at these palaces! Very beautiful—but do we need such costly materials? Must we hire such high-priced architects?" I wonder sometimes if some people *prefer* repulsive looking schools with poor heating, lighting, and acoustics, on the theory that bleak surroundings are better for children. "Kids have it too easy nowadays," they say. "When I was a boy, there was no nonsense about school. We worked. We learned that life isn't all fun. It was good for us."

You learn, as I learned and as 700 devoted PTA members in Arcadia learned, that when you work for the schools you have to put up a determined fight and learn how to reply to a lot of abuse.

Sooner or later every school argument gets around to the three R's. Around this trio there appears to be an unblushing campaign to belittle the public schools. Most lay members of boards of education—lawyers, doctors, housewives, businessmen—know this is tommyrot. But the general public doesn't always recognize what is often irresponsible and sometimes downright dishonest criticism. I often hear, accompanied by loud cheers from the audience, "Make 'em learn, like we did in the old days."

Sometimes I agree. I say, "I think I know what you mean. There was an editorial about it in a New York paper." Then I read it:

> When we were boys, boys had to do a little work in school. They were not coaxed; they were hammered. Spelling, writing, and arithmetic were not electives, and you had to learn.
>
> In these more fortunate times, elementary education has become in many places a sort of vaudeville show. The child must be kept amused and learns what he pleases. Many teachers scorn the old-fashioned rudiments; and it seems to be regarded as a misfortune to read and spell by the old methods. As a result of all the improvements, there is a race of gifted pupils more or less ignorant of the once-prized elements of an ordinary education.

This always gets applause. So I continue: "I've just read you an editorial from the *New York Sun* for October 5, 1902."

Evidently, to paraphrase Will Rogers, "The schools ain't what they used to be and probably never were."

## GOOD OLD DAYS

Good old days? More than 100 years ago the 40 best pupils in Cleveland took a special test. Recently the 40 brightest youngsters from Cleveland junior-high schools took the same test. The twentieth century youngsters heavily outscored the nineteenth century class in reading and arithmetic. They barely lost in American history, despite having 100 years more of it to study. The 1848 pupils won in grammar and geography, but overall our century's boys and girls outscored their predecessors by 955 correct answers to 924.

In Indianapolis a test that had been given in 1919 to high-school seniors was given again to a modern-day senior class. It covered 10 subjects. The 1919 class averaged 138 of a possible 190 points. The modern students averaged 152. Similar comparative tests are being made throughout the country. The results, favorable to present-day pupils, go unpublished except in educational journals.

The spelling deficiency is often thrown in my face. "Why don't schools have spelling bees nowadays?" parents demand. "When we went to school, we had to spell words like *circumambient, ammoniacal,* and *effumability.*"

I resist the temptation to ask how many times a day they use these words—and how well they can spell the *cereal* they eat in the morning, the *sincerely* they sign to their letters, the *deficiency* of which they accuse today's spelling teachers. I know that one weary school superintendent suggested a public spell-down between complaining parents and their own junior-high children. The kids were all for it. The parents declined to a man. Parents at Coulee Dam, Washington, were more reckless several years ago. In an old-fashioned spelling bee they were spelled down by the high-school sophomores ten to six.

The same is true of arithmetic. The old schools thought the way to make us learn was to punish us for failure. We worked, true enough, but the mind has a way of drawing a curtain over unpleasant experiences. Now we know that children who experience fear and punishment in their arithmetic class have learned to hate arithmetic but not to solve arithmetic problems.

We also know that neither threats nor prizes can propel a child as far as the drive that comes when he wants to know. Our better schools get wonderful results by tapping this eagerness to learn. Are youngsters having more fun in school than their parents had? Yes. Most of them are learning more, too.

The current attack on our public schools is unlike any in our history. So far, the result has been to undermine confidence in the personnel, the subject matter, and the moral and intellectual climate of the public educational system. Much of the criticism seems deliberately slanted. We hear a great deal about Blackboard Jungles and very little about the many good schools. Take the nationwide television system that sent a crew to spend a day at a high school. They shot hours of sound film portraying the magnificent job this school was doing. They also picked up a few minutes of some boys loafing outside the school, boasting of the easy time they had in a snap course—and used *them* on a nationwide broadcast.

A book comes out proclaiming that the public schools don't teach children to read. Any well-informed teacher can refute the book practically sentence by sentence, but the public doesn't know this.

A national magazine runs a full-page photo of a girl reading a "confession" magazine in class and readers are left to infer that this is typical.

These may just be instances of sensationalism intended to attract audiences. But they're used as pile drivers by agitators. These bell-wethers take one bad schoolroom and hold it up as typical of American school systems. They keep bobbing up at meetings and on the air, and in the public press, repeating the same demagogic criticisms even after they have been shown frequently and clearly that the facts do not bear them out. A number of organizations have names which imply that they are militantly patriotic and firm supporters of public education, yet these organizations are everywhere trying to spread the idea that the schools are bad and should be deprived of financial support. Maybe I'm overheated from the pummeling I've taken, but I say these groups are insincere. I think they may be covert foes of our democracy—something practically everybody in the school system sometimes is accused of being.

When you hear rumors about your schools, ask the speaker for facts and watch how fast he backs off. Don't let him put over halftruths about "frills" and "waste" and "no discipline." Make him be specific. When you stand up for your schools, it won't take many like you to halt the unjustified abuse.

And when you stand up for your schools, it won't take many—and it won't take long—to bring about the improvements that *are* needed, that are justified.

# Public Understanding and Support for Education*

## Propositions That Need Public Understanding

1. Most Americans now realize that our leadership, and indeed our national survival, is being challenged as never before in history. Most Americans must be brought to realize that the survival and well-being of this nation depend no less upon the strength of our educational system than upon the strength of our military establishment.

2. Educational institutions in a democracy are properly expected to meet the fundamental needs of society. If they are subject to passing whims and fancies, schools and colleges cannot perform this function. Responsible citizens share with educators a moral obligation to insist upon wise and careful planning to meet fundamental needs and to protect our educational institutions from hysterical demands and panicky reactions.

3. Critical analysis of our educational system is certainly in order, but mistaken efforts to place blame through name-calling and fault-finding should not be permitted to obscure the fact that our schools, colleges, and universities are seldom much better or worse than their respective publics want them to be. The best of our institutions certainly rise above the common levels of aspiration, yet the vast majority simply mirror the values most commonly held. If American education is to undergo a general improvement, the people at large must place a higher value upon intellectual achievement and must be prepared to uphold higher levels of educational performance.

4. Lip service to the value of education is not enough. The critical need is for material support. The American people can afford to spend more on education. Doing this, however, will necessitate assigning a much higher priority to the importance of teaching and research as crucial forms

---

* Reprinted by permission of the American Council on Education.

of enterprise in a dynamic society. There must be a willingness to practice self-denial in paying higher taxes and in making heavier voluntary contributions to provide greater material support for education.

5. The time factor is extremely important, and basic issues must be faced now. Nothing less than a massive national effort, launched immediately, will do. Local support and control will remain the best safeguards and guarantors of excellence for our diverse educational system. They can and should be preserved, but bickering over forms and sources of financial support necessary to meet the present emergency can be disastrous. Positive and immediate action on all levels—federal, state, local, and voluntary—is the first imperative.

6. Economic inflation has already levied a heavier toll on educational institutions than on most other forms of enterprise. Still further inflation would be a more serious threat. If this possible consequence of vastly increased governmental expenditures for education is to be avoided, investment in our schools, colleges, and universities must take precedence over existing expenditures which are of less importance to our national security.

7. The total economic resources available for higher education, whatever they may be, will necessarily exist in limited amounts. One demand upon those resources is to raise the general level of performance in all schools and colleges. If this is allowed to be the only call, however, a tragic mistake will be made. A second, and vital, call upon our economic resources is to strengthen our leadership in all important fields and to add to our best existing institutions the appreciable support needed to meet the demands for the highest order of quality. Statesmanship must see to it that adequate support for the attainment of both goals is provided.

8. A genius of American education has been its unity through diversity. This diversity should be preserved, with strengthening all along the line and greater stress on the importance of quality everywhere. In short, all our human resources must be vastly strengthened through the medium of improved education.

## PROPOSITIONS THAT NEED PUBLIC SUPPORT

1. The magnitude of the job to be done can hardly be exaggerated. We are not spending nearly enough on education. Modest measures will not do the job. In colleges and universities alone, the number of qualified students will be doubled by 1970, and a doubling of expenditures will not even perpetuate present inadequate quality levels. To do the job effectively, the following order of priorities should be observed:

- Salaries for teachers, scholars, and scientists should on the average be at least doubled;
- Existing institutions should be maintained more adequately and some of them greatly strengthened;

- Support for the establishment of new institutions will be necessary, but should not be supplied at the expense of existing institutions;
- Scholarship programs should stress quality rather than quantity, graduate as well as undergraduate study, and should be accompanied by a parallel system of grants to the institutions in which scholarship holders enroll.

2. Although federal support for educational activities already exists in many forms, excessive reliance upon it may weaken other sources of initiative. However this may be, we are in a national emergency, and prompt action of unprecedented magnitude is urgent. The truth seems to be that the Federal Government is the only agency which can act with sufficient speed and on a scale large enough to enable schools, colleges, and universities to accomplish their tasks. Action by the Federal Government need not, and should not, extend federal controls over education. Further, as a partial attack on a problem of such great size, it need not weaken initiative and action at the state, local, and voluntary levels. Federal support should be considered only as a necessary supplement to action by state and local entities, corporations, alumni, parents, churches, foundations, and philanthropic individuals. The initiative and interest of these agencies and individuals are the greatest asset of American education; they must now be exercised to an extent never before demonstrated.

3. Greatly increased amounts of money must be allocated to fundamental research and other forms of creative and scholarly activity. These can be carried on more effectively in our colleges and universities than anywhere else, because in the academic environment the creativity of central figures is reproduced by students who have worked with them.

4. If American education is to continue to serve the best interests of the nation, drastic measures to increase the supply of highly trained persons are required in many areas other than physical science and engineering. The need for teachers at all levels and in all fields is a compelling illustration. Continued progress in the humanities, the arts, and the social sciences, as well as in science and technology, is highly essential to our national survival and well-being.

5. Totalitarian methods are not necessary to counter the threats of a totalitarian power. These threats can be countered and overcome by our own American strengths, strengths which in education include academic freedom for teachers, scholars, and scientists; freedom of mobility and choice of programs of study and vocations by college students; diversity of programs, forms of control, and philosophies among institutions. These qualities of American education must receive continuous, vigilant support.

*The actions called for cannot be postponed. The priorities must be established immediately. Should we fail to do these things, the deferred costs will be too staggering to be met in time. If the nation is to survive and prosper, we must start making the basic provisions now.*